Soft Power Mad

Claire Seungeun Lee

Soft Power Made in China

The Dilemmas of Online and Offline Media
and Transnational Audiences

Claire Seungeun Lee
Inha University
Incheon, South Korea

ISBN 978-3-030-06593-5   ISBN 978-3-319-93115-9   (eBook)
https://doi.org/10.1007/978-3-319-93115-9

Cover credit: benoitb/iStock/Getty Images Plus
Cover design by Tom Howey

This Palgrave Macmillan imprint is published by the registered company Springer Nature Switzerland AG
The registered company address is: Gewerbestrasse 11, 6330 Cham, Switzerland

To my family and those who live with globalizing China

PREFACE

The rise of China is inevitably significant to China's neighbors—South Korea and Japan—as well as for Asia, and the world at large. Along this connection, this geopolitically and globally informed project began with a rather simple set of empirical questions: "As a neighboring country of China, how can we understand and navigate the rise of global China?" and "How can we understand China's soft power, sociologically and empirically?"

This study examines the ways in which China has evolved from a sleeping lion into an awakened rising power along the idea of soft power, and evaluates China's attempts to wield soft power regionally, internationally, and globally.

In the course of working on this project I have been asked, "Does China even *have* soft power?" As I developed this project from a PhD dissertation into a scholarly book, I found myself steering in increasingly different directions. I gradually realized that this book is about *why and how* China's soft power works (*or not*) in one of the seemingly best places to work with a powerful medium—TV series. The cases of Korean, Japanese, and American media, as well as that of the telenovela, have been well-documented. Yet, a research gap existed on the topic of Chinese televisual media. Thus, this book aims to tackle this simple but relatively unanswered question in the emerging field of Soft Power Studies, as well as China/Chinese Studies, and Sociology.

It was not clear to me what inspired this research interest, and that it was "destined," until I studied Chinese soft power planning and its global projections for rising China. As an undergraduate student in 2005, I won a Chinese Language Contest in Seoul, South Korea, sponsored by the

Ministry of Education of the People's Republic of China. Subsequently, I was awarded a month-long exchange program at Beijing's Language and Culture University. I later realized that this contest had been sponsored by the very first Confucius Institute in Seoul, and the name of the competition has since changed to "The Confucius Institute's Chinese Contest."

The establishment of the Confucius Institutes, and spread of Chinese education through these Institutes, is the most renowned example of China's soft power effort to date. Subconsciously influenced by this phenomenon, I came to study China's soft power through other mediums along my academic journey. All of which culminated in my first academic project.

As a sociologist, I am a big believer that research should be empirically grounded and relevant, not only to me as a researcher, but also to people in society at large. Discovering interesting topics for academic investigation in my everyday life and interactions, connections, and relationships with people across societies is always a blessing to me.

China, as the focus of my research, is located west of where I originally come from. Coincidentally then, *The Journey to the West*, was composed by the renowned Chinese novelist Cheng'en Wu, who shares a meaningful connection with me through our names' Chinese characters. Through these signifiers, I have come to believe that engaging in this research area is my destiny. I am very pleased that my first book is a step in the direction of communicating the inspirations behind my academic career and life to the world.

In the near future, I hope to see development in the changing contours of China's soft power in both my original field sites and other parts of the world.

Incheon, South Korea   Claire Seungeun Lee

ACKNOWLEDGMENTS

A book is both a journey and a snapshot of life that is filled with joy, inspiration, and opportunities—and of course, pain and suffering as well. This book's conclusion has been a concerted effort and made possible only through the continuous support of my teachers, informants, family, and friends.

This book could not exist without the contributions of many people. First and foremost, I am very grateful to those whom I met at the start of this project, as well as those who have supported me in finishing this book—some of whom I am not able to name here. In particular, I would like to thank my supervisor Chua Beng Huat, who has guided me and read multiple versions of this book from its most nascent forms. I also thank my professors Catelijne Coopmans, Qiushi Feng, Kurtulus Gemici, Kong Chong Ho, Ivan Kwek, and Eric Thompson at the National University of Singapore, and Sangmee Bak, Lifang Cheng, Jinseok Kang, Jun Young Kang, and Dageun Lim at Hankuk University of Foreign Studies. The Asia Research Institute and Tembusu College at the National University of Singapore has provided me with generous research funding and a vibrant research environment that greatly aided in the completion of this project.

My colleagues at Inha University deserve special recognition for their generous support and enormous interest in my teaching and research. I am very fortunate to find myself in my current academic "home" where I can comfortably discuss teaching, research, and life, in general. As an incoming faculty member, the collegiality and casual meetings I have enjoyed with my cohort at Inha University are gratefully acknowledged. Our Twenty "Seventeen" members who joined the University together in 2017 deserve special mention for their warm hearts and continuous support for encouraging each other's work and life. I also thank my students who inspire me and Lei Jin and Ran Shao for their research assistance in finalizing this book. I also thank my university's research support. This work was supported by Inha University Research Grant.

Some parts of this book and its earlier versions have been presented at conferences and workshops in Australia, China, South Korea, Japan, Germany, and the United States, at the Communication University of China, Hong Kong Baptist University, the National University of Singapore, Texas Christian University, Tübingen University, the University of Massachusetts Boston, the University of Melbourne, as well as at meetings of the American Sociological Association, the Eastern Sociological Society, the International Sociological Association, and the Korean Sociological Association. I am grateful for those who were among my audiences, providing valuable feedback to further develop this project. The engaging feedback and continuous support of scholars in the field, including Michael Curtin, Gao Jia, Michael Keane, Huei-Ying Kuo, Liew Kai Khun, Seio Nakajima, Soon Keong Ong, Philippe Peycam, Colin Sparks, Hayes Tang, and Xin Xin, were enormously helpful in the process of revisiting my PhD dissertation to create this book.

Many thanks to all the people in Beijing, Shanghai, Guangzhou, Shenzhen, Hong Kong, Taipei, Seoul, Tokyo and Yokohama, and Singapore who were willing to share their thoughts and experiences to support my research. Without their enthusiasm and generous help, this work could not exist. Although many who helped along the way shall remain anonymous for the sake of protecting their identities, I would like to express my gratitude by name to Shuwei Duan, Ranran (Yiqin Duan), Toth Gabor, Chris Han, Yun Long, Deqiang Ji, Iwabuchi Koichi, Xuehua Yan, and Wenqian Yu, who shared their insights and helped connect me with respondents and others who were interested in this project. I also thank Jeong-Hwa Ho, Sun Jung, In Kim, Sung Kyung Kim, Yuntae Kim, Sujung Nam, whom I met during my graduate studies, for their faith in me and my research and their emotional support.

In the United States, I would like to thank Professors Michale Ahn, Xiaogang Deng, Alexander Des Forges, Terry Kawashima, Paul Kowert, Lakshmi Srinivas, and Zong-guo Xia at the University of Massachusetts Boston, as well as Kiril Kochkov at Texas Christian University. I am thankful to all of the members of the newly established academic community Cybercrime Investigation & Cybersecurity Lab (CIC) at Boston University—Sinchul Back, Kyung-Shick Choi, Kevin Earl, Hannarae Lee, Jin

Ree Lee, Hyeyoung Lim, Marlon Mike Toro-Alvarez—who have come in contact with me through my newly invested research interests. In particular, I am grateful to Professor Kyung-Shick Choi for his guidance and encouragement. I also benefited greatly from discussions with and encouragement from Professor Pyong Gap Min at Queens College, City University of New York, who believed in my potential from early on.

My friends who were, and still are, in Singapore—Ambika Aiyadurai, Bubbles Asor, Thomas Barker, Minhye Kim, Chih Horng Lee, Eugene Liow, Stefani Nugroho, Fiona Seiger, Sunyoung Seo, Ping Shum—accompanied me throughout this entire project. I also thank my friends Minji Choi, Sung-a Jin, Hyejeong Kim, Jihye Kim, Sohee Kim, Yoonjeong Lee, Soryung Lim, Hyunju Park, Bora Sim, Hyeji Yun, and Seongmin Yun for their support and help with my research. In addition, I appreciate the unconditional help of Jaclyn Sakura Knitter and Alex Gordon, who strongly supported and encouraged me over the years, and who read and helped polish multiple versions of my manuscript.

Thank you to editor Ngeow Chow Bing for the generous permission to include parts of my article entitled, "Developing Social Science-based Chinese Studies in East Asia: Geopolitics, Discipline, Knowledge" from the *International Journal of China Studies.*

To my editor Shaun Vigil and assistant editor Glenn Ramirez at Palgrave Macmillan New York, thank you sincerely for your enthusiastic support and assistance from the moment I contacted you to suggest this potential book project. You have helped me from the very beginning, all the way into this publication's final stages.

Last but not least, I wish to thank my family in Seoul and Budapest for everything. I thank my beloved friend and husband, Benjamin, for his critical mind and unfailing support for my career, work, and life. This book is dedicated to my family.

Incheon, South Korea
August 2018

Romanization of Chinese, Japanese, and Korean Names, Places, and Documents

The guidelines for the Romanization of the names of persons and places in local languages—Chinese, Japanese, and Korean—as well as translations of documents in these languages which were used in the course of library research, field research, and dissertation writing are as follows.

Note on Chinese

For the Chinese transliterations, the Hanyu Pinyin system is used. Personal names of those whose origins are from Hong Kong and Taiwan follow their commonly used English transliterations. A single noun is usually written as a single unit in Pinyin (e.g. soft power: *ruanshili*, instead of *ruan shi li*).

Note on Japanese

The Hepburn system is used for the Romanization of Japanese.

Note on Korean

For the Korean Romanization system, the guideline of the "Romanization of Korean" provided by the National Institute of the Korean Language is used. Names of places and people with commonly documented English transliterations, which are different from the above, are used according to the common practice.

TRANSLATIONS

All translations are made by the author unless stated otherwise.

REFERENCES BY CHINESE AND KOREAN AUTHORS

Asian names, in particular Chinese and Korean names, tend to have a small range of variations of surnames. In order to avoid confusions, I use the initials of first names with surnames. The First and Last name order is kept except for cases widely used in a family-first name order (e.g. Deng Xiaoping).

CONTENTS

ABBREVIATIONS

CCP	Chinese Communist Party
CCTV	China Central Television
CTS	Chinese Television System (*Huashi*) (Taiwan)
CTV	Taiwan CTV (*Zhongshi*)
DOP	Department of Propaganda
FDI	Foreign Direct Investment
KBS	Korea Broadcasting Station of the Republic of Korea
KRW	Korean Won
MBC	Munhwa Broadcasting Station of the Republic of Korea
PRC	People's Republic of China
RMB	*Renminbi* (Chinese Yuan)
ROK	Republic of Korea, or South Korea
SAPPRFT	State Administration of Press, Publication, Radio, Film, and Television
SARFT	State Administration of Radio, Film, and Television
SBS	Seoul Broadcasting Station of the Republic of Korea
THAAD	Terminal High Altitude Area Defense
USD	US Dollar
WTO	World Trade Organization

List of Figures

LIST OF TABLES

CHAPTER 1

Introduction

Setting the Scene: China's Global Rise and Image Dilemma

"China is a sleeping giant. Let her sleep, for when she wakes she will shake the world." Napoleon Bonaparte staked this claim nearly two centuries ago, and today we observe an awakened China. On the 50th anniversary of Sino-French diplomatic relations in 2014, Chinese President Xi Jinping announced that, "Today, the lion has woken up." He quickly added, "But it is peaceful, pleasant and civilized." At this celebration of international ties, the Chinese leader underscored that the rise of China, the woken lion, is neither a danger nor harm to you.

In contrast with Xi's message, two contradictory and seminal advertisements by *The Economist* had already been circulating, which I encountered at King's Cross Station in London in June 2011, while waiting for the underground train in order to attend a conference on China. The advertisements were contrastively titled, "China is a Friend to the West" and "China is a Threat to the West" (see Gilroy 2011; Wade 2011).

The advertisement entitled "China is a Friend to the West" has three claims: (1) China makes a fifth of all the world's goods. It kits out the West's consumers and finances the West's borrowers; (2) China goes out of its way to emphasize that it wants a "peaceful rise." No other great power in history has done that; and (3) China is the world's biggest investor in green technology. On the other hand, "China is a Threat to the West" has three claims: (1) China spends about $100 billion on defense,

© The Author(s) 2018
C. S. Lee, *Soft Power Made in China*,
https://doi.org/10.1007/978-3-319-93115-9_1

almost three times as much as a decade ago, and nearly twice as much as Britain; (2) China has cracked down on minorities in Tibet and Xinjiang and persecuted campaigners like the Nobel Laureate, Liu Xiaobo; and (3) China's hunger for raw materials is exhausting the Earth and bolstering corrupt regimes in the developing world (The Economist 2011).

Framed to reflect two leading and opposing images of the People's Republic of China (PRC) that are circulating internationally, the advertisements depict both "China as an Opportunity" and "China as a Threat" (Cable and Ferdinand 1994; Zheng 2005). The perception of China as a dual source of opportunities and threats is predominantly a result of its worldwide geo-economic ascendancy, complicated by its creeping geopolitical expansionism in the Asian region. This Janus face of China's global rise reflects the coexistence of hopes and fears growing among other countries.

Cognizant of this situation, the official Xinhua News Agency—in advance of Xi's speech to present China as a peacefully rising country, to counter geopolitical anxiety—released a publicity film on the national image (*Guojia xingxiangpian*) of China for the first time in New York City's Times Square (People's Daily 2010; Reuters 2011). This was to coincide with former President Hu Jintao's state visit to the United States (Ministry of Foreign Affairs 2011).

Not only did it reflect China's endeavor to promote its soft power—which refers to "the ability to affect others through the co-optive means of framing the agenda, persuading, and eliciting positive attraction in order to obtain preferred outcomes" (Nye 2011)—but it also hints at the recent development of the Chinese media system and the production of media products along China's "going global" geocultural strategy.[1]

Views of China as a threat, a fragile power (Shirk 2007), or the partial power (Shambaugh 2013) still prevail, even though China's twenty-first-century leaders Hu Jintao and Xi Jinping have developed strategies for casting the PRC as a peacefully rising nation with desirable soft power offerings. Such ambivalent views of China exist not only in the West, but are also prevalent in Asia.

How would China, as an emerging superpower under an authoritarian regime, continue its ascendancy in the long run? One of the key elements may lie beyond sustaining its economic and societal development at home. Its continued growth is also stringently contingent upon mastering a way of communicating with others, via the formal and informal emulation of its soft power abroad. Attempts to account for this dilemma necessitate an understanding of the general predicament that China, as an emerging power under soft authoritarianism, faces in the task of building its soft power influence around the world. Since the early 2000s, China has developed a plan. But the ability of the PRC to convert its growing economic power into cultural influence in Asia and around the globe (Callahan 2013: 1) needs more work. China thus faces a dilemma with the geocultural projection of its soft power.

This book takes an unconventional approach to explain the untold truth of the aforementioned endeavors, to make sense of China's dilemmas with projecting its soft power on an ambitious international scale. *Soft Power Made in China* focuses particularly on the setbacks in China's effort to create a soft power field in East Asia, particularly South Korea and Japan, via the mediation of television products.

SOFT POWER BUILDING IN THE RISE OF CHINA

The recent history of the PRC's soft power engagements reflects its ambition to push China's global reach. It also underscores how the definition of the nation's wealth has undergone transformation, from a purely economic conceptualization to the inclusion of cultural wealth (State Council 2001; 2006; 2011).

In the first decade of the twenty-first century, during President Hu Jintao's administration (2002–2010), the Chinese government conceptually mapped the country's present and projected future in three Five-Year Plans: the Tenth (2001–2005), Eleventh (2006–2010), and Twelfth (2011–2015) Five-Year Plans. In 2004, the Tenth Five-Year Plan (2001–2005) proposed a strategic call for culturally "going global" (*wenhua "zouchuqu"*). In the plan, the term "cultural industries" (*wenhua chanye*) was first introduced and incorporated in a Chinese governmental project. Some scholars interpret the Tenth Five-Year Plan as the beginning of preparations for a system to export cultural products through the next Five-Year Plan (Esraey and Qiang 2011; Hong 2011; Su 2011).

In line with its global strategy, during the years of the Tenth Five-Year Plan (2001–2005) the Chinese government began promoting Chinese language and culture by establishing Confucius Institutes, which many scholars read as a means of developing China's soft power around the world (Cheng 2009; Chey 2008; Gil 2008; Hartig 2010; Hughes 2014; Lee 2009; Nye 2004; Paradise 2009; Starr 2009; Yang 2010). The East Asian region was strategically considered a test bed for such institutes.[2] The first Confucius Institute was established in Seoul in 2004, and the second in Tokyo the year after (Lee 2009). By 2013, there were more than 400 Institutes in over 100 countries (Confucius Institute Headquarters (*Hanban*) 2013), reflecting China's conviction about implementing its "going global" policy. As of December 2017, 525 Confucius Institutes and 1113 Confucius Classrooms exist in 146 countries (Confucius Institute Headquarters (*Hanban*) n.d.).

Subsequently, the Eleventh Five-Year Plan (2006–2010) focused on promoting Chinese culture (*zhonghua wenhua*) in a more explicit way as a means of enhancing China's influence around the world (*guoji yingxiangli*) and to project its cultural soft power (*wenhua ruanshili*). In July 2009, the State Council announced "A Plan for Promoting the Cultural Industries of China" (*Wenhuachanye zhenxingguihua*).

The Twelfth Five-Year Plan (2011–2015) emphasized China's rise to "cultural superpower" status with socialist characteristics (*Shehuizhuyi wenhua qiangguo*), making transparent its ambition of projecting both cultural soft power (*wenhua ruanshili*) and Chinese competitive cultural power (*Zhonghuawenhua de guojijingzhengli*) to build a "socialist cultural power" (*shehuizhuyi wenhuaqiangguo*). This plan asserts the importance of the cultural industries as a pillar industrial sector for the first time (Hong 2011), signaling that the Chinese central government views the cultural industries as a basic element in steering the country's economic development further.

In the Thirteenth Five-Year Plan (2016–2020), more focus is placed upon balanced development for building the nation into a cultural superpower. This plan includes strategies for developing traditional and new media, going culturally global, framing the cultural industry as a key industry, as well as preparing for the Winter Olympics (State Council 2016).

The state's ambition to develop Chinese soft power was presented in the context of furthering comprehensive national power (*zonghe guoli*) and the international competitiveness and influence of Chinese culture (*Zhonghuawenhua de guoji jingzhengli* and *yingxiangli*). The document also clearly indicates that the construction of a socialist cultural power requires a strengthening of cultural soft power, promotion of Chinese culture, and sustained cultural development with Chinese characteristics.

Having considered the development of China's policies along its ambition of internationally projecting soft power, attention will now turn to the empirical focus of this book with regard to the target countries of South Korea and Japan.

PATHWAYS TO CHINA'S TELEVISED SOFT POWER DILEMMA: SEARCHING FOR AN EXPLANATION FOR THE PUZZLE

In recent years, the study of China's soft power has become an academic fad and received great scholarly attention. The overseas expansion of Chinese media as part of China's "soft power" drive has emerged as a hot topic in media studies over the past decade (Zhao 2013: 6). Many works, which investigate *how* China projects its soft power, have appeared in disciplines such as political science, international relations, public diplomacy, and, more recently, media and communications studies. Less attention has been paid to *why* and how China's soft power works, *or not*. This book aims to tackle this simple but relatively unanswered question in the emerging field of soft power studies. To this end, this book presents an empirically grounded and comparative account that China's soft power strategy is targeting its audiences via media products.

Television products are arguably the most powerful medium of soft power among all types of media. There is evidence in the cases of America, Japan, and South Korea, and that of the telenovela. Aspiring to equip itself with a soft power reach proportional to its growing influence in economic, diplomatic and military arenas, China has been developing a domestic market and an ability to produce Chinese dramas of higher quality. Not only focusing upon domestic development, China has also, more importantly, worked on an export strategy for its television series.

This book explores the ways in which, and in what context, China's soft power fails to win over its audiences in the neighboring East Asian countries along its mediatized soft power strategy. Throughout this book, I use television series as a key soft power resource in the media realm, and refer to their influence as "mediatized soft power." The dilemma is that, despite the massive production of media products and the growing exports in the region, the influence of Chinese soft power has lacked proportional growth. In search of answers as to why this dilemma has occurred, this book addresses the following puzzles: Under what conditions and mechanisms would China's soft power via media experience a dilemma? How does the control of the Chinese government hinder China's turning into a successful soft power actor? What kind of actors do exist under such mechanisms? What are the processes and mechanisms of the predicament China's media faces, in projecting its soft power across South Korea and Japan? These questions probe the ways in which China's soft power is domestically produced and received in South Korea and Japan along different media circuits.

Pathways to (Dual) Dilemmas

For a country to fully realize its potential to wield soft power via projection and connection to potential audiences, it requires a well-designed process to come full circle. Such processes can be understood as media circuits, along which media products travel from production in one source country, to circulation (import, export), to reception in a receiving country. I argue that China's soft power dilemma is not a one-time problem. Rather, it is a problem that results from a chain of dilemmas, closely intertwined with the media circuit from production to reception. At the production level, a discrepancy between plans/infrastructures and reality inhibits China from effectively and successfully projecting its soft power. The ways in which "information" and the "content" of China's television series are controlled can be understood as the results of state "propaganda" and "censorship" mechanisms. Most of the content is censored to standards of the State Administration of Press, Publication, Radio, Film and Television (SAPPRFT)—formerly known as the State Administration of Radio, Film, and Television (SARFT)—to be able to cater to its own Chinese population. Yet, these same products are the ones being exported to foreign countries.

My overarching argument about the dilemma of cross-national soft power projection is that China, as a source country, has institutionalized barriers that limit its soft power projection. The processes and dynamics that I term "a pathway (or circuit) to a soft power dilemma" refer to the process by which the Chinese state has experienced its soft power projection as a broken chain of institutionalized paradoxes that come between its aspiration for projecting soft power and reality. This book illuminates the three main pathways along which soft power dilemmas have become instrumentalized into a constant circuit: (1) *Production* through *censorship* managed by the Chinese government to produce "healthy" media content; (2) *Circulation* through the gatekeeping role of media practitioners; and (3) *Consumption and reception*, and the paradoxes of historicized and politicized media products and unintentionally *outsourced* soft power, with co-ethnic and shared languages between the PRC, Hong Kong, and Taiwan. I argue that another dilemma of Chinese televised soft power in quasi-Sinophone East Asia is twofold. On the one hand, the dilemma lies in the unintended partial success of China's soft power in quasi-Sinophone East Asia with the help of Hong Kong and Taiwan. South Korean and Japanese audiences do not always differentiate the origin of products and

PRC products benefit from masked identities. However, in the long run, this would lead to an important, yet ignored dilemma and paradox that China's soft power encounters. This illuminates how the process of uniting resources, strategies, industries together to build China's soft power via media is hard to translate into a practice. On another hand, whereas cyberspace and digital media consumption are on the rise for ethnic Chinese communities living in South Korea and Japan, and Korean and Japanese people, new paradoxes emerge in the ways in which the flow of products, services, and platforms are manufactured and censored. Thus, there are hidden flaws in the blessing of digital media as a new platform for extending China's soft power in a transnational soft power field.

Along these lines, I contend that China's television series lack sophisticated *toolkits*, which leads the Chinese state to experience dilemmas with wielding soft power. The dilemmas include (1) a *discrepancy* between the forms of capital in the source country and those of the importing country and (2) a *lack of healthy conversion* between different forms of capital, to reach transnational audiences under non-authoritarian regimes (Fig. 1.1).

A Transnational Soft Power Field and Different Forms of Capital

"A transnational soft power field"—a soft power concept derived from an extension of Bourdieu's field of cultural production, Nakajima's extended theory, and Fligstein and Adam's field theory—focuses upon the production of soft power products in the source country and audiences in the receiving countries. This conceptual framework is useful for understanding why and how China's soft power struggles to reach East Asian

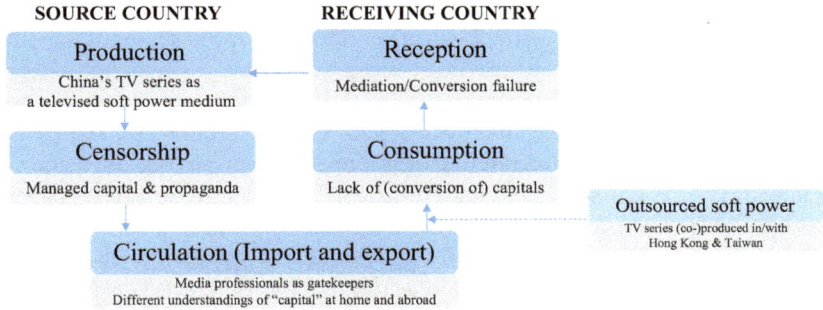

Fig. 1.1 Pathways to a dilemma of China's televised soft power

audiences, by elucidating the process and actors at local, trans-local, and transnational levels. Audiences are particularly important for the transnational soft power field as actors who are influenced as a consequence of the social actions—soft power projection—of China.

Borrowing from and extending Bourdieu's forms of capital, in this study I modify and develop different forms of capital: cultural capital, linguistic capital, political capital, celebrity capital, aesthetic capital, and virtual capital. Unlike Bourdieu's own study on capital and class, which applies the concept of capital at the personal level, I use these types of capital to contextualize, examine, and analyze Chinese TV series as a potentially powerful channel of soft power on a transnational level.

Political capital is a form of political knowledge or political influence that is embedded within the series (Bühlmann et al. 2013: 216). In the context of post-socialist authoritarian China, this can be ideological, educational, party-related content, as well as all formats and elements of propaganda. *Economic capital* is a value to be converted into economic returns or revenue from television drama production. In a transnational televisual soft power field, audience rating, market value, and product value in China and in the importing countries turn into economic capital in both the source and importing countries. *Cultural capital* refers to a form of knowledge utilized to appreciate or decipher cultural relations and cultural artifacts (Bourdieu 1993: 7). In the case of Chinese television series, history, as an important element of cultural knowledge, and its embodiment of cultural and linguistic capital is particularly important for South Korean and Japanese audiences in a transnational soft power field. In the source country, cultural capital can be converted to political capital, whereas in receiving countries the cultural capital is a tool for learning Chinese history and culture, as well as Chinese language, and not always viewed as political. *Aesthetic capital* consists of the beautified elements in the series. What the local audiences of Chinese television series recognize as aesthetic capital and convert it to might be different from those of transnational audiences in the importing countries, due to differences in definitions and standards of beauty. *Celebrity capital* refers to the popularity or strong presence of celebrities in the Chinese televisual subfields. There might be a discrepancy in the conversion of celebrity capital between the source and importing countries, again due to regional distinctions in the popularity of featured celebrities. *Virtual capital* is defined as the manner in which Chinese television series are consumed via online access and cyberspaces. Platforms such as streaming websites, smartphone applications, and websites, as well as digital media are spaces for cultivating virtual capital. These platforms are easy to access from anywhere and are continually growing. For young people, in particular, connectivity to spaces that have virtual capital are high access at low cost. In the transnational soft power field of China, these seemingly value-free platforms are oftentimes operated and influenced by the Chinese authorities, and the platforms and digital media where people can access Chinese television series are also controlled. Thus, the access value of Chinese television series via digital platforms, media, and televisual products might not always be realized, and this is not always easy to convert to virtual capital.

METHODS AND FIELDSITES: EAST ASIA IN THE EYE OF CHINA'S BEHOLDERS

Case Selections: East Asia

From a perspective of communities with shared language and culture, East Asia is divided into "Sinophone" Chinese-speaking communities, and "non-Sinophone" communities.[3] The "Sinophone world" refers to "a network of places of cultural production outside China and on the margins of China and Chineseness, where a historical process of heterogenizing and localizing continental Chinese culture has been taking place for several centuries" (Shih 2007: 4). Research endeavors regarding media audiences in Chinese societies (e.g. Sun 2006) have put forward the importance of soft power studies on China to further nourish the field. However, there is simultaneously a void of attention to the reception of Chinese media and the influence of soft power in non-Chinese societies, or the non-Sinophone world. In this book, I term South Korea and Japan as quasi-Sinophone East Asia. At a first glance, these two countries are non-Chinese societies and thus can be understood as regions of the non-Sinophone world. However, these nation-states share and are influenced by Chinese language, history, and culture from earlier periods, quasi-Sinophone East Asia characterizes these two societies better. Thus, I primary explore quasi-Sinophone East Asia, specifically examining South Korea and Japan as the two primary receiving countries of China's soft power. On the other hand, I approach Hong Kong and Taiwan as locations within Sinophone East Asia potentially serving as China's soft power targets, as well as producers of its outsourced soft power.

China's two important neighboring countries, South Korea and Japan, offer interesting but comparable case studies for analyzing China's soft power dilemma and its potential audiences. There have been concerted and institutionalized efforts by China to project its soft power across these two countries, making them veritable "testing points" (*shidian*) of such targeting. The first example of this state-led effort has been the establishment of more than 400 Confucius Institutes around the world with the ambition of combining language and culture as instruments of soft power. The first Confucius Institute (CI) was set up in Seoul in 2004 and the second was established in Tokyo in the following year (Lee 2009, 2015).

On an empirical and educational front, South Korea and Japan are the top source countries of international students, studying Chinese language in China. Language is an important gateway and soft power medium (Ding 2011; Nye 2011). Although this percentage of Korean and Japanese students has been decreasing over a decade (2004–2014), South Korea still remains the country that has sent the largest number of students to China, and Japan remains among the top five source countries (see Fig. 1.2).

Secondly, a more recent publication of the Ministry of Culture (2012) indicates an expansive, institutionalized approach to projecting Chinese soft power onto Hong Kong, Macau, and Taiwan, its neighbors South Korea and Japan, Southeast Asia, Europe, the Americas and Africa (see Fig. 1.3). In particular, the main export targets for China's soft power are

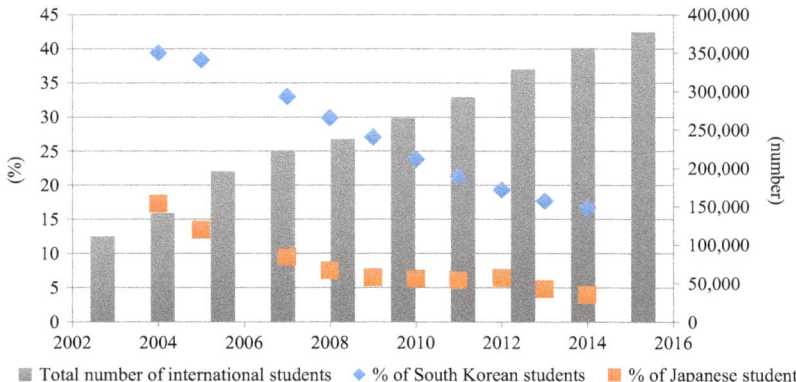

Fig. 1.2 China's international students from East Asia. Source: Institute of International Education (2016)

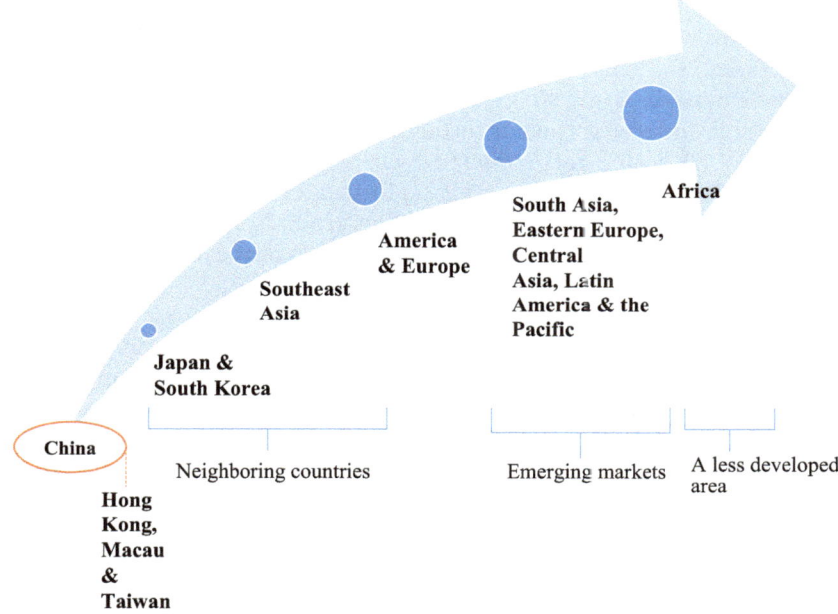

Fig. 1.3 The contours of the projection of Chinese soft power: institutionalized targets and objectives. Source: Ministry of Culture (2011; 2012). Note: This figure is based on an argument from the Ministry of Culture (2011). For the part regarding Hong Kong, Macau, and Taiwan, see the Ministry of Culture (2012)

Hong Kong, Taiwan, Japan, South Korea, and other Asian regions (Italian Trade Commission 2011).

Lastly, along the PRC's "One China" policy, Hong Kong and Taiwan are politically classified as part of China. However, looking from the perspective of media industry development in Greater China, these Sinophone East Asian communities have their own spheres of development, production, and consumers. Simultaneously, co-production between the PRC and Hong Kong, as well as cross-strait co-production between the PRC and Taiwan, have not only taken place, but share flows of capital and celebrities. Thus, joint media productions have become the industry norm in Greater China.

Considering China's efforts in establishing the first two CIs abroad in South Korea and Japan, as well as China serving as a home for the most international students from these two countries studying China and Chinese language, South Korea and Japan are ideal locations for studying Chinese soft power experiments through other platforms. Given the afore-mentioned rationales and contextual factors that make it possible for China's soft power to land in East Asia, the nearest neighboring countries of South Korea and Japan offer compelling grounds for looking into rea-sons behind why China's soft power drive via media does not par in excellence. Despite these efforts and strategized plans, South Korea and Japan are nuanced and interesting places to study the Chinese soft power dilemma. In the PRC's official plan, Hong Kong and Taiwan are also cat-egorized as soft power targets. However, these Sinophone communities have additional potential for playing an important role in helping to proj-ect PRC soft power to quasi-Sinophone East Asia or elsewhere. This book finds that China's soft power dilemma occurs in both quasi-Sinophone East Asia, with limited penetration, and in Sinophone East Asia with the aid of outsourced soft power.

Fieldwork and Data

Qualitative interviewing and archival research serve as valuable method-ological tools per the exploratory nature of this work. In particular, these approaches allow for understanding underlying mechanisms and reasons why Chinese soft power via media has encountered a series of dilemmas in target countries. This methodology provides opportunities for the researcher to attend to cultural and local meanings and explanations that are embedded in the receiving countries of China's soft power.

This book draws primarily from in-depth interviews that I conducted in the source and receiving countries of PRC soft power—China, Hong Kong, Taiwan, South Korea, and Japan. The majority of this research con-ducted was between November 2011 and July 2012, followed by subse-quent fieldwork trips in the summer and winter of 2013, October 2014, summer of 2015, and July 2016 (see Appendix A).[4]

Entry into the media industry as an outsider is particularly difficult, especially if the researcher is not local (Lee et al. 2006).[5] The issue of gain-ing access to the industry is a constant challenge, yet significantly impor-tant and time-consuming (Bruun 2016; Munnik 2016). In this vein, my work experience in the media industry played an important role in gaining access to potential interviewees. I, as a coordinator and interpreter of Chinese and Korean languages, have worked in the television industry in Hong Kong in 2008, and in the film industry in Taiwan in 2009 alongside colleagues hailing from China, Hong Kong, Taiwan, South Korea, and Japan. This not only helped me to become familiar with the industry, which is known to be a closed one, but also opened the door to former colleagues for introductions to media professionals in my fieldsite countries.

To explore China as a country set on exporting soft power, field research was carried out in four Chinese cities: Beijing, Guangzhou, Shanghai, and Shenzhen from December 2011 to July 2012, August 2013 (Beijing), December 2013 (Shanghai), and summer 2016 (Beijing, Hong Kong, and Shenzhen). In order to investigate how China's media is produced and exported through its television products, I interviewed thirty-two media practitioners in media and broadcasting companies and TV stations.

Field research in South Korea was largely conducted in metropolitan Seoul from mid-November 2011 to January 2012, in mid-March 2012, November 2014, and spring 2015. Seoul, the capital of South Korea, was selected for gathering a comprehensive, varied sample of consumers of Chinese media products. Field research in Japan was carried out in Tokyo and Yokohama from March to May 2012. Tokyo, the capital of Japan, provides a representative sample of interviewees. Yokohama, on the other hand, was chosen for its Chinatown, which hosts an immense Chinese population (Shu 1999). To obtain interviews, informants were recruited and snowballed via my personal network along with the informants' own introductions.

Two main groups of informants were interviewed in the receiving countries. One group of informants was comprised of media practitioners. Fifteen Japanese and seventeen Korean media practitioners were interviewed for two main reasons. First, access to different ranks of media practitioners can provide diverse and detailed views on the media production process. Second, it is important to include media professionals who are serving different positions in this media circuit, to understand the multifaceted and interactive nature of the processes and operations of media markets. Specifically, different types of media companies and TV stations have their own practices and unwritten guidelines.

Another group of informants were audiences and non-consumers of Chinese media products. Eighty-eight Korean audience members and fifty-nine Japanese audience members of Chinese media products were interviewed. These informants were chosen for the following reasons.

First, it is not a coincidence that most of the surveys on the media are largely sourced from young people. For surveys on media consumption and its effects, viewers between the ages of eighteen and forty-nine are very important. This is the age group that tends to have the most influence on public opinion and trends in consumption patterns. Thus, as any kind of influence coming from soft power through media is likely to affect this demographic it is crucial that it is given preference in surveys. Second, the sample used in this study consists of educated respondents. Given that South Korea and Japan have relatively higher populations of university degree-holders, the choice of younger generation respondents for this study did not create a significant educational bias. According to the World Bank (2011), Japan has a tertiary enrollment rate of 60 percent. The college entrance rate in 2012 for South Korea was 71.3 percent (Statistics Korea 2013: 31). Thus, it can be surmised that educated respondents are likely to have a larger influence on discourses of Chinese soft power, within the receiving countries. Lastly, the developmental pattern of Chinese media and the characteristics of young people signify valid reasons to select people in their 20s and 30s as the primary informants. On one end of the media circuit, they are arguably trend influencers, and enjoy being in the transnational consumption circuit. They also have a selective educational rapport with culture and language, in a cosmopolitan sense, and thus are the potential targets of soft power. On the other end, they are potential consumers of future, more highly developed Chinese media. Thus, they are generally considered agents of social, cultural, and global transformation, interacting with an influx of diversity and multiculturalism in their daily lives.

In addition to interviews, published statistics and local materials including government documents, newspaper articles, commercial magazines, posters, and pamphlets in Chinese, as well as locally published scholarly works in Chinese, Japanese, Korean, and English were collected for further analysis throughout the course of my fieldwork. These materials were analyzed through mixed methods, including content analysis, discourse analysis, and statistical analysis. During and after my fieldwork, I collected detailed information on imported Chinese television series from multiple websites and kept such information up to date, as current as 2016 (Appendix A). I supplemented my fieldwork with interviews with scholars, media professionals in the film industry,[6] journalists (China, Hong Kong, Taiwan, South Korea, Japan), scholars who research global and Chinese media and communication as well as different platforms of soft power, and

Chinese audiences in China, Singapore, South Korea, to achieve a fuller picture of Chinese views on soft power policies, media products, and consumption patterns as reference points. I conducted archival research on the topics of globalization, mediatized soft power, and China's global influence in the context of the changing world order.

China's policies and practices in general vary from place to place. Yet, when it comes to its soft power strategies and practices, they are largely state-coordinated, centralized, and top-down. This book, using two main receiving countries of China's soft power in quasi-Sinophone East Asia, draws broader implications for China's soft power dilemma and its outsourcing of soft power. It also juxtaposes different television industry circuits to shape a transnational soft power field (between source and receiving countries).

ROADMAP TO THE PATHWAYS AND THE DILEMMAS IN THE CIRCUIT OF MEDIA

In the following pages, this book explores the process by which China's soft power dilemma is formed in East Asia, which traverses the stages of production, censorship, circulation, and consumption of television products.

The dilemma of China's soft power influence is staked upon export regulations and different forms of capital that result from policies and censorship on the side of the PRC. It is also due to unintentionally manufactured capital ("propaganda for exports") in its contents, "controlled" circulation, and the local decisions of importing countries. As transnational media consumption serves as an essential basis and practice for projecting China's soft power, its successful accomplishment on the global stage necessitates greater attention to public opinion, making transnational communities important.

Part I explores the pathways of China's soft power via television series in East Asia. On the one hand, focus is on the production and circulation of Chinese television series that manufacture its soft power. On the other hand, the dimensions of consumption and reception of China's soft power by transnational audiences is also analyzed.

Chapter 2 provides context for the development of China's soft power by highlighting the embrace of culture in its developmental path during different historical phases, and contextualizes China's TV industry as both a soft powerhouse and a transnational soft power field to explore the ways in which soft power is exerted from source to receiving countries. While mass producing commercialized television series for domestic and Sinophone audiences, the state gradually realized the potential value of the export of television series and expanded to overseas markets. A concerted effort for China's soft power development via TV products is intertwined with local and global forces. Internally, the industry has undergone reforms, such as media commercialization, and experienced regulation to control content and its flow (i.e. censorship). Externally, the Chinese state has put forward strategies for culturally "going global" that have become cornerstones of the state's soft power projection since the 2000s.

Chapter 3 analyzes the role of media marketplaces and practitioners who reluctantly bring Chinese media products into their markets. This chapter explores the ways in which media products, which wield a considerable amount of potential soft power influence, are controlled and managed by the state, media institutions, and the market demands of the importing countries. In both South Korea and Japan, media professionals function not as cultural intermediaries, but as gatekeepers. The South Korean government, in particular, usually regulates foreign commercial media products in order to avert its citizens from unnecessary exposure to foreign countries, which may have negative effects on Korean society. The Japanese government, on the other hand, employs far less state regulation. Evidence also shows that foreign media products are not only managed by market structures and the engagement of media practitioners, but they are also filtered by the market demands of the importing society. As such, China's effort to build its soft power by exporting Chinese media products is constrained by foreign markets and media practitioners.

Chapter 4 comparatively explores contexts that China's soft power, via TV series, fails to reach among South Korean and Japanese audiences. For this exploration, I define "domestification," which refers to the ways in which certain kinds of media programs can be watched domestically or at home, as the characteristic of local embeddedness that occurs in both the source and receiving countries. This highlights domestic factors that further inhibit the foreign export of Chinese TV series, and suggests conditions under which such inhibitions could be overcome in the importing country. Whereas Korean audiences highly associate Chinese TV series with historical capital, but also a lack of high economic and cultural capital, Japanese audiences see Chinese TV series as highly politicized but with low cultural and economic capital.

Chapter 5 pays more attention to the mechanisms behind China's soft power failure, which are embedded in the lack cf convergence between cultural capital (language and culture) and economic and celebrity capital. Although there are a large number of Korean and Japanese people who are learning Chinese languages, there is a loss of translation in the ability to convert the fever for Chinese language and (traditional) culture into cultural and media consumption, which are lynchpins of soft power.

Part II turns in to take a closer look at the (potential) paradox of China's soft power vis-à-vis "outsourced soft power." Chapter 6 examines another dilemma of China's soft power building: Hong Kong and Taiwan's function as assistants in China's soft power projection—what I call "outsourced soft power." As an unintended consequence, PRC products from Hong Kong and Taiwan, or those co-produced with these sites, have reached South Korean and Japanese audiences. The unexpected gain of soft power influence for China with the help of products from Hong Kong and Taiwan might be a blessing. However, in the long run, this might evolve problematically into a competitive soft power ambush and produce surprise rivals for the PRC.

Chapter 7 explores another dimension of outsourced Chinese soft power in the realm of new and digital media. Whereas traditional consumption of television series on a physical television set is on the shrink, many—particularly young—people watch television series on devices. Against this backdrop, this chapter examines and asks how digital media and platforms emerge as a new, popular way of outsourcing Chinese soft power in a virtual transnational soft power field. Along this line, the mode of consumption creates "virtual capital," which is a form of capital tied to the virtual characteristics of television series. While Korean and Japanese people look for "free" virtual capital—no cost and uncensored in their countries—they rather often come across censored and manufactured virtual capital. On the other hand, ethnic Chinese communities living in South Korea and Japan are able to connect to platforms and apps that link them back to their homeland. As such, by using a similar set of virtually capitalized television series, locals and foreigners in the importing countries operate divergent pathways/strategies to the practice of outsourced Chinese soft power in a transnational soft power field at the margins.

Part III presents conclusions of the book and possible research areas for further investigation regarding theory, method and comparison. This part also presents envisioning the future of China's soft power.

The Conclusion brings China's soft power dilemma together along different circuits of media and different countries. The chapter returns to the question of what and why dual paradoxes of China's soft power exist via televisual products in the two closest geographically and culturally proximal importing countries—South Korea and Japan occur. It presents broader implications for findings and research areas for further comparative investigation. As building soft power requires constant and continuous effort, and is time-consuming, as well as rather unpredictable and largely dependent upon its audience, different models of soft power in developed countries—in particular the United States, Japan, South Korea—are important to discuss. By bridging locally sourced and outsourced soft power nodes within China's soft power strategy, and considering China's offline and online platforms together with media, we can not only better understand the value of soft power and the un/intended consequences of China's rise in the newly established world order, but we can also envision the future in which China may better position its global status and wield its soft power in the quasi- and non-Sinophone world, as well as in Chinese communities across the globe. This chapter ends with future imaginings on China's soft power development and continuous dilemma in the post-THAAD era where politics and the socio-cultural realm intersect.

NOTES

1. *Zouchuqu* can be translated as both "going global," in its liberal translation, and "going out" in its literal translation. The preference in this study is for the former expression because it engages with the transnational phenomenon of globalization.
2. However, the existing literature does not usually address such gaps that I note here. Attempts to consider soft power in a comparative context have yet to be explored. Regarding the Confucius Institutes, there is no research on how other countries perceive them, or China as their source.
3. This may be arguable in that Japan and South Korea have used Chinese characters to a certain extent, particularly in their premodern societies. However, there is no doubt that the Japanese and Korean languages have developed their own writing systems and Shih's discussion does not include the two countries; therefore, I would delineate Japan and South Korea as belonging to the quasi-Sinophone world.
4. Prior to conducting field research, prospective key informants were contacted via email (Emerson et al. 2011). Preliminary studies were conducted

in Beijing in December 2011, Seoul in November 2011, and Tokyo in February 2012.

5. In line with the argument, see Lee et al. (2006) on the difficulty of researching Chinese newspapers.

6. It is important to consider data from the Chinese film industry because there is a practice of boundary blending between cultural and media industries. In South Korea, the boundaries between the TV industry and the film industry, in terms of (creative) labor, are relatively rigid with not much overlap between different sectors. In China, however, such boundaries with regard to media personnel could be blurred. For instance, those who work primarily in TV could easily switch to film for future projects.

References

Bourdieu, Pierre. 1993. *The Field of Cultural Production: Essays on Art and Literature*. New York: Columbia University Press and Polity Press.

Bruun, Hanne. 2016. The Qualitative Interview in Media Production Studies. In *Advancing Media Production Research: Shifting Sites, Methods, and Politics*, ed. Chris Paterson, David Lee, Anamik Saha, and Anna Zollner, 131–146. New York: Palgrave Macmillan.

Bühlmann, Felix, Thomas David, and André Mach. 2013. Cosmopolitan Capital and the Internationalization of the Field of Bussiness Elites: Evidence from the Swiss Case. *Cultural Sociology* 7 (2): 211–229.

Cable, Vincent, and Peter Ferdinand. 1994. China as an Economic Giant: Threat or Opportunity? *International Affairs* 70 (2): 243–261.

Callahan, William A. 2013. *China Dreams: 20 Visions of the Future*. New York: Oxford University Press.

Cheng, Xu. 2009. Education: The Intellectual Base of China's Soft Power. In *Soft Power: China's Emerging Strategy in International Politics*, ed. Mingjiang Li, 103–124. Lanham, Boulder, New York, Toronto and Plymouth: Lexington Books.

Chey, Jocelyn. 2008. Chinese 'Soft Power': Cultural Diplomacy and the Confucius Institutes. *The Sydney Papers* 20 (1): 32–46.

Confucius Institute Headquarters [Hanban]. 2013. *Kongzixueyuan Niandu Fazhanbaogao [Confucius Institute Annual Development Report 2013]*. Accessed March 10, 2017. http://www.hanban.edu.cn/report/2013.pdf.

———. n.d. *Guanyu Kongzixueyuan/ketang [About Confucius Institutes/Classrooms]*. Accessed March 10, 2018. http://www.hanban.edu.cn/confuciousinstitutes/node_10961.htm.

Ding, Sheng. 2011. Branding a Rising China: An Analysis of Beijing's National Image Management in the Age of China's Rise. *Journal of Asian and African Studies* 46 (3): 293–306.

Emerson, Robert M., Rachel I. Fretz, and Linda L. Shaw. 2011. *Writing Ethnographic Fieldnotes.* Chicago: University of Chicago Press.

Esraey, Ashley, and Xiao Qiang. 2011. Digital Communication and Political Change. *International Journal of Communication* 5: 298–319.

Gil, Jeffrey. 2008. The Promotion of Chinese Language Learning and China's Soft Power. *Asian Social Science* 4 (10): 116–122.

Gilroy, Daniel. 2011. The Economist: Is China a Threat or a Friend? *ChinaSmack,* June 10. Accessed July 15, 2015. https://advertising.chinasmack.com/2011/the-economist-is-china-a-threat-or-a-friend.html.

Hartig, Falk. 2010. *Confusion about Confucius Institutes: Soft Power Push or Conspiracy? A Case Study of Confucius Institutes in Germany.* Paper presented at the 18th Biennial Conference of the Asian Studies Association of Australia in Adelaide, July 5–8.

Hong, Yu. 2011. Reading the Twelfth Five-Year Plan: China's Communication-Driven Mode of Economic Restructuring. *International Journal of Communication* 5: 1–20.

Hughes, Christopher R. 2014. Confucius Institutes and the University: Distinguishing the Political Mission from the Cultural. *Issues & Studies* 50 (4): 45–83.

Institute of International Education. 2016. *International Students in China.* Accessed March 23, 2016. http://www.iie.org/Services/Project-Atlas/China/International-Students-In-China.

Italian Trade Commission [Istituto nazionale per il Commercio Estero]. 2011. *China Television Industry Market Report.* June 3. Shanghai: Italian Trade Commission. Accessed November 30, 2013. http://www.ice.it/paesi/asia/cina/upload/174/CHINA%20TELEVISION%20INDUSTRY%20MARKET%20REPORT%202011.pdf.

Lee, Claire Seungeun. 2009. China's Cultural Diplomacy in the Hu Jintao Era: The Geocultural Role of the Confucius Institute. *Yonsei Journal of International Studies* 1 (1): 44–59.

———. 2015. A Comparative Study of Taiwan Academy and Confucius Institutes. *The Korean Journal of Area Studies* 33 (3): 147–167.

Lee, Chin-Chuan, Zhou He, and Yu Huang. 2006. 'Chinese Party Publicity Inc.' Conglomerated: The Case of the Shenzhen Press Group. *Media, Culture & Society* 28 (4): 581–602.

Ministry of Culture. 2011. *Wenhuabu guanyu cujin wenhuachanpin he fuwu "zouchuqu" 2011–2015 nian zongtiguihua [Ministry of Culture on the Promotion of Cultural Goods and Services "Going Out": 2011–2015 Overall Planning].* Beijing: Ministry of Culture.

———. 2012. *'Shi'erwu' shiqi wenhuachanye beizeng jihua [Plan to Make Cultural Industries Double during the '12th Five-Year' Period].* Beijing: Ministry of Culture.

Ministry of Foreign Affairs. 2011. *Hu Jintao Arrives in Washington, Kicking off His State Visit to the U.S.* January 19. Accessed August 21, 2012. http://www. fmprc.gov.cn/eng/topics/hjtzxdmgfw/t788243.htm.

Munnik, Michael B. 2016. When You Can't Rely on Public or Private: Using the Ethnographic Self as Resource. In *Advancing Media Production Research: Shifting Sites, Methods, and Politics*, ed. Chris Paterson, David Lee, Anamik Saha, and Anna Zoellner, 147–160. New York: Palgrave Macmillan.

Nye, Joseph. 2004. Soft Power and Higher Education. *Internet and the University Forum*. Accessed September 9, 2015. http://www educauseedu/ir/library/pdf/ffpiu043.

———. 2011. *The Future of Power*. New York: Public Affairs.

Paradise, James F. 2009. China and International Harmony: The Role of Confucius Institutes in Bolstering Beijing's Soft Power. *Asian Survey* 49 (4): 647–669.

People's Daily. 2010. *National Publicity Film to Boost Chinese Image*. July 30. Accessed June 22, 2012. http://english.peopledaily.com.cn/90001/90776/90882/7086378.html.

Reuters. 2011. *Zhongguo Xingxiangxuanchuanpian miaozhun 'ruan shili' dan liao nan gaibian meiguoren kanfa [China's Publicity Film for 'Soft Power,' It is Hard to Change Americans' Perception toward China]*. January 21. Accessed November 26, 2011. http://cn.reuters.com/article/CNAnalysesNews/idCNCHINA-3697220110121.

Shambaugh, David. 2013. *China Goes Global: The Partial Power*. Oxford and New York: Oxford University Press.

Shih, Shu-mei. 2007. *Visuality and Identity: Sinophone Articulations across the Pacific*. Berkeley: University of California Press.

Shirk, Susan. 2007. *China: Fragile Superpower: How China's Internal Politics Could Derail Its Peaceful Rise*. Oxford and New York: Oxford University Press.

Shu, Keirei. 1999. *Kakyō shakai no henbō to sono shōrai [Changes and Future of the Chinese Society]*. Kawaguchi: Duan Press.

Starr, Don. 2009. Chinese Language Education in Europe: The Confucius Institutes. *European Journal of Education* 44 (1): 65–82.

State Council. 2001. *Zhonghuarenmingongheguo guominjingji he shehuifazhan di shi ge wunian jihua gangyao* [The Tenth Five-Year Plan (2001–2005)]. Beijing: State Council.

———. 2006. *Zhonghuarenmingongheguo guominjingji he shehuifazhan di shiyi ge wunian guihua gangyao* [The Eleventh Five-Year Plan (2006–2010)]. Beijing: State Council.

———. 2011. *Zhonghuarenmingongheguo guominjingji he shehuifazhan di shi'er ge wunian guihua gangyao* [The Twelfth Five-Year Plan (2011–2015)]. Beijing: State Council.

———. 2016. *Zhonghuarenmingongheguo guominjingji he shehuifazhan di shisan ge wunian guihua gangyao* [The Thirteenth Five-Year Plan (2016–2020)]. Beijing: State Council.

Statistics Korea. 2013. *The Social Indicators of South Korea 2012*. Daejeon: Statistics Korea.

Su, Wendy. 2011. New Strategies of China's Film Industry as Soft Power. *Global Media and Communication* 6 (3): 317–322.

Sun, Wanning, ed. 2006. *Media and the Chinese Diaspora: Community, Communications and Commerce*. London: Routledge.

The Economist. 2011. *'China Is a Threat to the West' vs. 'China Is a Friend to the West'. Where Do You Stand? Campaign.*

Wade, Samuel. 2011. The Economist: China is a Threat to the West/China is a Friend to the West. *China Digital Times*, June 9. Accessed July 15, 2015. https://chinadigitaltimes.net/2011/06/the-economist-china-is-a-threat-to-the-westchina-is-a-friend-to-the-west/.

World Bank. 2011. *School Enrollment, Tertiary (% Gross)*. United Nations Educational, Scientific, and Cultural Organization (UNESCO) Institute for Statistics. Accessed May 15, 2013. https://data.worldbank.org/indicator/SE.TER.ENRR.

Yang, Rui. 2010. Soft Power and Higher Education: An Examination of China's Confucius Institutes. *Globalisation, Societies and Education* 8 (2): 235–245.

Zhao, Yuezhi. 2013. China's Quest for 'Soft Power': Imperatives, Impediments and Irreconcilable Tensions? *Javnost* 20 (4): 17–30.

Zheng, Bijian. 2005. China's 'Peaceful Rise' to Great-Power Status. *Foreign Affairs* 84 (5): 18–24.

PART I

Pathways to Soft Power

CHAPTER 2

China's Soft Power Building and Its TV Industry as a Soft Powerhouse

The extraordinary rise of China has produced significant global attention to this emerging power. The country is thus taking its image more seriously, both domestically and, to a greater extent, abroad. This has affected the orientation of China's policies, notably resulting in the twin strategy of "bringing in/absorbing" (*yinjinlai*, inward flow) and "going out" (*zouchuqu*, outward flow), which emphasizes the importance of both incoming and outgoing foreign investment. In this vein, engaging solely through "soft power" is not an easy task. The state agenda to wield China's soft power toward transnational audiences plays a potentially important role, but the policies supporting such vision require a set of both unwritten and written practices to achieve their purposes.

Analyzing Chinese soft power requires not only a comprehensive understanding of its core policy, but also a full grasp of its industrial development wherein generating soft power is an aim of the industry, as well as a mode for reproducing soft power. This chapter is essential for understanding how the Chinese state plans to achieve its soft power projection and to better elucidate the reality that China's soft power dilemma is tied to missing "toolkits." I frame the ultimate dilemma of soft power projection as an authoritarian and post-socialist China in the developmental stage.

In this chapter, I have two aims that are fundamentally connected to each other. First, I explore the issue of how the concept of soft power emerges alongside the country's industrial development, the evolution of "culture" in different government plans, and its evolving definition in the

© The Author(s) 2018
C. S. Lee, *Soft Power Made in China*,
https://doi.org/10.1007/978-3-319-93115-9_2

historical trajectory of post-socialist China.[1] Using Nye's concept of soft power as a baseline, I show that Chinese soft power is developed in notions of "culture," in its reproduction in Chinese discourse, as well as in China's institutionalizing cultural industry. I then demonstrate how China's television sector has developed as a newly established "soft powerhouse." This segment investigates China's involvement with commercial products and its approach to the export of television series. Finally, this chapter also contextualizes China's TV industry as a soft powerhouse, and theorizes the broader industry as a transnational "soft power field" by using a field framework that combines the theories of Fligstein, McAdam and Bourdieu to explore the ways in which soft power is exerted upon receiving countries, as well as to its source.

BUILDING SOFT POWER: BRINGING CULTURE BACK

China's economic and military growth—generally considered the product of a hard power policy (Nye 2005, 2011)—is recognized internationally. The unprecedented economic growth experienced by China has strengthened its aspiration to develop its cultural sectors. This is envisioned not only in terms of restructuring its internal cultural system, but also in projecting and diffusing its cultural soft power globally. Its cultural sector aspirations should be compatible with its economic power[2] to achieve a high level of comprehensive national power. In an attempt to explore the varying citations of "culture" in China's official discourse on building soft power, the following lines of inquiry will be highlighted. The first engages with industrial development and its supporting policies. It will be argued that the process by which China's soft power is built resonates with the other forms of Chinese industrial restructuring and development since the advent of its economic reform in 1978. In a related vein, the second line of inquiry highlights the involvement of key political figures and governmental bodies through a discourse analysis of China's soft power build-up. Both industrial developments and different stakeholders' involvements help to construct China's ambition of becoming "a culturally strong country (*wenhua qiangguo*)," through soft power building and the projection of a "better" image. The question of why culture needs to be brought back into the analysis of soft power is responded to here.

Secondly, it is important to consider how culture has been shaped and reinforced by industrial development. The path of industrial development has been both reinforced and reshaped by China's model of economic development dependency. Immediately after China's economic reform in the early 1990s, culture and cultural products were viewed as limited for the exclusive consumption of the citizenry. The cultural market, then, served domestic purposes. As industrial development expanded, the cultural industry entered the spotlight and strategically became a key pillar industry in 2001. This made it possible for this industry to enhance its infrastructure and become a system for "marketing culture," primarily along domestic purposes, with additional mechanisms tailored for exporting cultural goods to external audiences.

Third, how culture intersects with soft power is a significant juncture for understanding China's attempts at building soft power. The appropriation of culture in the official discourse on soft power is in line with the inclusion of the cultural industries as a platform on which culture is developed, and from which cultural influence is projected. In this sense, the building of soft power should be considered as a continuous process, rather than be regarded as having commenced exclusively during Hu's era (2003–2012). Throughout the years of Jiang Zemin and Hu Jintao, the field of soft power, including its enhancement and its international influence, has provided more than a mere testing ground for the implementation and dissemination of Chinese ideologies and culture to internal and external audiences.

More importantly, at a historical juncture in which China is bound to rise economically and militaristically, the country hopes to have a lasting cultural and "ideological" influence upon the world. As Thomas Friedman states, "China's main goal is to restore its greatness, what it sees as its place in history as a great economic power, a great cultural power, a great political and geopolitical power" (Friedman quoted in Pienovi 2010). As Chinese documents indicate, the government is aiming for an economic and political revival of the Chinese people and nation. China's infrastructural growth reflects a prevailing discourse on nation building, along with a nostalgic longing for an ancient, glorious past. With this understanding, then, the question needs to be posed: how can soft power assist China in its aspiration of becoming a strong cultural power?

China's Soft Power Strategy Under *Authoritarian* Rule

China, as a nation under an authoritarian regime, translates and projects its soft power onto other countries; in particular, non-authoritarian countries. How do we understand diffusions of soft power from authoritarian China, and what relevant distinctions should the Chinese state pay attention to?

Many theories about authoritarianism have focused on nondemocratic settings. In particular, these works and concepts look at how authoritarian governments control, facilitate, and negotiate to find a middle ground between citizens' wishes for democratic values and maintaining the regime ("modes of maintaining political power"). For example, responsive authoritarianism (Stockmann 2013), resilient authoritarianism (Nathan 2003), consultative authoritarianism (Truex 2017), and competitive authoritarianism (Levitsky and Way 2002). In sum, existing works explore questions about political regimes, the potential of and resistance to democratic power, and internal contestations around the authoritarian rules.

At the 18th National Congress of the Chinese Communist Party (CCP) in November 2012, President Hu Jintao of the People's Republic of China announced[3]:

> To complete the building of *Xiaokang* society[4] in all respects and achieve the great renewal of the Chinese nation, we must create a new surge in promoting socialist culture and bring about its great development and enrichment, increase China's cultural soft power, and enable culture to guide social trends, educate the people, serve society, and boost development. (Caixin 2012)

Notably, in examining the country's pursuit of greater soft power influence, the circumstances within China should be taken into account, for a unique feature characterizes China's soft power development and distinguishes it from soft power development in other countries. The 18th Party Congress was not the first occasion on which the CCP leader mentioned the idea of cultural soft power in an official speech to illustrate the central government's policy direction. Based on the Chinese government's logic and application of soft power, this chapter analyzes how the idea of "soft power" has developed along Chinese policies, and how it has become incorporated into soft power discourses over time. Unquestionably, the building of China's soft power aims to maintain internal stability and political legitimacy for internal and external purposes (Li 2008); soft power is something that the State desires.

In a 2008 speech, Li Changchun, the propaganda chief of the Communist Party of China (CCP), emphasized that the Chinese media needs to reinforce its communication capacity (*chuanbo nengli*).[5] He also pointed out that it is necessary for China to integrate culture, science and technology into advanced tools in order to enhance the creative, innovative, and communicative influence (*chuangxin nengli*) of its culture.[6] This message was reiterated during his visit to the Beijing International Film and TV Equipment Festival (*Beijing guoji guangbo dianying dianshi shebei zhanlanhui*) in August 2010 (The Central People's Government for the People's Republic of China 2010). Since then, the Chinese Central government has attempted to use the media to develop a policy of "international communication," believed to be essential for promoting Chinese culture and products abroad via the exportation of cultural products and services. In order to produce quality media, it is important to have quality infrastructure and the technical capacity of the industrial system. To achieve wider transnational audiences along these specifications, the Chinese state has exported commercial Chinese television series.

Making a Cultural Industry

Along the common understanding that developing the Chinese cultural industries was an important part of the Tenth Five-Year Plan (2001–2005), J. Wang (2004) and Flew (2012) agree that the notion of a "cultural policy" and that of a "soft power policy" had not existed before the twenty-first century.[7] In retrospect, it can be said that an inclusion of a cultural industry in the Tenth Five-Year Plan was a way of officially formalizing the development. On another level, it is crucial to note that the cultural industry had been included as part of "National Economic Plan,"[8] although there was an early attempt in 1992 to write the cultural industry— albeit without scholarly recognition[9]—into a publication of the State Council (State Council Information Office 1991; State Council Information Office et al. 1992). This moment can be read as the Chinese government's accordance of additional meaning to "culture," and can also be regarded as a means of preparation for the next stage. These previous attempts by the Chinese state to build up the cultural industry and conceptualize a developmental model illuminate the historical path Chinese culture has taken as a soft power resource, in a later stage of development at the macro level. Undoubtedly, the timing along which the Chinese state deployed the cultural industry's development—via cultural system restructuring and reform—has coincided perfectly with China's Tenth Five-Year Plan (2001–2005). Why, then, was this particular industry highlighted around this time?

Before this question is addressed in greater detail, attention now turns to discussing the transformation of the cultural industry under the Chinese government's policy. Domestically, the country has been investing in the first stages of cultural system development and the expansion of cultural affairs—infrastructure, in particular—in the less developed parts of the country. This was first documented in Jiang Zemin's speech in 1992, in the context of constructing a socialist culture. A similar line of argument can be found in his speech in 2002. Based on the CCP's 16th Party Congress Report, the Ministry of Culture published *The Cultural Market Development Plan (2003–2010)* in 2003 and spelled out a number of cultural products under development, such as choreography (*yanchu*), entertainment (*yule*), audio-visual products (*yinxiang*), internet culture (*wangluo wenhua*), films (*dianying*), and artifacts (*yishupin*).[10] Outwardly, the Chinese government is using its development of the cultural industry as a base for exporting its cultural products, premised on the belief that this industry can contribute economically. By bridging both internal and external demands, China wants to export its cultural products and bring cultural performance to an external audience through exhibitions of cultural products and cultural industry; for example, China (Shenzhen) International Cultural Industries Fair (Ministry of Commerce n.d.).[11] In the meantime, as with previous developmental paths to industrial sectors,[12] China has been willing to learn from others by looking to the United Kingdom, Japan, Singapore and South Korea's cultural and media industry development plans.[13] It is attempting to build its creative industries, creative economy, and creative society alongside each other.[14]

Cultural industrialization (*wenhua chanyehua*) can be articulated along three accounts: (1) Changes in the position of cultural industry in the Chinese economy; (2) changes and reform in the cultural system; and (3) the impetus to globalize Chinese culture. Following a continuous lineage of industrial development,[15] the Chinese government named the cultural industry as one of its eleven pillar industries in 2003 and treated it as a strategic industry. "Creative industries emerged as a policy concept in 2004, gaining particular momentum in the major cities such as Beijing, Shanghai, Shenzhen, and Guangzhou" (Flew 2012: 48).[16] In 2005, the concept of "cultural creative industries" (*wenhua chuangyichanye*) had gained acceptance and, "by the end of 2006, the creative industries or 'cultural creative industries' strategies were a part of the Eleventh Five-Year Plan draft for the cities of Beijing, Shanghai, Chongqing, Nanjing, Shenzhen, Qingdao, and Tianjin" (Flew 2012: 49). Scholars began recognizing the relevance of individual cities' policies, such as those of Beijing (Rossiter 2006). The relevant policies exist not only at the national level, but also in different sectors at the regional level as experimental testing points. Moreover, China then began emphasizing the move from a "Made in China" economic base to a "Created in China" paradigm (Flew 2012: 48).[17] During this period, utilizing the global cultural strategy that started in 2003, China intended to export its cultural products not only for profit, but also to gain recognition for PRC-made products.[18]

The Projection of "Imagined" Chinese Soft Power Through a Globalized Chinese Culture

How, then, does the idea of soft power play out? In order to conceptualize soft power, we should first consider the international political sphere. Although there were several attempts by the journalistic and scholarly fields to coin the concept, the use of the term "soft power" in an official sense is recent. An initial attempt was made in China through the Ministry of Culture's mention of "cultural power (*wenhuali*)" in 2005 (Ministry of Culture 2005).[19] In the same year, the State Council mentioned "cultural comprehensive power (*wenhua zongheguoli*)." In 2006, the general offices of the CCP and the State Council mentioned "cultural power" and "cultural influence (*wenhua yingxiangli*)." "Influence" has two related meanings; it is either used interchangeably with soft power itself, or is used to capture the achievement of soft power recognition.

President Hu Jintao included the phrase "cultural soft power (*wenhua ruanshili*)" in his speeches throughout the 17th CCP Congress in 2007 and the 18th Party Congress in 2012. These iterations on consecutive occasions can be regarded as attempts to set the agenda for national policies. In documents from 2010, Hu emphasized the need to increase China's competitiveness in cultural trade and cultural exports. He also highlighted the need for Chinese culture to be enhanced so that it will have broader international influence. Since then, the imperative to enrich "national (cultural) soft power"[20] has been mentioned several times in the 2011 documents of the CCP and the Ministry of Culture. Li Changchun, the chief of the Department of Propaganda, explicitly mentioned "cultural soft power" in a leading magazine in 2011. However, an emerging reluctance to use "soft power" in official discourse has been observed, as it began slowly disappearing from Hu Jintao's speeches.

Toward a Construction of Soft Power with Chinese Characteristics: "Socialist" Cultural Power and Repertories of Being "Chinese"

In constructing soft power, China not only seeks to enhance its influence internationally, but also to link all Chinese in the world to a "homeland." The soft power influence of a country can be expanded from inside to outside, to broaden international influence. The Chinese "*minzu*" (ethnic group) can be a PRC citizen or an overseas member of the Chinese diaspora, thereby bringing all "Chinese" together (*Zhonghua minzu/huaren*) on different occasions and CCTV New Year's Festival (*Chunjie Lianhuanwanhui*) is an excellent example,[21] regardless of their location.

The long-term objective is obviously to reinforce China's soft power as a part of its comprehensive national power. In particular, the country aspires to become a "socialist" cultural power (*shehuizhuyi wenhua qiangguo*) and to revive the Chinese people (*minzu fuxing*), or even the Chinese nation. At both the short- and mid-term intervals, it is important for the Chinese state to develop its cultural industry in order to achieve a more balanced percentage of Gross Domestic Product (GDP) earned by the cultural sector relative to other industrial sectors, and to reduce its deficit in cultural trade.

Soft Power, Industrial Development, Institutionalized Targets: Envisioning the Future

According to the WTO's (Doyle 2010) estimates of major exporters and importers of audio-visual products and related services among fifteen countries in 2007, the leading exporter was the United States (15 billion USD, 51.5 percent of the whole share), followed by the European Union (9.9 billion USD, 34.1 percent), and Canada (2 billion USD, 6.9 percent). China (0.3 billion USD, 1.1 percent) was the fourth largest exporter. Notably, the three largest exporters take up more than 92 percent of the total share. China pushed forward to engage more heavily with cultural trade in the Twelfth Five-Year Plan. One of the field-specific guidelines in this Plan was the document entitled *The Ministry of Culture's Plan (2011–2015) to Facilitate Globalizing Cultural Products and Services (Wenhuabu guanyu cujin wenhuachanpin he fuwu "zouchuqu" 2011–2015 nian zongtiguihua)* (Ministry of Culture 2010).[22] This was the very first attempt by any Chinese ministry to explicitly mention different targets and plans in relation to cultural exports and cultural soft power. Furthermore, it clearly states the ways in which the Ministry of Culture aims to implement the relevant policy inside and outside China.

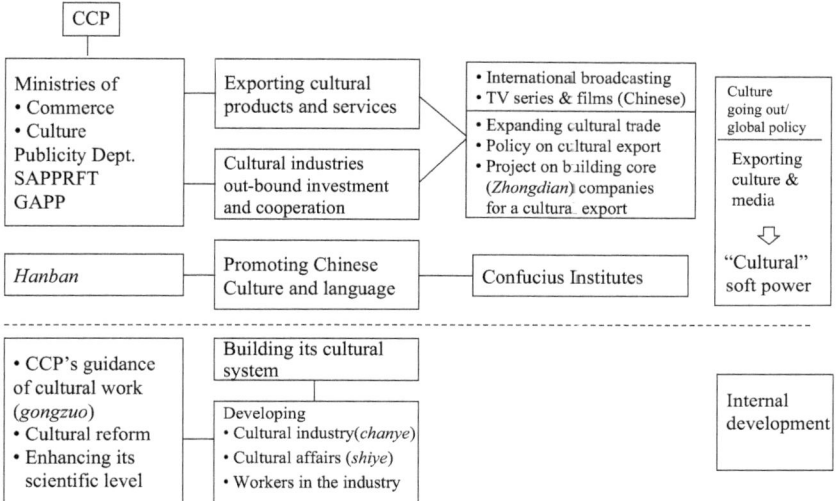

Fig. 2.1 China's soft power projection plan: "going out" and "entering in" policies through outward and inward development. Note: *Hanban* refers to the Chinese Language Council

The logic behind exporting culture and projecting soft power was framed in the following manner: "domestically, we try to build our culture, and facilitate the cultural industry as a new development engine of the national economy; internationally, in the framework of diplomacy, we try to enhance national cultural soft power, and increase Chinese international influence" (see Fig. 2.1; Ministry of Culture 2010, 2011a, b), "we try to enhance Chinese cultural products and services' influence in our neighboring countries, we make well-known brands in America and Europe, we do have an increased profit in emerging markets such as South Asia, Eastern Europe, Central Asia, Latin America and the Pacific, and we cultivate the African market."

Chinese TV Industry as a Soft Powerhouse and Globalizing Chinese Media Products

To pave the way for building soft power, the Chinese government has initiated a cultural industry along a broader agenda. As one Chinese academic, CM11, commented, "On the national level, the Chinese government wants to focus on the cultural industry. The 6th plenary session of the 17th Communist Party of China Central Committee (*Shiqi qi liu zhong quanhui*) is exemplary of what the government intends. This is surely also a means of making money, or commercialization." It is important to note that the Chinese state, like countries such as South Korea and Japan, regards the cultural industry to be a source of (sustainable) wealth for its own economy.

The Chinese cultural industry[23] has grown in recent years and it will continue to grow. In 2004, the economic value of the industry was 3400 billion RMB, which was 2.15 percent of the country's GDP. It has consistently maintained a growth rate of more than 2 percent of the GDP. In 2010, it surpassed 1.1 trillion RMB. In 2015, it was 2.7 trillion RMB, at 4 percent of the whole GDP for the year 2015 (Fig. 2.2). It is also estimated that the market size of China's cultural industry will surpass that of Japan in 2017 (Korea Creative Content Agency 2015; PwC 2012). This is reflected in the Chinese government's recent investment in the cultural industries and its ambition to project its soft power as the basis for, and through the mode of, industrial development.

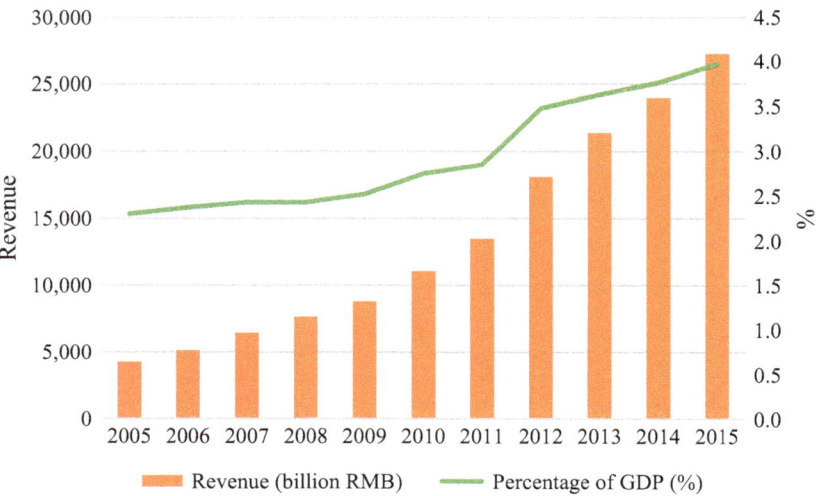

Fig. 2.2 Economic value of China's cultural industries. Source: Guangming Daily (2017), National Bureau of Statistics (2016)

Different Forms of Capital in Chinese TV Series

Chinese TV series,[24] according to SARFT (2008, 2012) and SAPPRFT (2017), are categorized by their position along the timeline of Chinese history, and by their main theme. I adapt SARFT's guideline for classifying Chinese TV series to "capitals" and "fields" to conceptualize different forms of classifying Chinese television dramas along the language of capital.

First, a historical subfield/capital includes all dramas that have historical themes and settings. This includes four distinct groups: (1) Ancient (*gudai*): before the Xinhai Revolution of 1911; (2) Pre-modern (*jindai*): from 1911 to 1949; (3) Modern (*xiandai*): from 1949 to 1978, and (4) Contemporary (*dangdai*): since China's economic reform from 1978 to the present (see Fig. 2.3).

Second, major thematic subfields include: "palace" (*gongting*), "martial arts" (*wuda*), "rural" (*nongcun*) and "urban" (*dushi*); "youth" (*qingshao*); "law" (*she'an*); "military" (*junlv*); "science fiction" (*kehuan*), and "others" (*qita*). A third category can be noted: "significantly important incidents (*zhongda*)," which includes major revolutions and historical events throughout Chinese history.

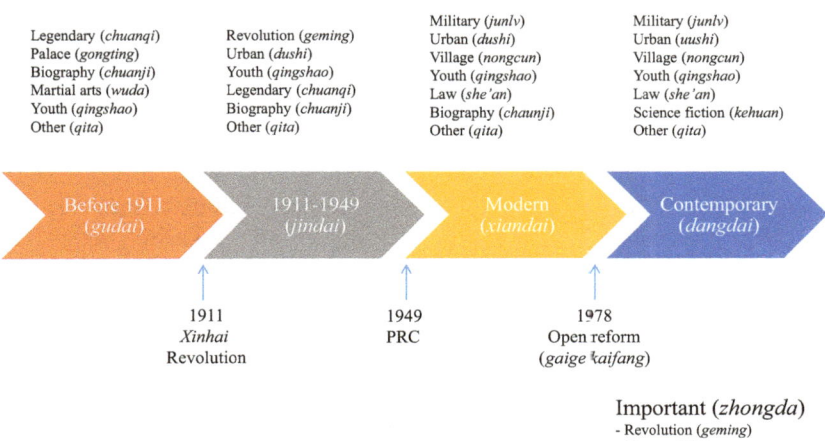

Fig. 2.3 Standard themes of Chinese TV series: what is produced. Source: SARFT (2008, 2012), SAPPRFT (2017). Note: The category of "Important" does not necessarily fall under the four historical timeframes

Lastly, there are the subfields of "biography," "time slip," and "main melody." The "biography" subfield usually depicts a famous Chinese historical or contemporary figure such as Confucius. The "time slip" subfield is a relatively new one that also possesses a historical element, trespassing temporal boundaries between historical and contemporary periods. The Chinese "main melody" subfield is a drama genre with politically laden themes that support the Chinese Party and state, centering events such as political revolutions or anti-Japanese movements (Table 2.1).

Themes that are not compatible with identified designated periods may not be approved for production. When local Chinese products[25] move beyond Chinese borders as foreign commodities to South Korea and Japan, they are unlikely to experience the same reception as in China.

Televised Soft Power Through Export

How much have China's television series, which embody such different forms of capital, been exported to and received by foreign audiences so far? Official annual statistical data from the Chinese government on the import and export of TV products features common categories including Europe, the United States, Japan, South Korea, Africa, and other countries.[26] These categories are also delineated by region. Along these lines, if one considers China's main partners in cultural trade (South Korea, Japan, and the United States), it may not be surprising to see these countries as a single category. Similar methods of categorization can also be observed in the corresponding data for South Korea. A significant difference in the reports between the years 2006 to 2010, and 2011, is the change in national and regional categories. For instance, data from 2006 to 2010 identifies Latin America as a category, while equivalent data from 2011 to 2015 only includes Americas with a subcategory of the United States (see Tables 2.2 and 2.3). This shows that Latin America was potentially seen as an important part of the world to export Chinese TV series, but the exchanges between China and Latin America in the transnational soft power field have yet to be significant.

The statistical data from 2011 in the Yearbook between 2012 and 2015 does not feature information on Latin America, but rather emphasizes the Asia Pacific region, that is Southeast Asia, Hong Kong, Taiwan, and Oceania as additional categories.[27] Despite the fact that annual statistical data does not explicitly indicate what the category "Other" might be comprised of, it is presumable that "Other" may include "unspecified

Table 2.1 Mapping the Chinese televisual field

Subfield	Historical	Martial arts	Biography	Time slip (chuanyue)	Premodern	Main melody (zhuxuanlu)	Contemporary
Key logic	Cultural logic, political logic	Cultural logic	Cultural logic, political logic	Market logic, artistic logic	Political logic	Political logic	Market logic
Important capital	Cultural capital	Cultural capital	Cultural capital	Economic capital, cultural capital	Political capital, cultural capital	Political capital	Aesthetic capital, cultural capital
Capital conversion	To economic capital	To economic capital		To economic capital			
Demand of production	High	Middle	Middle	Middle	Middle	High	Middle
Mode of import/ exchange	High	Middle	Middle	High	Low	Low	Low
Mode of consumption	High	High	Middle	High	Low	Low	High

Source: Compiled by the Author

Table 2.2 The value of exported Chinese TV series for main importing countries: 2006–2015 (Unit: RMB in thousands)

	Europe	Africa	United States	Japan	South Korea	Southeast Asia	Hong Kong	Taiwan	Oceania
2006	5680	N.A.	2360	18,010	3210	N.A.	N.A.	N.A.	N.A.
2007	70	N.A.	1010	N.A.	N.A.	N.A.	N.A.	N.A.	N.A.
2008	14,100	970	9120	12,730	1400	N.A.	N.A.	N.A.	N.A.
2009	770	1610	2460	3720	2980	N.A.	N.A.	N.A.	N.A.
2010	770	320	6900	6760	4070	N.A.	N.A.	N.A.	N.A.
2011	420	1480	65,010	9390	4560	N.A.	N.A.	N.A.	N.A.
2012	1560	510	7600	13,530	4820	24,520	11,570	51,900	22,650
2013	6230	5470	8680	15,450	11,260	15,160	5530	18,550	2000
2014	6770	60	3180	13,140	7670	N.A.	N.A.	N.A.	N.A.
2015	34,610	8720	20,660	19,660	12,170	93,140	71,490	64,050	12,730

Source: National Bureau of Statistics (2007, 2008, 2009, 2010, 2011: 942, 2012: 937, 2013: 848, 2014: 784, 2015: 182–183, 2016)

Note: N.A. refers to such categories are not available

Table 2.3 The number of exported TV series for main importing countries: 2006–2015 (Unit: season/episode)

	Europe	United States	Japan	South Korea	Southeast Asia	Hong Kong	Taiwan	Oceania
2006	6/180	5/218	23/735	10/355	N.A.	N.A.	N.A.	N.A.
2007	2/60	7/198	N.A.	N.A.	N.A.	N.A.	N.A.	N.A.
2008	11/239	12/898	19/801	9/304	N.A.	N.A.	N.A.	N.A.
2009	7/168	18/805	12/384	10/475	N.A.	N.A.	N.A.	N.A.
2010	8/338	89/2838	4/134	13/521	N.A.	N.A.	N.A.	N.A.
2011	3/130	87/3396	17/573	17/682	78/4851	28/1561	39/1750	2/67
2012	20/537	48/1759	9/257	14/590	78/3472	42/1861	45/2095	39/3876
2013	5/184	39/1564	13/575	19/828	93/3798	16/731	36/1609	5/201
2014	11/361	30/992	6/336	14/630	N.A.	N.A.	N.A.	N.A.
2015	17/373	31/1189	8/250	20/923	129/6522	44/1638	68/2603	8/49

Source: National Bureau of Statistics (2007, 2008, 2009, 2010, 2011: 942, 2012: 937, 2013: 848, 2014: 784, 2015: 182–183, 2016: 894)

Notes: (1) The Chinese words for (calculating) a season of TV series is *bu* and an episode of TV series is *jí*; (2) N.A. refers to such categories are not available

Asian countries" not included with the existing categories in the data. In this regard, Southeast Asian countries, Hong Kong, and Taiwan, which are newly updated categories in the 2011 data, have possibly been previously included under "Other." Jiang et al. (2013) argue this point, explaining that, "Major importers of our [Chinese] domestic TV series are Hong Kong, Taiwan, and Southeast Asia which take up about two thirds of the total amount of export." Along with the ethnic Chinese population in Southeast Asia, Japan and South Korea are considered easier targets for exporting Chinese domestic TV drama products, while the United States and Europe are "forbidden areas" (*jinqu*) for such exports (Jiang et al. 2013). Likewise, there is consensus about the regional disparity of and deficit in China's cultural trade.

South Korea, Hong Kong, Taiwan, and Southeast Asia have been primary export sites for Chinese TV series, particularly from 2012 and 2013 (National Bureau of Statistics of China 2012: 937, 2013: 848; see Tables 2.2 and 2.3). In recent years, TV series from Thailand have become a significant import market in China. Some observe that Thai dramas[28] could possibly replace South Korean dramas for China's audiences. Reflective of this trend, *Huaxiashibao* published a rather provocative newspaper article on June 21, 2008, titled, "Thai Wave sweeps over Korean Wave, Thai dramas[29] are going to overtake Korean dramas (*Tailiu laixi, Hanliu tuiwen, Taiju tiaozhan Hanju*)."[30] This illustrates China's anticipation of a newcomer to the cultural market. As such, the increasing popularity of Thai dramas in China could be one of the reasons why Southeast Asia is included as a single category in the cultural export data for 2011.[31]

Since 2006 the value of TV series imported from South Korea has significantly increased, whereas the value of Japanese TV series has decreased (see Table 2.2). South Korea is now the leading cultural exporter to China and the Chinese state is concerned with the emergent cultural trade deficit vis-à-vis South Korea; recent guidelines of SARFT and SARPPFT demonstrate China's regulation over popular foreign products.[32] The Chinese government not only deals with the cultural trade deficit by taking such actions, but its soft power development policy also aims to offset the imbalance in cultural trade.

In line with China's soft power policy, "Hong Kong, Taiwan, Japan, South Korea, and other Asian regions are still China's main export target at this moment, although the market has been expanding to Europe, the United States, and some Middle East countries" (Italian Trade Commission 2011: 24). It also intends to export Chinese TV series to Africa, evidenced by "Africa" remaining a single category in import-and-export trade data.

Thus, Chinese TV series have slowly been entering the African market. The United States, Japan, and South Korea are the three most regular buyers of Chinese TV series, despite monetary values fluctuating year by year. For example, in 2006, 2.3 million RMB of Chinese TV series (5 seasons, 218 episodes)[33] were exported to the US; in 2007 they were 1.01 million RMB (7 seasons, 198 episodes) and in 2011 it dramatically increased to 65.01 million RMB (3396 episodes). In 2006, 18.01 million RMB of Chinese TV series (23 seasons, 735 episodes) were exported to Japan; in 2011, it was 9.39 million RMB (573 episodes). In 2011, 4.56 million RMB (4851 episodes) of Chinese TV dramas were exported to South Korea.

It should be noted that Chinese TV series are sold at different prices in Japan and South Korea (National Bureau of Statistics 2007, 2008, 2009, 2010, 2011: 942, 2012: 937, 2013: 848, 2014: 784, 2015: 182–183, 2016: 894). 94.87 million RMB, equivalent to 24 seasons (767 episodes) of Korean TV dramas, were imported by China; 5.75 million RMB, equivalent to 1 season (23 episodes) of Japanese dramas, were imported.

On the export side, in 2011, 17 seasons (573 episodes) were exported to Japan, which corresponded to 9.39 million RMB, while 17 seasons (682 episodes) were exported to South Korea, which were 4.56 million RMB (see Fig. 2.4).

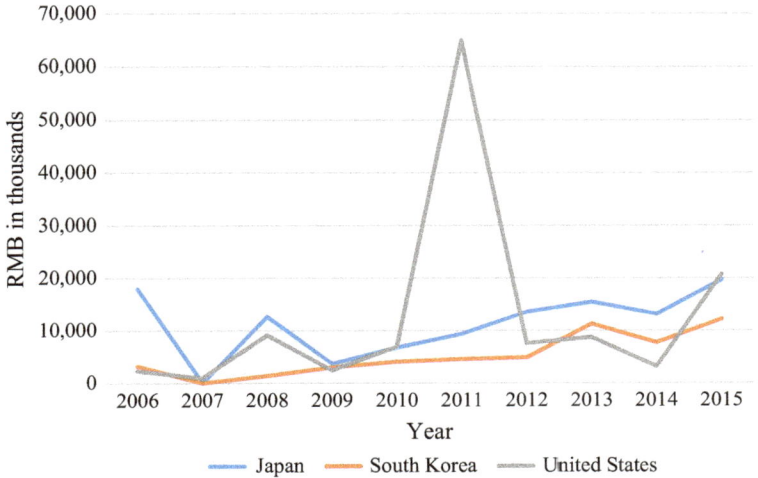

Fig. 2.4 Exported Chinese TV series to Japan, South Korea, and the United States: 2006–2015. Source: National Bureau of Statistics (2007, 2008, 2009, 2010, 2011: 942, 2012: 937, 2013: 848, 2014: 784, 2015: 182–183, 2016: 894)

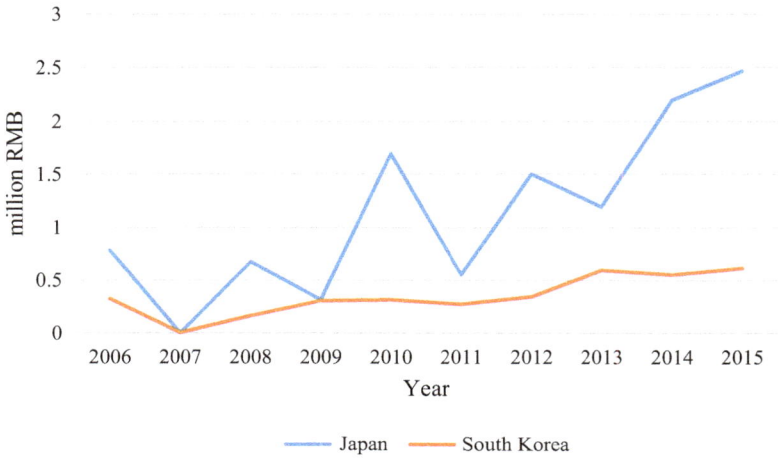

Fig. 2.5 Chinese TV series' prices per season: comparison of Japan and South Korea. Source: National Bureau of Statistics (2007, 2008, 2009, 2010, 2011: 942, 2012: 937, 2013: 848, 2014: 784, 2015: 182–183, 2016: 894)

The number exported to Japan and South Korea was almost same; however, Chinese TV dramas in Japan were sold at a higher price than in South Korea. From 2006 to 2015, Japan bought a Chinese television series on average 1.26 million RMB per season, while South Korea bought a Chinese television on average 0.38 million RMB per season for the same period (see Fig. 2.5).[34] The prices were also significantly different from prices that were set for exchanges with the United States.[35] From this it can be determined that South Korean television series were cheaper to buy than Japanese television series and American television series. Similarly, prices of Japanese programs are also higher for Chinese importers than for South Korean importers, while Korean programs are cheaper for Chinese importers than for Japanese importers. Apparently, the relationship and pricing practices between two paired countries are reciprocal.

CONCLUSION

This chapter examined China's "going global" strategy, its TV sector, as well as its approach to soft power development. The first aim of this chapter has been to rethink the institutional treatment of culture in post-socialist China, in the suggested timeframe. This chapter has also problematized the emergence of soft power in a rising China. By analyzing the state discourse on soft power, a perspective emerges that China's soft power construction is better understood as a progression of multifaceted meanings of culture, and the location of culture in its economy. This approach allows us to build upon an idea of culture that is presented rather loosely within the literature on soft power. It argues that culture is one of the resources embedded in China's soft power developmental plan, and is intertwined with the government's management of culture, economy, industry and vision for the future.

This chapter has presented three key findings. First, the changing role of culture has contributed to the development of China's soft power logic over two decades. In the 1990s, culture was commonly regarded in the context of the politicization of government propaganda. In recent years, culture has been used strategically along ambitions to enhance China's image, project influence, and further develop economic growth. Culture is therefore not only a channel for soft power, but also a by-product of soft power. Second, coupling economic development with culture reinforces the cultural logic of soft power. Locating culture in the economic sector helped to transform the cultural industry, which emphasizes creativity. Following the stages of economic development—from commodification and marketization, to commercialization and industrialization—culture has played integral roles at the different historical junctures presented in this chapter. Third, this chapter has highlighted soft power in an evolutionary pattern of change, with a progressive understanding of culture and its entrenchment in political leaders' vision for the future. The discourses of soft power mirror and reflect China's path of industrial development. Along this understanding, Chap. 3 will specifically examine how China's cultural globalization strategy has been playing out in the course of its accumulation of soft power.

In the second part of this chapter, I highlight China's involvement with commercial products and its approach to the export of television series in shaping its transnational soft power field abroad. I alluded that the export of Chinese media commodities to South Korea and Japan is rather difficult, and might expose a pathway to China's soft power dilemma. These barriers reveal weaknesses in China's soft power approach to "going global" when dealing with these two countries. The cultural "trade deficit," which China experiences with South Korea in particular, is likely to make it difficult for China to exercise its soft power policy there.

NOTES

1. The actors—who craft and implement policies at the governmental level—and the institutions would shape the development of China's soft power at critical junctures and historical configurations in post-socialist China.

2. In other words, the latter—China's cultural system reform and cultural influence projection—needs to show its capacity with commensurable economic power. This discussion is in line with China's discourse on the expansion of "comprehensive national power" (*zonghe guoli*).

3. See Caixin (2012).

4. This is a direct translation of *Xiaokang Shehui*, which refers to a "well-off society." See the United Nations Development Programme [UNDP] (2005).

5. This often refers to *chuanbo liliang* as well.

6. "…and communication capacity (*chuanboli*) as new engines, we need to develop our culture's creativity (*chuangzaoli*), communication capacity and influence (*yingxiangli*)" is a literal translation of such statement. ("*yao chongfen renshi keji jinbu dui wenhua fazhan de zhongyao zuoyong, jinjin zhuazhu xinxihua shenru fazhan de lishi jiyu, jiakuai tuijin wenhua he keji de ronghe, ba yunyong gaoxinjishu zuowei tigao wenhua chaungxin nengli he chuanbo nengli de xinyinqing, qieshi zengjiang woguo wenhua de chuangzaoli, chuanboli he yingxiangli.*")

7. For an examination of China's cultural policy in the late 1970s and early 1980s, see Pang (2012).

8. Depending on the source used, the date when the phrase "cultural industry" first appeared in an official Chinese document is different. For example, most literature indicate 2000, but Hu (2006) argues that it first appeared in 1992 (*A Decision Made to Develop the Third Sector*). However, the term was clearly included before the Eleventh Five-Year Plan started. Furthermore, I would argue that the official inclusion of the phrase "cultural industry" was done in preparation for further development, in line with the cultural industry argument in the Eleventh Five-Year Plan.

9. Most of the published literature, without taking account of any earlier attempts, informs us that the first inclusion of the phrase "cultural industry" was either in 2000 or in 2001.

10. There is no specification on the field of "international broadcasting" yet, although the English CCTV channel was launched in 2000. *The Cultural Market Development Plan* specifies that the Ministry and government aimed toward "*Wenhuachanye jibenfa*" (The Basic Law of Cultural Industry) in the year 2010.

11. From 2016, Shanghai started to host the Shanghai International B & B Cultural Industry Expo (*2016 Shanghai guoji minsu wenhuachanye bolanhui ji xiangcun lvyou zhuangbeizhan*), which has exhibitions related to cultural industry as well as travel.

12. Media reform is an example of this.

13. It is intriguing that it does not mention anything related to Hollywood.
14. For a more detailed discussion see Li, Wuwei. 2011. *How creativity is changing China* edited by Michael Keane, translated by Hui Li and Marina Guo, Bloomsbury London and New York: Bloomsbury Academic.
15. For example, in terms of the real estate industry, its industrial upgrading has been followed a similar step to this configuration.
16. This can be regarded as a result of the National Cultural Reform Testing Points Work Conference which was held in Beijing in 2003 (Flew 2012: 48).
17. See also Keane (2006).
18. Flew (2012) and Keane (2006) observed a desire of the government aspiring to move from "China fake" and "China manufactured" toward "China Created/China Inc."
19. Ministry of Culture (2005, 2007), "Opinions on further strengthening and improving the export of cultural goods and services." There are two versions using the same title. One is dated in 2005 and another is dated in 2007.
20. In the Chinese official documents, China's cultural power (*Zhongguo wen-huali*) is less observable than national cultural power. The latter appears as a different category because it further links to the function of the idea as a vehicle of nation building (*Zhonghua fuxing*).
21. On a slightly different note, China's "One Country, Two Systems" policy can be interpreted in this regard, as well. Bringing all ethnic Chinese into the program demonstrates this approach.
22. This version was released in October 2010.
23. Cultural studies include publishing, comics, music, films, game, animation, broadcasting, advertisement, characters, licensing, knowledge and information. This is based on the Classification of Culture and relevant industries (*wenhua ji xiangguanchanye fenlei*) (The Chinese government 2012) and also resonates with "Classifications of Contents, Media Industry" (OECD) and UNESCO Framework for Cultural Statistics (UNESCO).
24. By quantity, without a doubt, China is one of the largest TV drama producers in the world. In 2007 China produced 14,670 episodes (529 seasons), in 2008, 14,498 episodes (502 seasons). China produced 14,685 episodes (436 seasons) in 2010 and 14,942 episodes (469 seasons) in 2011 (SARFT 2012).
25. It is noted that there is burgeoning literature on the Chinese commercial media products (e.g., Zhu and Berry 2009). This has a tendency to focus on a single type or period. In part due to this, it may not be sufficient to present a systematic snapshot of the full picture of what kind of Chinese TV dramas are (not) to be produced in the Chinese domain.
26. Due to the availability and inconsistency of published data by the Bureau of Statistics of China, figures for "imported and exported TV programs during the year (hour)" are not included. This is because TV programs in these categories include both TV series and cartoon TV programs. It is not possible to separate one from the other.

27. This is the first appearance of such specific categories of the Asia and the Pacific in the corresponding annual data. Acknowledging such differences in the data, however, in order to make presentable and coherent figures, Southeast Asia, Hong Kong, Taiwan and Oceania are incorporated as others.

28. In 2003 a Thai TV drama *Qiaonvyong* was broadcasted in CCTV-8 for the first time. *Chutaode gongzhu*, which was aired on Hunan Satellite TV (*Hunan Weishi*) in 2008, was a great success (Nai Niu 2009). An increasing number of Thai TV series were shown on Chinese Televisions from 2010 to 2012. In 2010 eight Thai series were imported: three were in CCTV-8, five in Anhui Satellite TV (*Anhui Weishi*). In 2011, 17 Thai series were imported to the Chinese market. For example, two were in CCTV-8, nine were in Anhui TV, one in Jiangsu Satellite TV (*Jiangsu Weishi*), two in Zhejiang TV station (*Zhejiang dianshitai*), one in Yunnan Satellite TV (*Yunnan Weishi*), one in Hebei Satellite TV (*Hebei Weishi*), one on the Shanghai TV-Drama channel (*Shanghaidianshitai dianshiju pindao*). In 2012, 15 Thai TV dramas were shown on Chinese TV stations. Two were on CCTV-8, seven in Anhui Satellite TV (*Anhui Weishi*, one in CCTV-1, one in Beijing *Yingshi*, one in Zhejiang TV station, one in Sichuan Satellite TV (*Sichuan Weishi*), one 1 in Hubei Economic TV Station (*Hubei Jingshi*), and one in Xizang Satellite TV (*Xizang Weishi*).

29. For a detailed discussion of a Thai drama in China, see Deng (2013).

30. For a similar discussion, see Hua Chen (2010), Nai Niu (2009), and Ying Zhang (2008).

31. However, it is not straightforward to argue that whether this will be continued in the subsequent data.

32. A document of "No. 42 Provisions on the Administration of Import and Broadcasting of Overseas TV Programs (Article 18)" is important. The content of the document is as follows: "(1) The time for broadcasting overseas TV plays per day should be less than 25% of the total time for broadcasting TV plays in each TV channels; (2) The time for broadcasting other imported TV programs per day should be less than 15% of the total time for broadcasting in each TV channels and (3) During prime time (19:00–22:00) imported TV plays can only be broadcasted with the approval from SARFT (before 2004, it was 15% of the total programming during prime time) (Italian Trade Commission 2011: 21)." See also Globaltimes (2012).

33. This is consistent with the South Korean data which will be discussed in Chap. 5. The latter is presented based on both episode and USD calculation, but not by seasons.

34. It is noted that data from the year of 2007 for Japan and South Korea is unavailable. The average was counted for nine years for Japan and South Korea. However, data from the United States is available for all years from 2006 to 2015.
35. From 2006 to 2015, the United States bought a Chinese television series on average 2.54 million USD per season.

REFERENCES

Caixin. 2012. *Shibada zai Jing kaimu, Hu Jintao zuo baogao [The 18th Party Congress Held in Beijing, Hu Jintao's Report].* November 8. Accessed November 8, 2012. http://china.caixin.com/2012-11-08/100458021.html.

Chen, Hua. 2010. Taiju de liuxing dui woguo shouzhong de yingxiang [Thai Dramas' Influences on Chinese Audiences]. *Xinwen shijie [News World]* 5: 189–190.

Deng, Jing. 2013. *Taiju rebo Zhongguodeshouzhong jieshou xinlifenxi [Analysis of the Thai TV Drama's Audience Receptive Psychology in China].* Master's Thesis. Chengdu: Southwest Jiaotong University.

Doyle, Gillian. 2010. *Audio-Visual Services: International Trade and Cultural Policy.* Asian Development Bank Institutive Working Paper 355. Tokyo: Asian Development Bank Institute. Accessed October 19, 2012. http://www.adbi.org/workingpaper/2012/04/17/5049.audiovisual.srvc.intl.trade.cultural.policy.

Flew, Terry. 2012. *The Creative Industries: Culture and Policy.* Los Angeles, London, New Delhi, Singapore, and Washington: SAGE.

Globaltimes. 2012. *Foreign TV Dramas Restricted in China.* February 18. Accessed November 30, 2013. http://www.globaltimes.cn/NEWS/tabid/99/ID/696030/Foreign-TV-dramas-restricted-in-China.aspx.

Guangming Daily. 2017. *2017 nian Zhongguo wenhuachanye fazhan qushi [The Trend of the Development of Chinese Cultural Industry in 2017].* January 7. Accessed October 18, 2017. http://ex.cssn.cn/dzyx/dzyx_xyzs/201701/t20170107_3374116.shtml.

Hu, Huilin. 2006. *Wenhuachanyexue: Xiandai wenhuachanyelilun yu zhengce (Cultural Industries: Theory and Policies on Contemporary Cultural Industries).* Shanghai: Shanghai wenyi chubanshe.

Italian Trade Commission [Istituto nazionale per il Commercio Estero]. 2011. *China Television Industry Market Report.* June 3. Shanghai: Italian Trade Commission. Accessed November 30, 2013. http://www.ice.it/paesi/asia/cina/upload/174/CHINA%20TELEVISION%20INDUSTRY%20MARKET%20REPORT%202011.pdf.

Jiang, Mengwei, Yang Lu, Yuanyuan Wu, and Jianbin Li. 2013. Zhongguo dian-shiju ruhe baituo 'jing jinkou' [How Chinese TV Series Escape from 'Net Import']. *Beijing Business Today [Beijing Shangbao]*, April 2. Accessed December 2, 2013. http://news.hexun.com/2013-04-02/152743010.html.

Keane, Michael. 2006. From Made in China to Created in China. *International Journal of Cultural Studies* 9 (3): 285–296.

Korea Creative Content Agency. 2015. *Sinheung sijang gweonyeokbyeol sijang jin-chulbangan yeongu [A Study on Strategies of Emerging Markets by Regions]*. Naju: Korea Creative Content Agency.

Levitsky, Steven, and Lucan Way. 2002. The Rise of Competitive Authoritarianism. *Journal of Democracy* 13 (2): 51–65.

Li, Mingjiang. 2008. *Soft Power in Chinese Discourse: Popularity and Prospect.* RSIS Working Paper No. 165.

Ministry of Culture. 2005. *Opinions on Further Strengthening and Improving the Export of Cultural Goods and Services.* Beijing: Ministry of Culture.

———. 2007. *Guanyu jinyibu jiaqiang he gaijin wenhuashangpin chukou de yijian [Opinions on Further Strengthening and Improving the Export of Cultural Goods and Services]*. Beijing: Ministry of Culture.

———. 2010. *Wenhuabu guanyu cujin wenhuachanpin he fuwu 'zou chuqu' 2011–2015 nian zongtiguihua [The Ministry of Culture's Plan (2011–2015) to Facilitate Globalizing Cultural Products and Services]*. Beijing: Ministry of Culture.

———. 2011a. *Wenhuabu guanyu cujin wenhuachanpin he fuwu 'zou chuqu' 2011–2015 nian zongti guihua [Ministry of Culture on the Promotion of Cultural Goods and Services 'Going Out': 2011–2015 Overall Planning]*. Beijing: Ministry of Culture.

———. 2011b. *Cultural Export Declaration of the Year 2011: Incentive Funds by the Central.* Beijing: Ministry of Culture.

Ministry of Commerce. n.d. *China (Shenzhen) International Cultural Industries Fair.* Accessed October 25, 2016. http://english.mofcom.gov.cn/article/zt_icif/.

Nathan, Andrew J. 2003. Authoritarian Resilience. *Journal of Democracy* 14 (1): 6–17.

National Bureau of Statistics. 2007. Quanguo dianshijiemu jinchukou qingkuang (2006) [Basic Statistics on Imported and Exported TV Programs 2006]. In *2006 Zhongguo wenhua ji xiangguan chanye tongji nianjian [China Statistical Yearbook on Culture and Related Industries-2006]*. Beijing: China Statistics Press [*Zhongguo tongji chubanshe*].

———. 2008. Quanguo dianshijiemu jinchukou qingkuang (2007) [Basic Statistics on Imported and Exported TV Programs 2007]. In *2007 Zhongguo wenhua ji xiangguan chanye tongji nianjian [China Statistical Yearbook on Culture and Related Industries-2007]*. Beijing: China Statistics Press [*Zhongguo tongji chubanshe*].

———. 2009. Quanguo dianshijiemu jinchukou qingkuang (2008) [Basic Statistics on Imported and Exported TV Programs 2008]. In *2008 Zhongguo wenhua ji xiangguan chanye tongji nianjian [China Statistical Yearbook on Culture and Related Industries-2008]*. Beijing: China Statistics Press [*Zhongguo tongji chubanshe*].

———. 2010. Quanguo dianshijiemu jinchukou qingkuang (2009) [Basic Statistics on Imported and Exported TV Programs 2009]. In *2009 Zhongguo wenhua ji xiangguan chanye tongji nianjian [China Statistical Yearbook on Culture and Related Industries-2009]*. Beijing: China Statistics Press [Zhongguo tongji chubanshe].

———. 2011. Quanguo dianshijiemu jinchukou qingkuang (2010) [Basic Statistics on Imported and Exported TV Programs 2010]. In *2010 Zhongguo wenhua ji xiangguan chanye tongji nianjian [China Statistical Yearbook on Culture and Related Industries-2010]*, 942. Beijing: China Statistics Press [Zhongguo tongji chubanshe].

———. 2012. Quanguo dianshijiemu jinchukou qingkuang (2011) [Basic Statistics on Imported and Exported TV Programs 2011]. In *2011 Zhongguo wenhua ji xiangguan chanye tongji nianjian [China Statistical Yearbook on Culture and Related Industries-2011]*, 937. Beijing: China Statistics Press [Zhongguo tongji chubanshe].

———. 2013. Quanguo dianshijiemu jinchukou qingkuang (2012) [Basic Statistics on Imported and Exported TV Programs 2012]. In *2012 Zhongguo wenhua ji xiangguan chanye tongji nianjian [China Statistical Yearbook on Culture and Related Industries-2012]*, 848. Beijing: China Statistics Press [Zhongguo tongji chubanshe].

———. 2014. Quanguo dianshijiemu jinchukou qingkuang (2013) [Basic Statistics on Imported and Exported TV Programs 2014]. In *2013 Zhongguo wenhua ji xiangguan chanye tongji nianjian [China Statistical Yearbook on Culture and Related Industries-2013]*, 784. Beijing: China Statistics Press [Zhongguo tongji chubanshe].

———. 2015. Quanguo dianshijiemu jinchukou qingkuang (2014) [Basic Statistics on Imported and Exported TV Programs 2015]. In *2014 Zhongguo wenhua ji xiangguan chanye tongji nianjian [China Statistical Yearbook on Culture and Related Industries-2014]*, 182–183. Beijing: China Statistics Press [Zhongguo tongji chubanshe].

———. 2016. Quanguo dianshijiemu jinchukou qingkuang (2015) [Basic Statistics on Imported and Exported TV Programs 2015]. In *2015 Zhongguo wenhua ji xiangguan chanye tongji nianjian [China Statistical Yearbook on Culture and Related Industries-2015]*, 804. Beijing: China Statistics Press [*Zhongguo tongji chubanshe*].

Niu, Nai. 2009. Shenxian? Yaogui?—Jinkan zouqiao Yazhoude Taiguo Dianshiju [Closely Looking at Thai TV Series]. *Dazhong Dianying [Popular Cinema]* 3: 50–51.

Nye, Joseph S., Jr. 2005. Soft Power and Higher Education. *The Internet and the University* 33–60. Accessed April 28, 2014. http://www.educause.edu/ir/library/pdf/ffpiu043.pdf.

———. 2011. *The Future of Power*. New York: Public Affairs.

Pang, Laikwan. 2012. Post-Socialism and Cultural Policy: The Depoliticization of Culture in Late 1970s' and Early 1980s'. In *Popular Culture and the State in East and Southeast Asia*, ed. Nissim Otmazgin and Eyal Ben-Ari, 147–161. London and New York: Routledge.

Pienovi, Andrew. 2010. *Building a Global Empire, The Chinese Way*. November 19. Accessed October 6, 2012. http://www.globalenvision.org/2010/11/19/building-global-empire-chinese-way.

PwC. 2012. *Global Entertainment and Media Outlook 2012–2016*. London: PwC.

Rossiter, Ned. 2006. Creative Industries in Beijing: Initial Thoughts. *Leonardo* 39 (4): 367–370. Accessed October 24, 2012. http://nedrossiter.org/wp-content/uploads/2011/06/39.4rossiter.pdf.

SAPPRFT. 2017. *Guangdianzongju guanyu 2017nian 3yue quanguo paishe zhizuo dianshiju bei'an gongshi de tongzhi [Notice on the Statistical Information on the Authorized Filmed TV Series in March 2017]*. Accessed May 17, 2017. http://dsj.sarft.gov.cn/tims/site/views/applications/note/view.shanty?appName=note&id=015b65d82c9c04be4028819a5b5c3982.

SARFT. 2008. Dianshiju ticaide fenlei biaozhun [Standard Themes of TV Series]. May 1. Accessed February 14, 2013. http://www.chinasarft.gov.cn/articles/2008/05/01/20080430191753470537.html.

———. 2012. *Guanyu 2012 nian diyiji quanguo guochan dianshiju faxing xukezheng banfa qingkuang tongji jieguode tonggao [Notice on the Statistical Information on the Authorized Domestic TV Series in the first quarter of 2012]*. Accessed February 14, 2013. http://www.chinasarft.gov.cn/articles/2012/05/08/20120508165936620990.html.

State Council Information Office. 1991. *A Report on the Cultural Affairs of a Number of Economic Policy Consultations by the Ministry of Culture*. Beijing: State Council Information Office.

State Council Information Office, the Department of Propaganda, the People's Bank of China, the Ministry of Commerce, the Ministry of Culture, the State Administration of Radio, Film, and Television (SARFT), the General Administration of Press and Publication, the China Banking Regulatory Committee, the China Securities Regulatory Committee, and the China Insurance Regulatory Committee. 1992. *Major Strategic Decisions to Speed Up the Development of the Third Industrial Sector*.

Stockmann, Daniela. 2013. *Media Commercialization and Authoritarian Rule in China*. Communication, Society and Politics Series. Cambridge: Cambridge University Press.

The Central People's Government. 2010. Li Changchun's Visit to International Film and TV Equipment Festival [Li Changchun canguan guoji guangbo dianying dianshi shebei zhanlan]. August 23. Accessed July 1, 2014. http://china.cnr.cn/news/201008/t20100824_506938358.shtml.

Truex, Rory. 2017. Consultative Authoritarianism and Its Limits. *Comparative Political Studies* 50 (3): 329–361.

United Nations Development Programme [UNDP]. 2005. Supporting the All Round Xiaokang Society. Beijing: UNDP China. Accessed November 27, 2012. http://www.undp.org.cn/projectdocs/33756.pdf.

Wang, Jing. 2004. The Global Reach of a New Discourse: How Far Can 'Creative Industries' Travel? *International Journal of Cultural Studies* 7 (1): 9–19.

Zhang, Ying. 2008. Taiju Tiaozhan Hanju [Thai TV Series Challenges Korean TV Series]. *Beijing Jishi* 9: 63.

Zhu, Ying, and Chris Berry, eds. 2009. *TV China*. Bloomington and Indianapolis: Indiana University Press.

Zhu, Ying, Michael Keane, and Ruoyun Bai, eds. 2008. *TV Drama in China*. Hong Kong: Hong Kong University Press.

CHAPTER 3

Foreign Markets and Professionals: The Gatekeepers

INTRODUCTION

The dilemma regarding the soft power impact of media products concerns the obstacles to accessing foreign and transnational markets that are within reach for some but not for all. Among these obstacles are the management activities of the media professionals in the importing country, who, as this chapter will show, more often impede rather than facilitate the import process. This chapter will account for the gatekeeping role of media professionals in the importing country by exploring the manner in which the import and distribution of Chinese television series intersect with different forms of capital that are embedded within them and are transformed into mediatized transnational soft power fields in South Korea and Japan. To undertake this inquiry, the operation of foreign television markets and the gatekeeper role of media professionals in South Korea and Japan are critically examined.

The starting point for any discussion about China's media projection into potential import countries necessitates an understanding of the Chinese state's rationale for promoting such an undertaking. As critically discussed in Chap. 1, many scholars have analyzed soft power policies and resources (Esraey and Qiang 2011; Su 2011; Wang 1993; Wang and Lu 2008; see also Chap. 2). However, the mechanisms or paths for transmitting China's mediatized soft power into the media field of another country are complex and riddled with obstacles at the export stage. Cognizant of the need to analyze the latter, this chapter argues that the reasons for the

© The Author(s) 2018
C. S. Lee, *Soft Power Made in China*,
https://doi.org/10.1007/978-3-319-93115-9_3

failure of China's projection of its mediatized soft power have to be understood at the level of the televisual market, with regard to the special gatekeeping role of media professionals in the importing country.

Attention to the domestic institutional level in this comparative study of the processes and mechanisms of China's soft power dilemma is important. As this chapter explains, the embrace of television series—a soft power medium—by media practitioners is conditioned not only by the market structures of the potential import countries. Their actions in South Korean and Japanese media markets also reflect their evaluations of the impact of Chinese television series on potential values for audience ratings, economic capital, and consumption by local audiences in the importing countries. These actors are rarely the focus of empirical investigation, as previous research on soft power often implicitly considers the importing countries and domestic institutions. Addressing this gap in the body of literature can generate a clearer understanding of the conditions under which soft power policies either facilitate or discourage the successful importation of foreign television programs into the receiving countries.

The Market Level: The Making of China's Soft Power in Receiving Countries

This chapter aims to explain the role that meso-level markets and institutions play in the construction of China's soft power dilemma. It sheds light on the conditions and mechanisms at the market level that contribute to the failure of Chinese television products to reach a significant portion of East Asian audiences.

South Korea and Japan, the two receiving countries in this comparative study of Chinese soft power, have similar television markets. These countries have dual market systems based upon terrestrial and cable TV stations, but it is primarily the cable television stations that serve as venues for airing foreign television products. Despite similar institutional arrangements between the television markets in South Korea and Japan, the patterns and conditions for the formation of a Chinese soft power field have diverged between these countries because of the different forms of capital that, in practice, shape their televisual fields into mediatized transnational soft power fields.

This chapter then addresses the following linked question: What role do South Korean and Japanese media professionals play as gatekeepers in these media markets and what rationales motivate them? Responding to these two questions requires consideration of the different forms of capital which constitute Chinese televisual subfields, and placing of them conceptually in the respective transnational soft power fields in South Korea and Japan. This situating model will elucidate the similar institutional arrangement of the two television markets and their import processes, with regard to the divergent patterns of capital, and will highlight the rationales and roles of media professionals in constructing such divergences.

In Nakajima's (2016) recent theorization of the Chinese cinematic field, he uses a field and organizational analysis approach. The different forms of capital he analyzes are as follows: (a) *political capital*, which refers to both political and financial connections to, and support from, the state; (b) *economic capital*, referring to financial success in the market economy, evidenced by tools of measurement including box-office receipts; and (c) *cultural capital*, either in the form of an award in an international film festival or knowledge of modern and contemporary Chinese history (Nakajima 2016: 92, 94).

Such operationalization of the Chinese cinematic field works within the boundary of China, but understanding the Chinese televisual field within larger mediatized transnational soft power fields in South Korea and Japan requires a different set of definitions for different forms of capital. This chapter, thus, will extend Nakajima's analysis of the Chinese cinematic field and explore different forms of capital present in Chinese televisual subfields.[1] The latter is supported by concrete interview content obtained from media professionals.

As defined in Chap. 1, I use the following modified definitions of five different forms of capital: (a) *political capital* is a form of political knowledge and political influence that is embedded in the Chinese televisual subfields (see Bühlmann et al. 2013); (b) *economic capital* is a value representing economic returns or revenue from a television drama production; (c) *cultural capital* refers to a form of knowledge required for appreciating or deciphering cultural relations and cultural artifacts (Bourdieu 1993: 7). In the case of Chinese television subfields, cultural capital refers to important/ referential knowledge of the culture and history of China; (d) *aesthetic capital* represents beautified elements of a series; (e) *celebrity capital* refers to the popularity or strong presence of celebrities in the Chinese televisual subfields; and (f) *virtual capital* refers to the ways in which Chinese television series are consumed via online platforms and virtual communities. This implies that the flexibility of time and space has a potential for further developing Chinese soft power in a transnational soft power field.

Given this brief summary of the theoretical approach to be used in this chapter, the remainder is organized into the following four sections. The first section shows what the respective television markets and import processes of South Korea and Japan have in common. The second and third sections explore in detail the export and import processes, along with the roles of media markets and professionals. These sections identify conditions of the formation of transnational Chinese soft power fields via mediatized Chinese televisual subfields in the two receiving countries. Finally, the fourth section compares the similarities and differences in the construction of a transnational Chinese soft power field in the two receiving countries.

From Export to Import: The Pathways and Mechanisms

Understanding China's soft power dilemma vis-à-vis the two receiving countries of South Korea and Japan requires initial consideration of the processes involved in the export of Chinese television series, although the focus of this book is largely the reception side of these transactions.

Exports Behind the Scene

How does China export its media? In a state-coordinated market economy, the export of television products starts with the SAPPRFT of the PRC,[2] a government agency responsible for cultural and media activities and industries. The distribution and sale of Chinese programs to foreign buyers (overseas distribution, *haiwai faxing*) can take a number of routes, particularly with the involvement of individual television stations and media professionals (the Korea Creative Content Agency 2011). First, deals are made through major companies, such as the CCTV International Television Company (CITVC) (*Angshi guoji gongsi*), which is affiliated with CCTV. With its government backing and advantages in priority channeling, the company is "the largest exporter" of television programs (Italian Trade Commission 2011: 24). *Shanghai Wu'an Chuanbo*, based in Shanghai, is another example, according to CM20.[3] Second, some deals are made with individuals through social networks (*guanxi*) and personal channels (*geren qudao*). CM36[4] said that "*Guanxi* is important to get things started and get things done, particularly in the cultural and media sectors." This is also evident in the importation process in South Korea and Japan. Third, deals can also be made through departments or personnel within media companies that do marketing and distribute media products. Fourth, venues such as exhibitions and festivals[5] of such goods are also important. On these occasions, media companies show prepared samples (*yangpin*) of what they intend to sell in their booths. In addition, catalogues that contain details about the products[6] and audience ratings for potential customers are also prepared. Although big events are gathering points for buyers and sellers, the latter often visit potential customers at places like television stations, where they leave materials (*liu ziliao*) and contact details (*lianluo*) for consideration.[7]

Imports Behind the Scene

Importing Chinese programs into South Korea and Japan entails entanglement with multiple institutions at each step in the process, from regulation and decision-making to scheduling. The various actors in the process are interlinked. In the next section, the circumstances under which Chinese programs are imported are considered (Fig. 3.1).

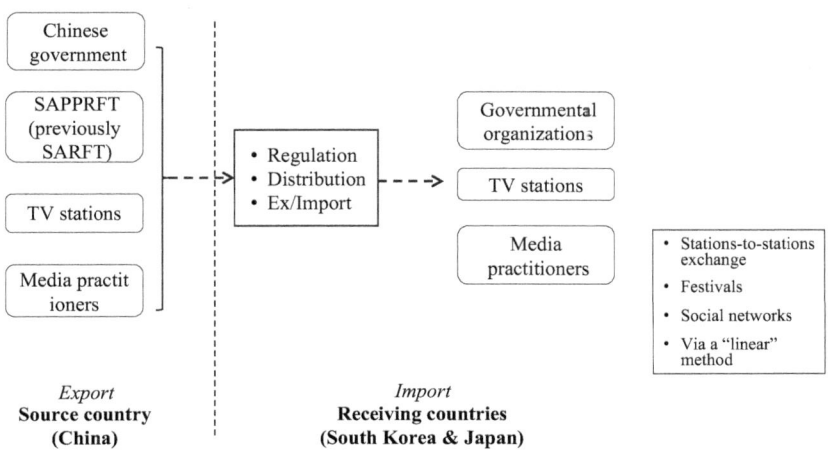

Fig. 3.1 Export and import behind the scene. Source: Compiled by the Author

What are the potential routes by which foreign media can enter recipient countries? One is official occasions, such as film and television festivals, the main events for trading media products. During festivals, dramas and movies are showcased either openly or on the fringes of the festival location. The booths in the festivals are venues for meeting people from the various media companies, and provide spaces where basic information about the programs can be introduced and discussed. Asia TV Forum and Market and China (Shenzhen) International Television Drama & Television Program Fair are examples of such events (Asia TV Forum and Market 2016; Asia Content Marketing Association n.d.; China Television Drama Production Industry Association 2015).

Unofficial occasions serve as another route. This often occurs when managers and producers of television stations exchange their products with each other, or through unofficial channels where a broadcasting station uses a contact's name to sell the product and avoid paying a commission or introduction fee. This way of making contacts is popular among established media professionals, according to JM6, a television producer at Nippon TV.[8] Direct transaction expands departments[9] at television stations where key business can be done in-house. A similar practice is found with Chinese programs imported to the South Korean market. The second "unofficial" mode is the exchange of products by "cultural intermediaries" or a "broker."[10] Although this is considered the "traditional" mode of transaction, used mostly in the 1980s and 1990s, it is less frequent today. KM1,[11] who worked for a producer in China and Hong Kong dealing mainly with Chinese and Hong Kong products for the South Korean market, explained, "That is why people like me have less of a chance to do business now. Nowadays, TV stations have experts or a special department to manage this issue; they are smart, and they do not give us the opportunity to make money." Others do their business on a "freelance" basis; transactions are worked through the social network of the person who has experience in distribution. These days, those who know the import/export routes, and have the products and information, directly approach TV stations to sell products using their existing social networks, to maintain and build business contacts. Prior to the development of in-house departments, they benefited from locating niches in the televisual market. As the media product exchange becomes more institutionalized, the traditional role of brokers as cultural intermediaries exploiting a face-to-face business format is becoming more limited.

DUAL MEDIA MARKETS AND PROFESSIONALS
AS GATEKEEPERS

Media Professionals as Gatekeepers

As already illustrated with the import process, media professionals, i.e. producers and managers who work for media organizations, are crucial actors in the media trade and distribution circuit. In the processes of exporting and importing products, they act as "gatekeepers" who have the capacity of excluding or promoting products or events (Janssen and Verboord 2015) or "cultural intermediaries," who are involved in "the work of mediation in commercial cultural fields" (Bourdieu 1993). Their roles are reflections of the push to accommodate market demands along market structures (Edwards 2012; Moor 2012; Smith Maguire and Matthews 2012) and they frame issues that impact society and consumers (Smith Maguire and Matthews 2012: 554).[12] In the case of media professionals in South Korea or Japan, and in regard to the shaping and unmaking of a transnational Chinese soft power field, this research finds that these individuals play an important role as gatekeepers, rather than cultural intermediaries. Media professionals in the two target countries decide what to invite into the media market, and control media flows by utilizing decisions based upon personal taste and their companies' guidelines.

The Dual Media Markets in South Korea and Japan

Understanding a Chinese mediatized soft power field requires consideration of media markets as institutions and (sub)fields of a transnational soft power field. In addition, the dual media market structure in South Korea will be examined with special reference to terrestrial and cable station priorities to underscore the ways in which Chinese television programs are imported. What follows will demonstrate that South Korea and Japan share similar institutional arrangements regarding their dual market systems and functions. Furthermore, in the case of terrestrial and non-terrestrial television stations, the former usually houses domestic television products and the latter usually houses foreign television products.

In South Korea, terrestrial (*jisangpa*) television, cable television, satellite television (*wiseong bangsong*), and program providers (*bangsong chae-neol saeopja*) are key players in the country's broadcasting system (Korea Communications Commission 2011). Unlike terrestrial television, cable stations in South Korea broadcast foreign programs to some extent, from American shows and films to Asian dramas and movies.[13] Cable stations seek profit through diverse advertising and subsidies from their parent companies.[14] Some Asian drama and movie channels deliver only Chinese programs, setting these programs apart from other foreign products that rarely have such specialized channels. Chinese dramas and Hong Kong action movies are the two core genres within this subfield.

Table 3.1 shows the number of Chinese television series on Korean terrestrial television. It ostensibly suggests that Chinese television series are not popularly nor regularly imported into the terrestrial television stream. Across twelve years, 94 series were imported in 2003, 31 series were imported in 2007, 19 series were imported in 2012, and 3 series were imported in 2015. Interestingly, even though China has put forward its soft power strategy determinedly, the main South Korean television stations—terrestrial television channels every household has subscribed to—

Table 3.1 Chinese television dramas in South Korea (2003–2015)

	Terrestrial TV			Cable TV		
	Series (number)	Price (1000 USD)	Price per series (USD)	Series (number)	Price (1000 USD)	Price per series (USD)
2003	94	293	3117	453	320	706
2004	0	0	0	89	78	876
2005	0	0	0	973	1016	1044
2006	0	0	0	577	310	537
2007	31	98	3161	533	670	1257
2008	0	0	0	477	453	950
2009	0	0	0	496	727	1466
2010	0	0	0	184	274	1489
2011	0	0	0	209	325	1555
2012	19	159	8368	321	162	505
2013	0	0	0	378	617	1632
2014	1	900	900,000	374	791	2115
2015	3	41	0	869	1466	1687

Source: Korean Broadcasting Commission (2002, 2003, 2004, 2005, 2006, 2007), Korea Communications Commission (2008, 2009, 2010, 2011, 2012), Ministry of Science, ICT and Future Planning and Korea Communications Commission (2013, 2014, 2015, 2016)

successfully manage the flow of Chinese television series into the country. On the one hand, this is due to the nationalistic and protectionist sentiments in the Korean media marketplace, shaped by both the Korean government's policy and media practitioners' gatekeeping role. On the other hand, as presented in this chapter and Chap. 4, limited acknowledgment and good reputations of diverse televisual subfields can also inform gatekeeping, instead of intermediating.

Similar to South Korea, Japan has terrestrial and cable stations, broadcast satellite (BS), and communications satellite (CS) (Tōyōkeizaishinpōsha 2012). Like the cable channels in South Korea, BS and CS channels charge on a monthly basis.[15] Considering the way these channels are managed and used by consumers, Japan's television market can be said to have its own dual market structure. Parallel to the South Korean market, foreign programs are predominantly located on the BS and CS channels, with the exception of Korean-related programs.[16] The Japanese media market is largely dependent on BS and CS channels such as WOWOW, BS-FOX, and J Sports ½ and other famous channels, which broadcast Chinese programs such as Channel Ginga and Neco.

South Korea and Japan, the two receiving countries in this comparative study of Chinese mediatized soft power, have a similar television market. These countries not only have a dual market system of terrestrial and cable TV stations, but also have cable TV stations that are structured as venues for accessing foreign television products. Despite similar the institutional arrangements of television markets in South Korea and Japan, the patterns and conditions of embracing Chinese soft power have diverged between countries because of different forms of capital that are in use. Yet, these patterns and conditions shape both of their televisual fields into transnational soft power fields. Taken together, cable television is a venue for foreign programs in these two countries with similar institutional arrangements, including those from China.

A CHINESE SOFT POWER DILEMMA IN MARKETS

As explained in Chap. 2, different forms of capital are important not only as tools for analyzing Chinese television series per se, but more importantly they provide a means by which to interpret the import of Chinese television series in South Korea and Japan, and the resultant shape of the transnational soft power fields in these two receiving countries.

The following sections shed light on how media professionals in South Korea and Japan "perceive" Chinese television series, how they import them, as well as what they believe has led to China's soft power dilemma at the market/institutional level, as transferrable capital is embedded within these series. In what follows, imported Chinese television drama subfields are analyzed along the different forms of capital operating within them, and in the accounts given by media professionals.

South Korea

Among the many cable television stations in South Korea, the three main channels that predominantly import Chinese television programs are Junghwa TV, Channel CHing, and AsiaN. The biggest player, Junghwa TV, was established in 2005 as part of CJ E&M. Channel Ching (CHing), operated by Hyundai Media, started in 2009. AsiaN, broadcasting Asia-focused programs, launched in 2002 (AsiaN n.d.; Channel Ching n.d.; Junghwa TV n.d.).

Over the past ten years, the main cable television stations in South Korea imported 9.5 dramas per year (Fig. 3.2). Imports peaked from 2011 to 2013, due to the fact that about ten historical dramas were imported in each of these years. Although the Chinese historical drama remains the

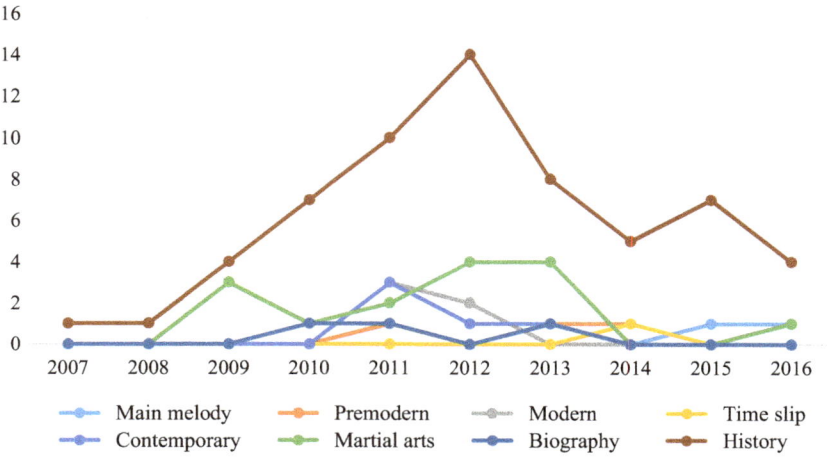

Fig. 3.2 The number of Chinese television series at three main cable stations in South Korea (Unit: number of series). Source: Compiled by the Author

dominant China-imported genre on the South Korean television market, each station utilizes a different scheme to bring in their featured Chinese television dramas. Junghwa TV has imported predominantly history-themed dramas, including *Palace* (*Gungsaesimok*), *New Journey to the West* (*Shin Seoyugi*), and *Beauty World* (*Miyincheonha*). This was the case, particularly in 2012 and 2013. Similarly, CHing also imported mostly history-themed dramas, in the largest volume between 2011 to 2015, and history-related time slip dramas, particularly in 2012 and 2013. This channel also broadcast martial arts and contemporary dramas. AsiaN imported historical and martial arts dramas (Fig. 3.3).

Historical Subfield
The subfield of Chinese historical drama in South Korea divides into high cultural capital, high economic capital and low political capital. In contrast with those in China, Korean media professionals do not see this subfield as a highly political, capital-engaged genre/field, nor that this genre is a unique import for South Korea. Many historical dramas are based on novels and events that are also well-known in South Korea. For example, *Three Kingdoms*, which aired 95 episodes in 2013, was produced by South Korea's public television station KBS. Others are biographical, such as *Confucius*. A newer genre, "time slip" or "time travel," has also emerged in which stories begin in a contemporary setting and move into a historical period, such as the Tang or Qing dynasty. *Scarlet Heart* is an example of this genre that gained enormous popularity in South Korea.

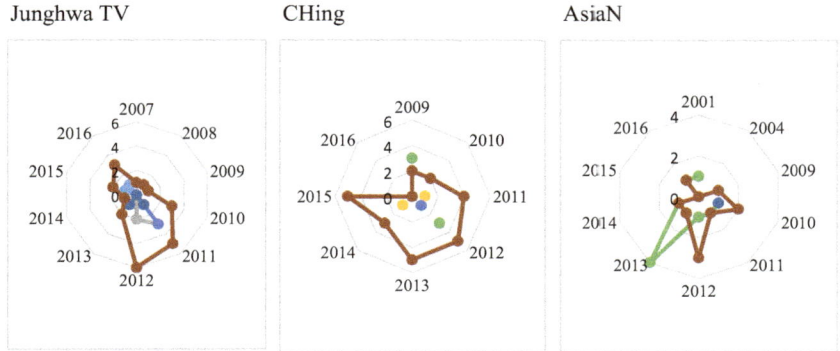

Fig. 3.3 Three major cable stations and imported Chinese television series. Source: Compiled by the Author

The characteristics of a Chinese historical drama, based on Bourdieu's field theory, are as follows. First, the "key logic on the production side" of historical dramas is cultural as well as political because the key rationale for television series production in China is not only cultural and historical, but also engages a rather implicit political attribute. Second, the most important form of capital in the South Korean televisual field is cultural capital. This is also the selling point owing to the cultural, historical and linguistic elements in Chinese period dramas. Third, this historical drama subfield can potentially produce a high level of economic capital, which can materialize in the form of revenues or audience ratings, for media professionals and markets in South Korea. Also, South Korean media professionals can convert cultural capital to economic capital with less consideration of the country's market demands. Two main factors associated with the conversion of cultural capital to economic capital are exemplified in interviews with Korean media professionals. KM1 said, "The rich Chinese history and culture are represented in Chinese historical dramas. These elements easily appeal to South Korean audiences who are usually familiar with some level of the history from their school years."

As mentioned, media practitioners play an important role in bringing foreign media products into the South Korean media market and cultivating local tastes. Another factor is revealed to a greater extent at the individual level. KM9[17] mentioned, "I personally like to engage with historical dramas. Given that my company is intended to reach those who want to consume Asian media products, I mostly deal with Chinese products and Japanese products, too. In addition, as I am the only person who manages this import work in my company, I have room for what to choose and what to import." The producer who works for the Asian Media Network in South Korea says that she is flexible in choosing products if they are within the boundary of "Asia." The media professional's personal taste should be in line with the media company's guidelines for importing such products, as well as guaranteed to generate a certain number of audiences. At this point, senior practitioners often play a role in introducing "new" and "state-of-the art" culture to their home society through the import of cultural products. They have to do this under heavy consideration, however, so as not to cross sensitive lines which may provoke national sentiments, given that South Korea and China's histories overlap and have been entangled in nation building conflicts and political interests. Fourth, in a related vein, if the mode of import by South Korean media professionals is of a "high" status then the mode of consumption is "high" (see Chap. 4).

One of the most important practical considerations in the media industry is meeting a budget. Chinese products are considered "competitive" not in quality but in price, which allows them to be used for "filling a space" in the market and television schedules. This is true in the case of historical dramas, which usually have more than 40 episodes. In this regard, KM4 commented, "Chinese programs function as substitutes because they are the best value for money—cheap, but with bulky episodes."[18] KM4[19] continued: "Chinese programs do not always vouch for good quality. That's why sometimes we are reluctant to import them into our market. However, everything is about money. We are pushed by the top management in our TV station to cut on costs. Thus, the lower quality gives us some benefits. As they are not of good quality, you can buy them at a lower, reasonable price." In KM4's eyes, Chinese television series may not be seen as the best entertainment option for the market, his TV station, and potential audiences. However, decisions are also made by multiple factors including quality, cost, running time, and profits for the company. Considering all these at the same time, importing Chinese television series is a good idea. In the process, Korean media professionals play an important role as cultural intermediaries while managing the flow of imported programs into their markets.

Martial Arts Subfield

On a scale from high to low cultural and economic capital, the subfield of Chinese martial art dramas in South Korea is located at the position of medium cultural capital and medium economic capital. First, the key logic on the production side is fairly cultural. In contrast with those in China, where martial art dramas are often considered a subset of historical dramas, South Korean media professionals do not see the martial arts subfield as belonging within historical dramas and do not regard them as having high cultural capital. Second, the important form of capital for this subfield is cultural capital, although at a lower level than for the historical subfield. Third, a core audience that is always interested in martial arts makes it is possible for the genre to be converted into economic capital. Thus, the mode of import and consumer demand exist.

One of the salient reasons for importing this programming is that the subfield itself enjoys a stable "mania pool" that can always be tapped into. For example, the martial arts subfield is popular among those who collect different versions of cultural products, from DVDs to books. A TV producer mentioned, "These programs are not only supposed to appear on

TV but, more importantly, other additional forms (such as DVDs and VCDs) are included and thus appear on the market. However, since VCDs and DVDs are in small demand in South Korea, contrary to the Japanese situation, South Korean media producers do not want to buy a full package, but rather purchase as a rearranged package." As such, occasional purchases are made to collect goods of value (*sojang gachi*)— e.g., limited edition products, famous artist collectibles, and rare items— or for educational purposes, such as screening in class or during lectures. On the other hand, well-known characters, or some stories taken from traditional Chinese literature (*gudian xiaoshuo*)[20] or martial arts novels (*wuxia xiaoshuo*)[21] are preferred by media practitioners and audiences (see Chap. 4). Martial arts dramas are also often sold as part of a package, along with products of a number of similar genres. This is the way for South Korean media professionals and television stations to save on budgets. On this approach, KM1[22] commented, "Phoenix TV has almost all the Hong Kong or martial arts programs' copyrights (*pangwon*) that were popular in the 1980s and 1990s, to the best of my knowledge. They are sold in ten to twenty programs as a package."

Main Melody Subfield

The Chinese main melody subfield refers to dramas with politically laden themes, and those that capture support for the Chinese party and state. Two typical themes exist in the subfield: revolution and anti-Japanese movements. The Chinese main melody dramas in South Korea are located in the position of high political capital, but low cultural and economic capital. First, the key logic on the production side is high political capital, embedded through Chinese educational and cultural elements. Second, ostensibly the most important type of capital for this subfield is political capital. Third, due to these characteristics, it is less likely to be converted to economic capital in South Korea. Fourth, the highly political and ideological dimensions of this subfield are usually difficult for South Korean media professionals to import, but some interesting exceptions are observed. Certainly, the main melody subfield has a limited audience in South Korea (see Chap. 4). KM17 commented, "Due to South Korean audiences' mixed and complex views on Japan, this subfield is imported."[23] As such, in 2015 the main melody drama *Nirvana in Fire* (*Langyabang*), based on the story of a Chinese spy in the anti-Japanese regime, gained popularity by offering a way to look back on Korean history critically and to reflect on alternatives for Korean agency see Lee 2016) (Fig. 3.4 and Table 3.2).

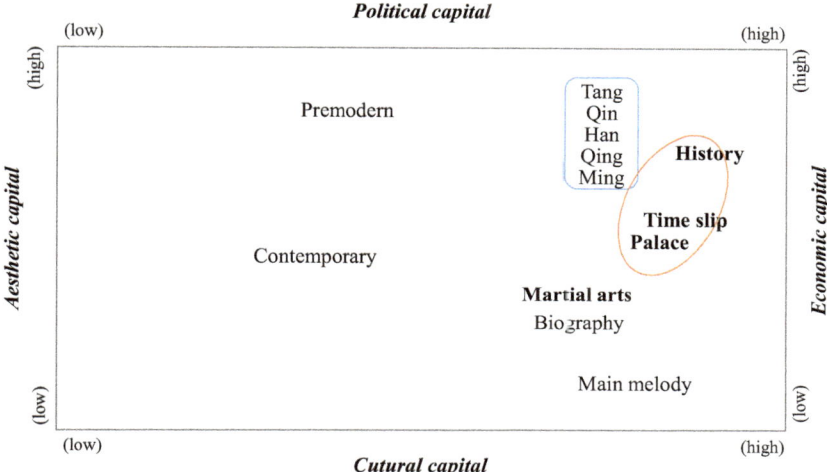

Fig. 3.4 Chinese televisual field in South Korea: capital. Source: Compiled by the Author

Table 3.2 Chinese televisual subfields in South Korea

	Historical subfield	Martial arts subfield	Main melody subfield
Key logic on the production side	Cultural logic, political logic	Cultural logic	Political logic
Important capital	Cultural capital	Cultural capital	Political capital
Capital conversion	To economic capital	To economic capital	
Demand of production	High	Middle	High
Mode of import	High	Middle	Low
Mode of consumption	High	High	Low

Source: Compiled by the Author

Note: The attributes are modified from Nakajima's (2016) analysis on Chinese cinematic field

Japan

SKAPA, as part of the BS platform, has a WOWOW channel. On the CS platform, the Ginga and Neco channels are the leading importers of Chinese products (Biglobe n.d.; Chinese Drama Legend n.d.; Ginga n.d.; Neco n.d.). Ginga has a special segment on historical drama (*Nitchūkan rekishi dorama · eiga*), whereas, Neco has a dedicated section on martial arts (*Bukyō dorama*), Chinese Wave products (*Karyū sakuhin*), and a "Jackie Chan Theater" (*Jakkī chen gekijō*) (Ginga n.d.; Neco n.d.). In recent years, Cinem@rt has emerged as a broadcast platform for Chinese television dramas, along with Asian dramas, making it equivalent to the AsiaN channel of South Korea (AsiaN n.d.; Cinem@rt n.d.).

Unfortunately, the value and size of Chinese dramas imported by Japan fluctuated (see Chap. 2). "This is because of quality and theme of dramas that are available for import," according to JM5.[24] However, what is clear is that Chinese historical and martial arts subfields are imported regardless of the broadcast year. As a note, although Hong Kong television dramas are an important part of the martial arts subfield, these productions exist outside the boundaries of mainland Chinese dramas; thus, they do not receive attention in the discussion below.

Historical Subfield

As in the case of South Korea, the subfield of Chinese historical dramas in Japan is located in the position of high cultural capital, high economic capital but low political capital. One popular subgenre of historical dramas is biography, or rather stories about heroes. A series featuring *Shu Genshō* (朱元璋) of the Ming dynasty is an example. Another subgenre is built upon "stories in the palace"; for example, *Ō no kōkyū* (王の後宮) and *Futari no ōjo* (二人の王女). Notably, the time slip genre, in such series as *Scarlet Heart*, is less popular in Japan than in South Korea.

The characteristics of Chinese historical drama in Japan can be summarized here: first, the "key logic on the production side" of historical dramas is cultural as well as political because the key rationale for television series production in China is not only engaged with its culture and history, but also with a rather implicit political attribute. Second, the most important form of capital in Japan is cultural capital, which is a selling point that is related to representations of culture and history in Chinese historical dramas. Third, this subfield of historical dramas has the potential to attract a high level of economic capital, in the form of revenue and/or audience ratings for media professionals and markets in Japan. Additionally, Japanese media professionals can convert cultural capital to economic capital. Three main factors which are associated with the conversion from cultural capital to economic capital were mentioned in interviews with Japanese media professionals. Foremost, the *balancing of budgets*: companies exist for profits and therefore they need to enhance profits over costs. JM5[25] said, "In general, Chinese products are cheaper than producing a Japanese program in Japan in the first place; that was the reason for Japanese production companies to buy Korean products." Once products of another country of origin are established and they can guarantee a certain level of quality, Japanese producers will favor those options rather than explore new options, such as importing media products from elsewhere. In the past, broadcasting companies in Japan did not have to consider the budget issue seriously, as they had enough funding to utilize money for producing programs; however, nowadays they have to manage money and resources as they plan what to make and how to sell it (Korea Creative Content Agency 2010).[26]

Given this situation and the exporting "doldrums" of Japanese cultural products, Japan offsets its profits by importing overseas programs. With bulky episodes, the historical subfield is welcomed by Japanese media professionals for the following reasons.

Some Japanese media professionals point to a different issue here—the quality of products that they are importing to the Japanese marketplace. As JM11,[27] a producer at Nippon TV, said, "There are Rank S, Rank A and Rank B products and so forth in the Japanese media market. From Rank B to Rank S, the price will go higher, but they're less risky. Yet, if one goes for Rank B, instead of Rank S, it can be much cheaper, but with lots of risks." Price, in general, vouches for a certain quality, yet quality and cost make up a double-edged sword. Tied to the impression that Chinese television dramas do not always vouch for high quality, which emerged in interviews with Korean media professionals earlier in this chapter, these series are purchased to fill time on a low budget. As in South Korea, foreign media programs often function as a substitute in Japan. This is evident when the products are not from a country that produces popular media products. As JM2,[28] a journalist working in Japanese media, said, "In terrestrial television, Korean dramas used to be function by filling the available time. But, after the Korean Wave hit Japan, it was not the case anymore." This corresponds to the two previous points, evincing that filling available time is akin to saving of money in order to enhance profits. Once a media product is purchased, it can be circulated over time, especially when the product has a ready audience.

Martial Arts Subfield
The subfield of Chinese martial arts dramas in Japan is located in the position of medium cultural capital and high economic capital. The key logic on the production side is fairly cultural because it is embedded with cultural values. The important form of capital for this subfield is cultural capital, although the level of this capital is not as high or as cemented as in the historical subfield. Due to a core viewership that is always interested in martial arts, cultural capital is, like in South Korea, potentially convertible to economic capital. Thus, the modes of import and consumption exist. One of the salient reasons to import martial arts is because this subfield itself has a stable fandom that is always attracted to this subfield. DVDs and VCDs are important sources and constitute a novel characteristic of the Japanese media market (Culture Convenience Club 2012; JVA 2011, 2012). Marital art dramas are popularly demanded by Japanese audiences, according to a Tsutaya Shibuya manager. Thus, the potential for cultural capital to monetize is well recognized by Japanese media professionals. There are many DVD and VCD rental shops in Japan, unlike in South Korea. Among them, GEO and Tsutaya, which have more 1400 stores, are among the biggest. Japanese and Western movies and dramas exist in separate sections (Culture Convenience Club 2012). South Korean, Chinese, and other Asian products, on the other hand, are classified under the "Asia" section, stocking around 15 percent of the shops. Classifications and inventory numbers are indicators of marketability and salability. Producers tend to buy a single program in a "package," which makes it easy for them to explore several combinations of products from only one program. Broadcasting rights regarding terrestrial, satellite and cable channels are grouped, while regulations for producing and circulating VCDs and DVDs remain separate. In the process of combining products to sell to the general audience, media professionals manufacture local tastes by giving local people choices to explore; however, it seems that this strategy does not play out very well. Another selection factor is that media professionals regard the martial arts subfield to be a hallmark of Chinese television dramas. In this manner, Japanese media professionals also use martial art dramas to manufacture local tastes. JM4,[29] a Japanese interviewee who works for a media company commented, "In other parts of Asia, some Asian dramas have been popular among some people. Martial arts dramas and films are such examples. We, Japanese producers, have this in mind when importing them." Foreign media products are imported not just because of Japanese audiences' tastes, but they are also a response to what others watch (Fig. 3.5 and Table 3.3).

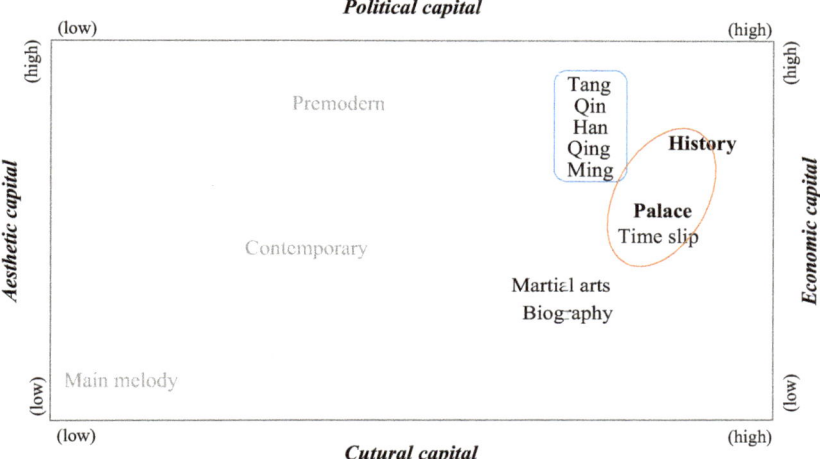

Fig. 3.5 Chinese televisual field in Japan: capital. Notes: Gray refers to those genres (subfields) that exist in South Korea but not in Japan. Source: Compiled by the Author

Table 3.3   Chinese televisual subfields in Japan

	Historical subfield	Martial arts subfield
Key logic on the production side	Cultural logic, political logic	Cultural logic
Important capital	Cultural capital	Cultural capital
Capital conversion	To economic capital	To economic capital
Mode of import	High	Middle
Mode of consumption	High	High

Source: Compiled by the Author

Note: The attributes are modified from Nakajima (2016)'s analysis on Chinese cinematic field

COMPARATIVE PERSPECTIVE

In recent years, the television markets in South Korea and Japan have similar institutional arrangements and allocations of Chinese programs on cable television channels, but through these products they establish divergent patterns in (un)making a transnational Chinese soft power field. There are three main reasons for this.

First, although the development of such market systems differs between these two countries, "cable" television channels are landing sites for Chinese programs in the similarly institutionalized television markets of South Korea and Japan. In South Korea, the institutionalization of Chinese television products occurs on cable television, with channels that strongly represent such programs. In Japan, BS and CS channels, which are functionally equivalent to South Korea's cable networks, house Chinese programs.

Second, although South Korean and Japanese media professionals utilize the same import mechanism, these two countries differ in terms of rationales and allocations for certain Chinese televisual subfields. Higher opportunity costs, with numerous episodes at a reasonable price are the main reasons for importing Chinese television products in both countries. In terms of distinctions, the personal taste of a media professional is highlighted in the case of South Korea, while the potential for audience expansion guides on the role of media professionals in Japan. In addition, in recognition of limited celebrity capital, which is often lamented by Korean and Japanese audiences (see Chaps. 4 and 6), Chinese televisual subfields market celebrity capital to South Korean and Japanese media professionals differently. Whereas celebrity capital in Korea is magnified when a Korean co-star or a famous Chinese celebrity stars in Chinese televisual subfields, mixed Japanese celebrities are often welcomed in Japan. These differences occur out of the patterns and making of audiences in the configurations of transnational Chinese soft power fields in South Korea and Japan. They are affected by the careful import selections of media professionals, who mediatize the forms of capital in Chinese televisual subfields. This, with a focus on audiences, will be further discussed in Chap. 4.

Third, the historical and martial arts subfields play a predominant role in the Chinese televisual subfields in South Korea and Japan. As a result, South Korean and Japanese media professionals have similar interpretations of the corresponding forms of capital. However, South Korea and Japan select quite different (if limited) Chinese televisual subfields. In South Korea, the main melody and contemporary subfields are occasionally broadcast. The first links Chinese and South Korean viewers who are familiar with anti-Japanese sentiments; the second is imbued with locally attractive Korean celebrity capital. In contrast, these two subfields hardly exist in Japan (Shanghaiist 2015; Yu 2015). By importing provocative and controversial televisual subfields, South Korean media professionals maximize the economic capital of these subfields.

In China's soft power policy (see Chap. 1), South Korea and Japan are listed as the very first target countries. The existing literature does not usually examine the roles and processes of markets and of media professionals as gatekeepers in these two countries, who block the influence of Chinese soft power, particularly at the audience level, and shape a limited transnational soft power field in the two receiving countries. As explained in this chapter, the similar institutional arrangements of television markets, such as cable television as the only venue for foreign media products, certainly offer a base for comparison. Altogether, there are subtle discrepancies in the ways that media professionals make sense of the forms of capital operating in the televisual fields in South Korea and Japan. And, as shall be seen later in this study, local audiences shape the divergent pathways of China's effort to build soft power fields in these two neighboring countries in northeast Asia.

Conclusion

This chapter has elaborated upon the ways in which television markets and media professionals in South Korea and Japan function as gatekeepers of the mediatized projection of China's soft power via television channels.

Regarding the engendering of mediatized televisual fields in South Korea and Japan, the first characteristic to note is the dual media market system, wherein foreign television products are intentionally broadcast exclusively on the terrestrial market and predominantly via "cable." Markets are the key institutions for the possible penetration of soft power. However, the analysis in this chapter has shown that there is a missing link between China's mediatized projection and the markets of receiving countries.

On one level, in terms of content, the characteristics of television products are transformed when they move from a domestic market to a transnational market. In other words, SAPPRFT does not translate well into the South Korean and Japanese televisual fields. In a related vein, the different forms of capital mediated through television content shape the content's import desirability among media professionals and its propensity for consumption by audiences. In particular, the celebrity capital of imported Chinese television series is relatively weak, while also relying on pan-Chinese and local actors. This translates, in Japan, to the starring of a Japanese-Taiwanese actor. In South Korea, Korean actresses and actors who are popular and work predominantly in Chinese media are typically cast in place of Chinese celebrities to satisfy alternative/modified needs for celebrity capital. On another level, the accumulation of forms of capital in the Chinese televisual field does not occur to the same degree in South Korea and Japan.

Many subfields, as detailed in Chap. 2, such as premodern, contemporary, and main melody dramas, have basically disappeared only to be imported and presented in the Chinese transnational soft power fields in South Korea and Japan. According to the logic of import, media professionals in South Korea and Japan do not necessarily import subfields that signify lower economic capital and depleted cultural capital, as they know well that this will lead to smaller audiences.

The import of media products is not only constrained by market structures and media practitioners, but must also accommodate the market demands of the importing society. Priority is generally given to domestic media products, as in the cases of South Korean and Japanese terrestrial television systems. On the other hand, cable television stations are often reserved as venues for imported foreign media products. Annual data from the Korean Communications Commissions show that market demands encourage South Korean media professionals to import profitable foreign programs. By the same token, cheaper Chinese programs with a large number of episodes have been exported to South Korea. In the case of Japan, media professionals do not have overt control over the inflow of Chinese programs, as these do not typically enjoy a broad audience base. The next chapters will analyze the audience reception of Chinese television products in South Korea and Japan, and demonstrate that the institutional dimension of importing Chinese media products and consumers' choices influence China's ambition to accomplish its mediatized soft power aspirations in the two countries.

Second, the mechanism of selective appropriation of Chinese television products by local media professionals into the televisual fields of the importing countries operate along several themes. Media professionals in the South Korean market function not as cultural intermediaries, but as gatekeepers via a systematic process of selective "filtering out." In a related manner, the process of importing and the roles of media professionals are important. As this chapter has shown, South Korean media practitioners are rather open to importing Chinese programs, as they tend to be cheaper in bulk and relatively easy to place within the cable stations market. Japanese media producers, on the other hand, tend to play safe by favoring quality South Korean programs that are popular with viewers, over Chinese programs.

Chapter 4, based on ample empirical data, explores how and why China's soft power dilemma occurs at the audience level in the televisual fields of South Korea and Japan.

NOTES

1. For more on field analysis in Sociology, see Hanquinet and Savage (2015) and Savage and Silva (2013).
2. It is formerly known as the State Administration of Radio, Film, and Television (SARFT). It is under the State Council and to administer and supervise the state-owned enterprises engaged in the television, radio, and film industries.
3. CM20, interview with a Chinese academic, February 28, 2012, Shenzhen, China.
4. CM36, interview with a Chinese academic, August 4, 2013, Beijing, China.
5. Such events held in China include Beijing International TV Week, Shanghai TV Festival, Sichuan TV Festival, and *Quanguo guochan dianshijiemu zhanshi jiaoyihui* (Domestic TV Programs Exchange). Venues outside of China include Asia TV Forum & Market in Singapore, Tokyo International Film Festival in Japan, Banff World Media Festival (formerly, Banff World Television Festival) in Canada, BRITDOC Foundation (formerly Channel 4 BRITDOC Foundation), Celtic Media Festival (Celtic Film Media Festival) in the United Kingdom, DISCOP, Burgh International Television Festival, Festival International de Programmes Audiovisuals, FesTVal in Spain, ITVFest (Independent Television Festival), Monte-Carlo Television Festival, New York Television Festival, MIPTV & MIPCOM in France.
6. Details of the products include the number of episodes, featured actors or actresses, similar products that were on the market, and potentially attractive sales points.
7. CM21, interview with a Chinese media professional February 28, 2012, Shenzhen, China.
8. JM5, interview with a Nippon TV producer, May 10, 2013, Tokyo, Japan.
9. This related matter is often handled by the Global Business Department, although the actual name can vary.
10. A "broker" or an "agent" is *junggaein* in Korean and *chukajin* in Japanese.
11. KM1, interview with a South Korean producer, December 20, 2011, Seoul, South Korea.
12. This can be also found in other types of cultural markets such as news media, the art worlds (Becker 1982), and the fashion industry (Mears 2011).
13. Here television channels that are available in South Korea through a linear method are not included. A linear service is one in which program providers determine the program scheduling. A non-linear service is one where program providers provide catalogues and viewers decide viewing time based on the catalogues. A linear method prevails on satellite or foreign

channels, which directly broadcast from a source country to other countries. CCTV and TVB are the examples of a linear service.

14. KM4, interview with a Korean television producer, January 19, 2012, Seoul, South Korea.

15. If viewers want to watch Western channels such as HBO and Discovery, they need to subscribe to an extra service that includes these channels.

16. Korean-related programs not only include dramas, movies, and variety shows from South Korea, but also entertainment and variety programs that are made in Japan.

17. KM9, interview with a South Korean producer, March 17, 2012, Seoul, South Korea.

18. This is a prevailing idea among both producers and audiences in South Korea.

19. KM4, interview with a South Korean TV producer, January 19, 2012, Seoul, South Korea.

20. See for the phenomenon of *Three Kingdoms (Samgukji)* in South Korea in Chapter 3. *Three Kingdoms, Huangbihong* and *Shuihuji* are examples.

21. See the phenomenon of *muhyeop* novels in South Korea. Jin Yong's novels are famous in South Korea.

22. KM1, interview with a South Korean producer, December 20, 2011, Seoul, South Korea.

23. Ibid.

24. JM6, interview with a Japanese media professional, May 10, 2012, Tokyo, Japan.

25. JM5, interview with a Japanese media professional, May 10, 2012, Tokyo, Japan.

26. In this line, see Korea Creative Content Agency (2010).

27. JM11, interview with a Japanese media professional, May 16, 2012, Tokyo, Japan.

28. KM2, interview with a South Korean media professional, December 22, 2011, Seoul, South Korea.

29. JM4, interview with a Japanese media professional, May 8, 2012, Tokyo, Japan.

References

Asia Content Marketing Association. n.d. Accessed April 14, 2014. http://asia-contentmarketing.net/.

Asia TV Forum and Market. 2016. Accessed February 17, 2017. http://www.asiatvforum.com/.

AsiaN. n.d. Accessed April 14, 2014. www.asiantv.co.kr.

Becker, Howard. 1982. *Art Worlds*. Berkeley and Los Angeles: University of California Press.

Biglobe. n.d. Accessed April 5, 2014. http://broadband.biglobe.ne.jp/contents/china_sp.html.

Bourdieu, Pierre. 1993. *The Field of Cultural Production*. New York: Columbia University Press. Translated in English.

Bühlmann, Felix, Thomas David, and André Mach. 2013. Cosmopolitan Capital and the Internationalization of the Field of Business Elites: Evidence from the Swiss Case. *Cultural Sociology* 7 (2): 211–229.

Channel Ching. n.d. Accessed July 15, 2017. ching.hyundaimedia.com.

China Television Drama Production Industry Association. 2015. Notice on 2015 China (Shenzhen) International TV Drama & TV Program Fair. Accessed September 15, 2017. http://jyh.ctpia.com.cn/en/Overview/content_1.shtml.

Chinese Drama Legend. n.d. Accessed July 15, 2017. http://www.chuka-drama.com/lineup/.

Cinem@rt. n.d. Accessed July 15, 2017. http://www.cinemart.co.jp/dramax/.

Culture Convenience Club. 2012. TSUTAYA、Taiwan・Taojplishi nai ni hatsu shutten Taiwan CMC gurūpu to no kokusaitekina entateinment jigyō ni kansuru senryakuteki teikei no ikkantoshite 「ageikageoto (yaiinin)」 ga kamei、12gatsu27nini minkenten ōpun [Information regarding the business and capital Joint Venture between Culture Convenience Club Co., Ltd. and the CMC Magnetics Corporation of Taiwan]. Accessed November 5, 2013. http://www.ccc.co.jp/company/news/2012/20121226_003534.html.

Edwards, Lee. 2012. Exploring the Role of Public Relations as a Cultural Intermediary Occupation. *Cultural Sociology* 6 (4): 438–454.

Esraey, Ashley, and Xiao Qiang. 2011. Digital Communication and Political Change. *International Journal of Communication* 5: 298–319.

Ginga. n.d. Accessed July 15, 2017. http://www.ch-ginga.jp/program/.

Hanquinet, Laurie, and Mike Savage, eds. 2015. *Routledge International Handbook of the Sociology of Art and Culture*. London and New York: Routledge.

Italian Trade Commission [Istituto nazionale per il Commercio Estero]. 2011. *China Television Industry Market Report*. June 3. Shanghai: Italian Trade Commission.

Janssen, Susanne, and Marc Verboord. 2015. Cultural Mediators and Gatekeepers. In *International Encyclopedia of the Social & Behavioral Sciences*, ed. James D. Wright, 2nd ed., 440–446. Oxford: Elsevier.

Japan Video Software Association [JVA]. 2011. *Bideo Sofutowea Tōkei Chōsa Repōto 2001–2011 [Video Software Statistical Survey Reports 2001–2011]*. Tokyo: Japan Video Software Association.

———. 2012. JVA rentaru shoppu no dōkō rentaru shoppu ni kansuru [The Trend of JVA Rental Shops]. *JVA nenji chōsa [JVA Annual Survey on Rental Shops]*. Tokyo: Japan Video Software Association.

Junghwa TV. n.d. Accessed July 15, 2017. zhtv.interest.me.

Korea Creative Content Agency. 2010. *Ilbon ui contentsu sanoep [Japan's Contents Industry]*. Issue Paper 27. Seoul: Korea Creative Content Agency.

———. 2011. 2010 nyeon bangsong contents suchulip hyeonhwang gwa jeonmang [The Current Situation of and Prospects for Exports and Imports of Media Contents in 2010]. *KOCCA Focus* 5 (3): 1–23.

Korean Broadcasting Commission *[Bangsong Wiewonhoe]*. 2002. *2002 nyeon Bangsong Siltae Sanoepjosa Bogoseo [A Report of Broadcasting Industry of 2002]*. Seoul: Korean Broadcasting Commission.

———. 2003. *2003 nyeon Bangsong Siltae Sanoepjosa Bogoseo [A Report of Broadcasting Industry of 2003]*. Seoul: Korean Broadcasting Commission.

———. 2004. *2004 nyeon Bangsong Siltae Sanoepjosa Bogoseo [A Report of Broadcasting Industry of 2004]*. Seoul: Korean Broadcasting Commission.

———. 2005. *2005 nyeon Bangsong Siltae Sanoepjosa Bogoseo [A Report of Broadcasting Industry of 2005]*. Seoul: Korean Broadcasting Commission.

———. 2006. *2006 nyeon Bangsong Siltae Sanoepjosa Bogoseo [A Report of Broadcasting Industry of 2006]*. Seoul: Korean Broadcasting Commission.

———. 2007. *2007 nyeon Bangsong Siltae Sanoepjosa Bogoseo [A Report of Broadcasting Industry of 2007]*. Seoul: Korean Broadcasting Commission.

Korea Communications Commission *[Bangsong Tongshin Wiewonhoe]*. 2008. *2008 nyeon Bangsong Siltae Sanoepjosa Bogoseo [A Report of Broadcasting Industry of 2008]*. Seoul: Korea Communications Commission.

———. 2009. *2009 nyeon Bangsong Siltae Sanoepjosa Bogoseo [A Report of Broadcasting Industry of 2009]*. Seoul: Korea Communications Commission.

———. 2010. *2010 nyeon Bangsong Siltae Sanoepjosa Bogoseo [A Report of Broadcasting Industry of 2010]*. Seoul: Korea Communications Commission.

———. 2011. *2011 nyeon Bangsong Siltae Sanoepjosa Bogoseo [A Report of Broadcasting Industry of 2011]*. Seoul: Korea Communications Commission.

———. 2012. *2012 nyeon Bangsong Siltae Sanoepjosa Bogoseo [A Report of Broadcasting Industry of 2012]*. Seoul: Korea Communications Commission.

Lee, Sae-sam. 2016. Jungguk dramarel sayonghaneun bangbeop [How to Use 'Chinese Dramas']. *Donga Ilbo*, April 19. Accessed June 27, 2017. http://news.donga.com/3/all/20160419/77654374/1.

Mears, Ashley. 2011. *Pricing Beauty: The Making of a Fashion Model*. Berkeley: University of California Press.

Ministry of Science, ICT and Future Planning and Korea Communications Commission *[Bangsong Tongshin Wiewonhoe]*. 2013. *2013 nyeon Bangsong Siltae Sanoepjosa Bogoseo [A Report of Broadcasting Industry of 2013]*. Seoul: Korea Communications Commission.

———. 2014. *2014 nyeon Bangsong Siltae Sanoepjosa Bogoseo [A Report of Broadcasting Industry of 2014]*. Seoul: Korea Communications Commission.

———. 2015. *2015 nyeon Bangsong Siltae Sanoepjosa Bogoseo [A Report of Broadcasting Industry of 2015]*. Seoul: Korea Communications Commission.

———. 2016. *2016 nyeon Bangsong Siltae Sanoepjosa Bogoseo [A Report of Broadcasting Industry of 2016]*. Seoul: Korea Communications Commission.

Moor, Liz. 2012. Beyond Cultural Intermediaries? A Socio-Technical Perspective on the Market for Social Interventions. *European Journal of Cultural Studies* 15 (5): 563–580.

Nakajima, Seio. 2016. The Genesis, Structure and Transformation of the Contemporary Chinese Cinematic Field: Global Linkages and National Refractions. *Global Media and Communication* 12 (1): 85–108.

Neco. n.d. Accessed July 15, 2017. http://www.necoweb.com/neco/program/category.php?id=3.

Savage, Mike, and Elizabeth B. Silva. 2013. Field Analysis in Cultural Sociology. *Cultural Sociology* 7 (2): 111–126.

Shanghaiist. 2015. Even More Anti-Japan War Dramas Will Fill China's Airwaves in Run-up to Victory Day Celebrations. *Shanghaiist*, August 30. Accessed July 22, 2016. http://shanghaiist.com/2015/08/30/more_anti_japan_dramas.php.

Smith Maguire, Jennifer, and Julian Matthews. 2012. Are We All Cultural Intermediaries Now? An Introduction to Cultural Intermediaries in Context. *European Journal of Cultural Studies* 15 (5): 551–562.

Su, Wendy. 2011. New Strategies of China's Film Industry as Soft Power. *Global Media and Communication* 6 (3): 317–322.

Tōyōkeizaishinpōsha, ed. 2012. *Gyōkai chizu 2013-nenban [Map of Industry 2013]*. Tokyo: Tōyōkeizaishinpōsha.

Wang, Huning. 1993. Zuowei Guojia Shili de Wenhua: Ruanquanli [National Culture Power: The Soft Authority]. *Fudan Daxue Xuebao [Fudan University Journal Social Sciences Version]* March: 23–28.

Wang, Hongying, and Yeh-Chung Lu. 2008. The Conception of Soft Power and Its Policy Implications: A Comparative Study of China and Taiwan. *Journal of Contemporary China* 15 (56): 438.

Yu, Miles. 2015. China's Bizarre Anti-Japanese TV and Movie Kitsch Backfire. *Washington Times*, May 21. Accessed July 22, 2016. http://www.washingtontimes.com/news/2015/may/21/inside-china-anti-japanese-tv-propaganda-dramas-ba/.

Local Embeddedness, Domestification, and Capital Displacement: The Case of Offline Media

INTRODUCTION

On March 8, 2006, a Korean newspaper *Sekye Ilbo* published an article titled "*Hualiu catching up with Hallyu dramas… only half of broadcasted Hallyu* dramas were aired on Japanese TVs (Kim 2006)."[1] What is discussed in the article is clouded by the fear that South Korean media might lose its presence in Japan. It claims, "with Japanese terrestrial stations—which were used to broadcast Korean dramas—now decreased, Korean dramas have now lost slots over *Hualiu* dramas, such as those from China, Hong Kong, Taiwan." Another report titled "The current situation and prospects for Korean dramas in Japan" by the Korea Broadcasting Institute claims "The number of Korean dramas on Japanese terrestrial stations is now decreased from 64 last February to 36. …In contrast, TV series from the PRC, Taiwan, and Hong Kong have recently gained popularity in Japan, and aired 19 dramas across 18 broadcasting stations." Less than one month later, on April 4, 2006,[2] another Korean newspaper *Hankook Ilbo* reported under the title "*Hualiu* is emerging while *Hallyu* is sleeping in Japan," comparing *Hallyu* with *Hualiu*. The article argues, "While *Hallyu* has not been able to find new momentum in Japan, *Hualiu* has started to win over Japanese minds (Lee 2006)." All of the articles concern the diminishing of Korean drama exports to Japan, alongside the emergence of "Chinese" dramas. Such stories did not stop in 2006, and

© The Author(s) 2018   81
C. S. Lee, *Soft Power Made in China*,
https://doi.org/10.1007/978-3-319-93115-9_4

continued for two more years. In 2008, *Munhwa Ilbo* wrote that "The explosive growth of *Hualiu* ... is getting ready to 'attack Korea' (Yoo 2008)." Likewise, this urged the Korean industry to be prepared to compete with a "new" player.

These three stories present snapshots of an emerging "Chinese" player in the inter-Asian media flow between South Korea and Japan. While the Korean Wave was deemed to be constrained in its export, there was a debate within South Korean and Japanese academic circles and the journalistic field, especially in the early 2000s, about identifying the next player in the televisionsphere and marketplace.[3] These discourses show not only different flavors of insecurities and fears about the (dis)continuity of the Korean Wave, but they also suggest a competition that could be introduced by a newcomer. As such, Korean journalists have expected to see the Chinese Wave (*Hwaryu* in Korean, *Karyū* in Japanese) rise as an alternative to the Korean Wave.

Against this backdrop, this chapter specifically looks to local contexts for why China's TV series-mediated soft power has difficulties in reaching South Korean audiences. In doing so, I utilize the concept of "local embeddedness" combined with "domestification," which refers to the ways in which certain kinds of media programs can be watched domestically, or at home (Ivy 1995).[4] Whereas the original definition of "domestification" regards the location of the consumption that takes place, the working definition in this study accords greater attention to the local embeddedness, both in the source and receiving countries that inhibits the reception of Chinese TV series and spread of soft power in South Korea. "Domestic(ation)," in the case of Chinese televised soft power, is used to indicate different things depending on the context. This concept highlights domestic factors that might inhibit the further export of Chinese TV series to the target country, as well as under what conditions such could happen in the importing country.

As the source country, China possesses "local" factors that inhibit the consumption of Chinese TV series by South Korean and Japanese audiences (see Chap. 3). On the import side of this dynamic, transnational audiences' consumption behavior is similarly influenced by the perceptions of other Koreans and Japanese toward China and Chinese products. "The domestication of the foreign," in the words of anthropologist Marilyn Ivy (1995: 3), explains the internationalization and embrace of foreign culture by a host society alongside desires to disseminate its own culture into the world. Here, it applies to how South Korean and Japanese consumers negotiate their choice to watch Chinese series and I use the term of "the local embeddedness of the foreign" by modifying from Ivy's concept. To that end, this chapter illuminates how existing "national" characters/motifs in complete Chinese TV dramas obstruct a transnational soft power field in South Korea and Japan, and in turn fail to reach Korean and Japanese audiences.

In what follows, this chapter delves into the soft power paradox to explain the problematic local embeddedness of the foreign in South Korea and Japan, with specific reference to the local construction of "Chinese" media. Responding to the question of "why Chinese TV encounters difficulties in circulating among transnational audiences," it is necessary to compare the end-products of "domestication" against the "domesticated" factors from the source country. These dynamics are viewed by Korean and Japanese respondents and play a role in constructing perceptions about China in their respective receiving country. The chapter will contend that local embeddedness and the dual absence of crucial forms of capital in certain subfields create limits for Chinese TV series to facilitate the creation of a transnational soft power field in South Korea and Japan. This chapter highlights similarities and differences between China's soft power dilemmas in these two quasi-Sinophone importing countries.

"Stepping Off on the Wrong Foot": Absence of Distinct Subfields of Chinese Television Series

Televisual subfields, like genres in any other type of media, serve as "the container of media (Kolker 2009: 25)." TV dramas are no exception. In this chapter, I apply a field theory to create a space to discuss and devote attention to the pathways and mechanisms used not only for (un)forming different forms of capitals, but also for (un)creating a transnational soft power field.

The televisual subfields of Chinese television series—historical, martial arts, biography, time slip, premodern, main melody. and contemporary—are well-defined genres in China (see Chap. 2); however, when it comes to their recognition by non-Chinese consumers, it is a rather different story. Why are the perceptions of other East Asian consumers different from those of their counterparts in China? How do these distinct subfields disappear at the micro level in the importing countries? This leads to two interrelated explanations: on the one hand, interviewees have pointed to an absence of (inter-cultural) understanding and audience negligence of the distinct subfields of Chinese television series. On the other hand, Korean and Japanese respondents feel that an underdevelopment of subfields creates issues for potential East Asian audiences.

KV85, an informant who enthusiastically identifies as a fan of Chinese dramas, was asked "what kind of Chinese television series do you watch?" Puzzled, she answered, "I only know historical dramas… Is there any other kind of Chinese drama?"[5] JV12[6] mentioned in a similar vein, "I watched the drama *Journey to the West* and am only aware of historical Chinese series." KV85 and JV12's responses are typical for my Korean and Japanese informants, whether at the heart of Tokyo or Seoul. Their understanding of what Chinese television series *are* revolves around their knowledge of the subfields of Chinese television series. This simple question of preference capitulates the entrance to Chinese soft power pathways, and implies the very first soft power dilemma here. "Stepping off on the wrong foot" describes this paradox well.

In sharp contrast with Korean and Japanese viewers' (mis)interpretation of a lack of diversity in the available range of TV series subfields, the guidelines of the SARFT (2012) and the produced thematic subfields of Chinese television series offer us a different story. The production of Chinese TV series in China is based upon both the situation of the series in Chinese history and the main theme of the series. As presented in Chap. 2 and Fig. 2.3, the ways in which Chinese TV series are managed and produced are juxtaposed along a historical timeline—from ancient to contemporary—with thematic subfields. In fact, there are a number of subfields that are produced exclusively in China. From the Korean audiences' lamentation of a shortage of diversity in Chinese TV drama genres, however, we can see that what is imported across borders encompasses only a small part of the whole range of what is produced in China.

As such, several distinct subfields exist within Chinese TV dramas as a medium, but in reality Korean and Japanese audiences do not seem to be aware of this and are therefore usually exposed to a limited range of Chinese content. Concerns about the mistranslation of televisual subfields into South Korean and Japanese markets, and related discontents, are predominant in interviews with Koreans and Japanese informants.

> Most of the Chinese dramas (that are imported) are historical or martial arts types. Even with Korean dramas, those who are manic for historical types only watch such dramas. Likewise, historical dramas that are from China garner much less audience in South Korea. In particular, because the Chinese version is not very interesting nor has a lot of 'things to see,' people feel it's not worth much of their interest.[7]

KV43's narrative captures, in particular, his misunderstanding of what is imported to the Korean televisionsphere compared to what is produced in China, demonstrating inconsistencies between what Korean audiences (as non-Chinese speakers) think is produced in China and what they believe they could consume in South Korea.

It is worthwhile to expose that locating Chinese media consumers in Japan is not an easy task because of the limited range of Chinese programs that are imported into the country. As Chap. 6 presents, Taiwanese and Hong Kong-produced television series are much more popular than Chinese television series in Japan. Furthermore, the favorable relationship between Taiwan and Japan shapes, to a large extent, a transnational Chinese soft power field via outsourced (Taiwanese) soft power in Japan. Consequently, it was difficult to find attentive viewers of exclusively "Chinese" television series; those who watch "PRC" Chinese media products in Japan were few among my interviewees. They lamented that many of the premodern and modern Chinese televisual subfields portray anti-Japanese sentiments and revolutionary themes, making them difficult to export to Japan. Thus, these thematic Chinese media products were by and large missing not only from Japanese TV schedules, but also from my fieldwork data. Such observations were also generally noted among Japanese media professionals. The underdevelopment of imported subfields specifically for the Japanese market impacts the problematic local embeddedness that leads to dilemmas for China's soft power.

Given the similarly limited thematic range and restricted distribution of imported Chinese programs in Japan, their consumption by Japanese audiences is inherently constrained. In response to the same question about her preferred Chinese television series, JV17⁵ told me, "maybe TV series based on historical or classical novels? I can only think of those." As in the case of my Korean informants, Japanese informants were also limited in the variety of Chinese television series they could access in Japan.

Others in South Korea described the less developed Chinese subfields on the Korean market, but in more detail and a rather different manner than I encountered with my interviewees in Japan. In fact, we cannot blame the informants for their perception of a limited range of genres because there is evidence that most of television series imported from China to South Korean and Japanese marketplaces *are* historical subfields. For example, many of the recently imported TV serial dramas to South Korea are historical dramas (see Chap. 3). As Fig. 3.3 has already shown, historical subfields series have been imported every year for the last ten years, and the proportion of these imported historical subfields was always at least double the number of remaining subfields of Chinese television series on Korean cable TV stations. Following behind historical subfields, martial arts programs are the second most frequently imported Chinese television series to the Korean marketplace. This trend is similarly observed in the case of Japan.

As such, there is evidence of ruptures between China's transnational soft power field that the Chinese create, and Chinese transnational soft power field that quasi-Sinophone East Asian import countries shape. The underdevelopment of Chinese televisual subfields impedes China's transnational soft power field from being fully realized, while setting more for backgrounds for Chinese soft power creates paradoxes for both import contexts.

DUAL SIDES OF "LOCAL" EMBEDDEDNESS

Lost in Translation: Chinese Particularities in Foreign Contexts

Discrepancies exist between Korean and Japanese audiences' expectations of Chinese dramas and what Chinese TV series deliver. The ruptures are from local particularities and different trajectories in the development of Chinese dramas. This also links to the limited chance of converting existing Chinese series, and their characteristics, to other forms of capital.

Unlike American, Japanese and Korean TV series, Chinese dramas do not usually divide into multiple seasons with a smaller number of episodes.[9] KV67,[10] who enjoyed watching a new version of *Three Kingdoms*, said, "It was exciting, as I like history a lot. But even to me it was too much. 95 episodes for one season? I could not see all of them. Though I did not finish watching the episodes, I find this version of *Three Kingdoms* the best of the different versions." The value of the historical subfield, arguably the only Chinese televisual subfield which appeals to transnational audiences in quasi-Sinophone East Asia, is recognized by some audiences. However, the excessive number of episodes in this particular historical subfield drama puzzles even the most attentive consumers.

In terms of content, KV14 mentioned, "In China [Chinese television series], what is still prevalent in terms of themes is nationalism and patriotism. This makes Koreans who (wish to) watch Chinese [series] rather uncomfortable."[11] Distaste for the overtly nationalistic sentiment of Chinese television series is widely shared by other Korean informants.

Another informant, who works for an international trading company and had studied abroad and worked in China from 2002 to 2011, said, "Patriotic content is still very popular in China and is predominantly for Chinese content. I think this creates an adverse effect for Koreans who have initial interest in [only] the culture and language."[12] The patriotic sentiment of Chinese media products plays a detrimental role for Korean transnational audiences.

As the local embeddedness of the foreign fosters locally embedded consumption, similar subfields of Chinese TV series or particular cases might be interpreted divergently. Whereas Chinese and Koreans have not shared severe or ongoing major historical or political conflicts, until very recently with the installation of THAAD missiles which I will mention in Chap. 8, Chinese-Japanese relations have a much more complicated historical and political background. This conflicting situation results in commentary on slightly different emphases and seemingly different features, between what Korean and what Japanese audiences of a Chinese televisual subfield perceive as "nationalistic" and "patriotic."

As such, Chinese television series are also understood as politicized products, particularly to Japanese participants in my study. JV40's narrative epitomizes this: "I feel a reluctance towards Chinese television products because many of the products, even in China, are banned from TV." His antagonistic sentiment toward Chinese television series stems from local particularities of the series and the media system itself. He kept telling me, "I don't understand why the Chinese still produce anti-Japanese themes."[13] As his business is related to China and often allows him to travel to both small and big cities in China, particularly Dalian and Qingdao, he watches Chinese TV when he is on business trips. What he observed on Chinese TV unfortunately advocates against his own motherland and stirred feelings of being upset.

In 2012 when I was doing fieldwork in Tokyo and Yokohama, there was a moment when the Senkaku and Diaoyu Islands frequently appeared on TV. At the heart of the "war," many Japanese informants mentioned that political, historical, and territorial issues overrule everything that Japan does with China. In this vein, JV32[14] also reported that the Senkaku issue conjures up and even worsens China's image, in their eyes. JV11[15] indicated, "You know, a crewman was killed in a boat near China over the related issue of the Senkaku Island dispute. How China responded to this incident really made my friends and I think 'yappari'[16] China.'" Her narrative was highly emotional at this point, and implied that "China is different from Japan."

This line of thinking was prevalent among my Japanese informants and set tight boundaries for their consumption of Chinese television series against the heavily linked political, cultural and social factors in the media landscape.

JV11, JV32, JV40, and others in my study show how complicated historical and political relationships between the source and receiving countries of soft power play a critical role in determining which foreign—Japanese—audiences are willing to give Chinese television series a try. As such, there is evidence that Chinese television series have politicized peculiarities, but the dynamics are more complicated and highly elevated in Japanese respondents' narratives than in those of South Korean informants.

Local Embeddedness in Context

Some participants in South Korea described different dimensions of "local" embeddedness vis-à-vis Chinese television series. KV71 tried to maintain emotional distance to make a neutral statement: "Social prejudice or particularities in a society that are too strong make it difficult for products to travel."[17] What she told me brings us to another point; that local particularities are twofold in creating a transnational soft power field. On the one hand, the particularities lie in the contents of exported Chinese televisual products, that might primarily offer other forms of capital such as political and historical capital. On the other hand, the particularities can be located in the ways local people in the receiving countries perceive the contents and decode intended capital in the imported Chinese television series.

Likewise, the Chinese transnational soft power field in South Korea is particularly difficult to manage, whereby various intertwined historical, cultural and political issues and nationalistic sentiments exist. In other words, exported political capital—or Chinese nationalism—might be misunderstood or unacceptable to Korean publics and/or might trigger complicated sensitivities. In this regard, KV77[18] told me:

> Average Chinese dramas and films do not share Korean interests. [Their] stories are not particularly close to us. Contents are rather hard to understand because they're different from Korean dramas [local products].

He highlighted the difference between Chinese dramas and Korean dramas by implying that Chinese series' failure to meet the standards of Korean dramas is problematic. While KV82 consumes foreign—Chinese—television series, he expects the new series to be at least of a similar quality to what he is used to watching.

> First of all, from a Korean's point of view, there is a prejudice (or actually true…) that China-made products are like 'this' or 'that.' On the other hand, Koreans are trendy and easily adapt to change…. I think we have a strong sense of this… Compared to this, Chinese pop culture does not follow the pace and speed of Koreans. Also, the targets are still missing.[19]

Some of the local embeddedness often produces commentary on a lack of developments in Chinese television series. This informant pointed to an opinion that Chinese dramas have difficulty with fulfilling Koreans' expectations. Korean and Chinese dramas are not in a tug-of-war that requires a comparable level of developments, but rather Korean expectations and Chinese end-products are rather hard to reconcile.

While Japan has experienced the "the two lost decades (*wushinarareta 20 nen*)," China has experienced unprecedented economic success and marked itself as a rising power, not only in the region but on the global stage. Although my research does not explicitly focus on the geo-economic aspect of China's soft power, Japanese respondents propped up the economic rivalry as a background rationale for why China is experiencing a soft power dilemma in Japan. JV44,[20] a Japanese woman who works in the banking industry, feels strongly about the paradox of China's rise. She said, "I guess since the early 2000s, like 2001 or 2002, there was a sentiment in Japan that China is rising." She continued, "before I went to China, the images of China I carried were of the Tian'anmen Incident, corruption and the growing military. All of bad events, and becoming bigger and bigger (*ōkiini naru*). But later I could see more aspects of an economically-rising China." What Aoki implicitly and explicitly indicates is that the rise of China affects Japan. This embedded sentiment of a rivalry with, and a fear of, China plays a role in Japanese participants' attitudes about making contact with China's soft power.

HIGHLY HISTORICIZED CAPITAL IN THE HISTORICAL SUBFIELD AS EMERGING SUBFIELDS

Based on the typology of media products produced in China, as documented in Chap. 2, the following section will explore which Chinese media products South Koreans consume, and examine how their consumption behavior relates to the making of Chinese soft power in a transnational soft power field.

"Chinese television series genres are not diverse. I only recall 'history'."[21] This is one of the most frequent and short yet powerful answers provided my Korean and Japanese informants. The historical subfield was highly recognized by transnational audiences in quasi-Sinophone East Asia.

A large proportion of South Korean and Japanese history textbooks contain Chinese history, largely because of the country's rich history and civilization, as well as its interactions with the other countries in East Asia. This has resulted in many South Koreans taking an interest in Chinese history. KV81[22] said, "History was my favorite subject in school. To me, history is like a story. My friends were tired of memorizing details from our history textbook, but I liked it. Maybe this is why I often watch historical dramas. When I visit my parents in my hometown, I watch historical dramas on cable television. Unfortunately, I do not have a TV in my rented room near the university, so I watch downloaded programs on my laptop. I understand Chinese history after watching dramas and films. Having done this for many years, I am well-versed in Chinese history." This response indicates that China's rich culture and heritage are strongly represented in Chinese dramas. Chinese culture and history play an important role in attracting Koreans to learn more about China. And, notably, mass media simultaneously plays a role in providing exposure to history.

One of the most famous Chinese historical novels is the *Three Kingdoms* (*Samkukji*), and different versions of the story having been told through novels, films, and dramas. KV21[23] said, "Since my youth, I have liked Chinese history. Have you ever read the *Three Kingdoms* (*Samkukji*)? Most likely yes, right? If you are a South Korean who grew up in the country. Or you may even have come across the South Korean version in the form of Lee Munyeol's novel. We are all familiar with or have heard the idiom '*Samgochoryeo*,'[24] and of the characters of the novel, like *Yubi*, *Kwanwu*, *Jangbi*.... Many Chinese dramas tell historical stories. I watch them because they help me understand history better." A South Korean producer told me that his TV station imported and broadcast the latest version of *Three Kingdoms*[25] not for its length—95 episodes—but for its quality.[26] This series brings together elements of history (*lishi*), costume (*guzhuang*), and war (*zhanzheng*).

Three Kingdoms media products are regionally renowned, Chinese novel-originated and were also frequently mentioned in interviews with Koreans. This is the case particularly because a translated Korean version of this novel is one of the foundational books recommended by universities and publishers. As in South Korea, historical themes are the most popular types of Chinese media in Japan, as well. JV10[27] mentioned, "I have encountered every type—books, games and manga—of *Three Kingdoms*." JV12[28] also mentioned, "I watched the drama *Journey to the West*." Both are regionally famous, Chinese novel-originated cultural products and were also mentioned in interviews with Koreans, including informants KV19[29] and KV67.[30] These television series were in fact mediatized, based upon their original classical novels. Not only is the original classical literature still popular, but it is also widely available in quasi-Sinophone countries.

Historical subfields are popular with some South Korean and Japanese respondents, not only because of their cultural capital and historical capital in content, but also because of their accessibility and familiarity. Although this study is qualitative in nature, the data suggests that the male interviewees are more inclined to enjoy Chinese history than female informants. However, this gendered division in consumption behavior may not apply to the martial arts subfield.

A female informant, KV18, said, "Most Chinese television series are based on history or martial arts. Even in Korea, historical dramas are predominantly watched by fans; not by all generations. Because of this, historical Chinese dramas cannot easily appeal to foreigners."[31] KV43,[32] whom I interviewed in winter 2011 in Seoul, commented that, "Most of the content is old stories. Content is pretty much based on the classics. They are historical." He highlighted the historical capital in most of the Chinese television series he consumed, both before and now. Like KV43 said, the scripts for Chinese TV series that are imported to South Korea and Japan are in fact based predominantly on historical texts or novels.

The sheer length of China's history, in turn, is usually framed by transnational audiences in both import countries as uninteresting. Many Korean audiences in my research tended to equate history with stories that are "dull and tedious." Yet, watching a foreign-produced media program is different from watching a local program. When trying something foreign is considered trendy or fashionable, foreign products might have different connotations. For example, what audiences see as "trendy" in their local media products, or what local media presents to them, may not be the same as what a foreign program delivers. Despite this, the sense of "foreign" as trendy and "local/domestic" as average does not always translate quickly into an adopted practice of watching foreign TV dramas every day. Their lack of understanding of foreign dramas could lead to such dramas being considered inaccessibly "foreign," but Korean audiences simultaneously hold Chinese dramas to expectations similar to those they hold for their local media. These expectations and realities poses difficulties for the "foreign" to permeate Koreans' everyday lives.

In sum, historical subfields predominate as the most welcomed and frequently imported series in South Korean and Japanese marketplaces. Cultural and historical capital in the subfield strikes a chord with their understanding of Chinese culture and history. The lavish historical representations of these forms of capital are also part of the reasons why this is only type that is frequently consumed, making it possible for Chinese mediatized soft power to partially *succeed* among Korean and Japanese audiences. It is a win-win situation on both the exporting and the importing side because demand for, and the quantity of production of, this television series subfield is high. Equally, the import traffic and consumption of this subfield remains high. However, the absence of other popular types of subfields and capital shows that China's mediatized soft power faces dilemmas.

CAPITAL DISPLACEMENT AND ITS DISCONTENTS[33]

Looking for Aesthetic Capital and Celebrity Capital

Aesthetic, celebrity, and technological capital are, remarkably, widely recognized by the Korean participants in my study. As key elements in any subfield of television series, well-known characters and good stories, which lead to attractive aesthetic capital, are seemingly important. In the case of Chinese TV series, stories are often adapted from traditional Chinese novels (*gudian xiaoshuo*)[34] or martial arts novels (*wuxia xiaoshuo*)[35] and transformed into TV serial dramas.

While it is largely true that Chinese historical and martial arts themes are the most popular, as attested by the majority of the interviewees, there are some other intriguing genres. The Chinese drama *Dwelling Narrowness* (*Woju*), which is set in Shanghai, has been analyzed from the perspective of China's neoliberal development policy (Liang 2010; Yu 2011). KV39[36] said, "I happened to watch a drama titled *Dwelling Narrowness* when I was in China. My Chinese friend went to buy DVDs with me and suggested it. She said it reflects the reality of China, 'what we Chinese in our 20s and 30s are concerned about.' When I watched some [other] Chinese news and drama programs, the first thing that came to mind was that this did not seem to be the China I had visited or where I had lived. But *Dwelling Narrowness* felt like *real* China. Later, I learnt that the State had banned it from broadcasting because the drama was seen as harmful to society." She later realized that the drama was not available either on TV or the Internet. As a student of Chinese Studies, KV39[37] wanted to know the "real" China and every hidden aspect of the country.

In contemporary thematic TV dramas, Beijing and Shanghai are the major background locations. *The Modern Family of China* (*Jiayou'ernv* of Beijing),[38] which was broadcasted by *Beijing dianshitai* (BTV), is a 20-minute sitcom (*qingjingxiju*) about two divorced couples and their families. Season 1 aired in China in 2005, and after four seasons the series has ended. There is also an animated sister version (*Jiayou'ernv xinzhuan*) that is unrelated to the four seasons. The first season of this drama (*Motmalrineungajok* in Korean) was also aired on Junghwa TV in South Korea in 2008. A male respondent KV54 said, "Since this was a sitcom, it's short and situational and easy to understand. It made me keep watching it."[39] What mattered for the respondent was not the "Beijingness" of the drama, but rather the format of the media product.

IPartment (*Aiqing gongyu*)[40] is produced by the Shanghai Film Group Co. Ltd. (*Shanghai Dianyingjituangongsi*).[41] This series consists of four seasons and will be turned into a movie. Season 1 aired in August 2009, Season 2 in January 2011,[42] Season 3 in July 2012[43] and Season 4 was aired in the summer of 2013. "*IPartment* makes me understand the joys and sorrows of the young people in Shanghai who are my age," according to KV40, who studied in China. She also added, "I like Shanghai very much. It was also enjoyable to see the scenery of Shanghai in this drama." Obviously, audiences consume media products selectively, according to their own experiences.

On the other hand, a Korean informant named KV68[44] pointed to a perceived lack of aesthetic capital in Chinese television series. He said, "Stories are very important for foreign audiences. In other words, foreign content or other supporting elements—music, costumes and so on—have to be catchy. I sometimes searched for some critics' comments on the series before I go into watching them. I found *Haishang dianying* and *Douban* useful for this matter.[45] Music, costumes and so on ... every single thing in the drama can be a point and a source of trendiness. Despite this expectation, Chinese dramas are too far behind in fashion." The informant uses his linguistic capital in an attempt to connect more with the Chinese local's view of Chinese television series. That way he can minimize any risk of absence of aesthetic capital in Chinese products.

Compared to celebrities with Japanese and Western foreign origins, Koreans do not necessarily know much about Chinese celebrities. This is due to the absence of celebrity capital in Chinese television series. As such, a respondent, KV40,[46] commented,

> Why isn't much Chinese content imported to South Korea? Why do Korean viewers not watch it? Well, the immediate and arguably most convincing answer is that there are no famous celebrities from 'China.'

The Korean TV market for foreign media is arguably devoted to airing American, Japanese, and Chinese programs (see Chap. 3). As such, marketing is more effective at producing sales and higher audience ratings when Korean celebrities are featured in the products. There are also rare instances when Chinese celebrities are known as Koreans due to "noisy marketing," or using negative features to promote celebrities. As KV88 mentioned, "Chinese celebrities are 'infamous' and known for no-good stuff."[47] This was also mentioned by another Korean informant. She said, "if a Chinese celebrity becomes famous for scandals, people start to take an interest in finding out who this person is and what programs she or he was in."[48] Interest spurred by unfortunate events is also potentially effective at generating new transnational audiences for Chinese soft power via offline television series. However, such interest does not last long. Partly due to the adverse effect of celebrity capital, some Korean audiences find that Chinese TV dramas do not have attraction for them without Korean celebrities.

Looking for Cultural Capital

To Korean audiences, watching Chinese TV dramas is like a hide-and-seek game for quality. This is because Korean audiences cannot always anticipate the level of quality of a Chinese production; some Korean people view Chinese dramas as a way to kill time. However, by and large, this characteristic of Chinese dramas makes audiences not only less likely to continue watching them, but also gives the Korean audience a higher chance of coming across TV dramas it does not like. Such unexpectedness, which implies an inconsistent level of quality in the content being consumed, is mainly due to the varying quality of the storylines: "Chinese programs do not have to be that funny in order for them to survive and to be aired among the crowded local and foreign programs… I have rarely encountered a Chinese program that I think is going to be successful in Korea."[49]

In this regard, KV86 said, "It's pretty much like a third-rate film to me… It's immature and lousy. It's not funny at all and cheesy. Because of these factors, it is not that popular yet."[50] Similarly, KV85 said, "Plots, content … are not diversified and are childish."[51] My informants, who were critically awaiting Chinese television series that would be popular among their peers, condemned the series as lacking cultural capital.

When it comes to the content, as mentioned earlier, Korean viewers have critical opinions about Chinese dramas. KV46 said, "Chinese TV series have wide variations in quality. Watching Chinese dramas is almost like a gamble. Odds that you could find interesting dramas are very slim."[52] She pointed out that the products have an unequal level of guaranteed appeal. This point resonates with KV36's interview statement, "They are good or bad, all or nothing… It's like a lucky draw where you can't gauge what's going to happen."[53]

Like these participants, KV1[54] also said, "Most people who have an interest in Chinese dramas are learning Chinese. Otherwise, ordinary people do not have any interest in Chinese culture. There is a prevalent view that the shows are of bad quality." KV1, who spent nine months in Ha'erbin as a Chinese Studies major, felt she had an obligation to gain exposure to Chinese television series. However, even for her, it was not merely for joy but rather came from a place of pure interest and intellectual attraction. In contrast, the dominant idea of Chinese television series does not vouchsafe quality. The quality level of typical Chinese television series pushes the local embeddedness of the foreign in a problematic way.

With that said, KV18 also mentioned, "For contemporary television series, the Korean ones are already enough. Under the pretense that Chinese television series are not very interesting, I think people might believe there are no reasons to watch them."[55]

The idea of contemporariness is one of the words that I often heard from my respondents, regarding what is missing but should be present in Chinese television series. As KV53 said, "Koreans usually think that Chinese things are lagging behind. [Thus] something from China, in particular Chinese pop cultural products, cannot be popular."[56] Like her, a male respondent delivered his opinion as, "A sense for modern and cutting-edge [things] are missing. Chinese television series do not share anything with Korean ones and there are no stories in them."[57] It is difficult for transnational audiences to relate what is shown and depicted in Chinese television series to their own lives.

In a similar vein, KV4 also mentioned that, "China is not a trendsetter. People do not prefer this."[58] By narrating this, she implied that China is behind the trends. This is important, not only in a time when Korean audiences consume Chinese television series, but also for targeting a level of contemporariness that produces cultural capital.

Others discuss the lack of contemporariness as a characteristic of offline media. A Korean female respondent in her early 20s, KV18, who considered majoring in Chinese language after enjoying a Chinese drama, well-articulated the predicament of offline media. She narrated, "What I can watch on TV is limited. Imported offline Chinese television series are less diverse. Newer and ongoing series should be immediately imported into the market, it seems it is not like that."[59]

Linking to the previous informant, KV65 also commented along this line that, "Imported Chinese dramas are very much limited and delayed. Now, with the development of the Internet, we could watch something online and catch up on trends very quickly, even if it's outside of our country. The most recent programs should be immediately imported. Only recently is it going in that direction. But it's still not enough."[60] This informant emphasized the "contemporariness" and "simultaneousness" of imported foreign TV series. The postponed access, due to the import of foreign offline media to another country and the longer circuit of offline media, is managed differently on online platforms, as Chap. 7 discusses. As such, Korean audiences pay attention not only to the subfields of television series, but they also take "freshness" into account.

China is arguably infamous for playing "copycat." "Shanzhai," literally meaning "a small mountain village" but used to describe Chinese cultural and social phenomena, is now associated with fakes.[61] I define "fake" as exaggerated Chinese versions of "cultural capital" that are problematically shaping Chinese television series and a transnational soft power field.

"Faked in China" is a well-known phenomenon, not only among foreigners and local Chinese people. When I walked down a street in Shenzhen for lunch with a media scholar after our interview, she pointed at a dumpling stall and told me, "in China, you cannot eat anything. Did you see the news report about fake dumplings?" Whereas Chinese informants agreed on the problem of "faked in China" by highlighting everyday life issues such as food security, transnational audiences pointed to cultural and social behaviors to conclude that a standard for copyrights is difficult to locate in China. With offline media consumption, a Korean Chinese-learner, KV33, in my study criticized such phenomenon: "As I started to learn Chinese language as a minor, I wanted to watch some good Chinese dramas at home. But what I found was quite devastating. Many storylines are very similar to Korean dramas. I feel the Chinese producers copied Korean ones."[62]

A Japanese respondent, JV12, who started to learn Chinese language for work-related reasons, also told me, "They [Chinese] do copy things a lot. This is what they are famous for."[63] The lack of genuine cultural capital, fronted by the "Chinese" fabricated version of cultural capital, paints a dark picture of Chinese television series.

Following this line of logic, Korean audiences compare "similar" accounts of Chinese TV dramas to the Korean originals. A male respondent, KV58, lamented that, "Chinese products imitate Korean ones. I hope there are no more sons from rich families. It seems like a copycat of Korean dramas."[64] He pointed out that copying and repeating what he's familiar with—Korean television series—clearly shows an absence of "creativity," while the Chinese government is ironically propagating the idea of moving from "Made in China" to "Created in China (Keane 2007)."

Another male informant, KV49, lamented that China is copying Korean products and said, "I see a lot of songs that used Korean songs."[65] As Bicket (2005) argues, "Almost everywhere, the programmes audiences like to watch the most are their own country's" (The Economist 1997: 72 in Bicket 2005). Likewise, this analysis shows that all reference points for Korean viewers to watch foreign Chinese products were Korean media products. No matter to what extent, Chinese programs have overlapping accounts of "original" Korean products reported about them; it is natural for Korean consumers to imagine the similarities and compare products.

I heard that *Huijia de youhuo* (*Temptation of Going Home*) is a remake of the Korean drama *Qizi de youhuo* (*Wife's Temptation*). But isn't it still copying the Korean drama?[66]

Most Korean viewers do not know about "remake" copyright purchases or format exchanges between the two countries. Such misunderstanding is perhaps drawn from the Korean association of China with "copying." KV56 said, "In terms of culture, Koreans have a tendency to think that Korean culture is superior to Chinese culture. There are two things: people usually are ignorant of Chinese culture or China. At the same time, they looked down on China."[67]

Views about China as a country rampant with copying and misunderstandings about some Chinese dramas that were based on formats purchased from South Korea may arise from attitudes of cultural superiority. The idea of superiority, which is underlined in locally embedded consumption, jeopardizes the potential for Chinese soft power to reach South Korean and Japanese audiences via television series.

Looking for Technological Capital

Young people are advanced users of technology and they are looking for technological aspects in the potential media products—technological capital—they consume. While the technological capital is often pointed out as missing by both male and female Korean respondents, a gendered response about technological capital emerged in my study.

Young Korean men in their 20s who watch Chinese TV dramas were knowledgeable about special effects, computer graphics and technical characteristics. When they watch and/or talk about foreign dramas, technological concerns come first, and obvious downfalls were spotted as fallacies on which to further comment. Likewise, young Korean men in this analysis had a tendency to enjoy their technological knowledge about media, and their aspirations for watching technologically advanced media. This truly applied to instances where the subject of Chinese TV dramas arose. Some male informants pinpointed perceived overall technological gaps between China and Japan/South Korea. One male participant, KV86, said:

> At the moment, Chinese technology for making cultural and media products has not developed equally with those of Japan and Korea. If the technology catches up, films as well as dramas will be of better quality.[68]

Others were more interested in particular technologies used in the Chinese TV dramas. Many informants offered their reasons and insights regarding why they have problems with Chinese dramas, with specific reference to different aspects of technology. Computer graphics were the most frequently discussed aspect among the young male respondents. For example, young Korean male interviewee, KV57, pointed out technological aspects of Chinese dramas:

Advancement of technology. I mean, overall technological development, by all means. In particular, computer graphics should be developed further. Even for a non-expert, I could see wires and colors that do not match.[69]

An upgrade for better technology in the televisual subfields is welcomed. A male Korean informant, KV44,[70] who lived in China for 18 months as a primary school student, vividly remembered what he saw on TV as a child in China. To my follow-up question of "what aspects of technology should be improved?" after his comment that "Chinese media products are not advanced in technology," he said without hesitation, "there are many areas to be improved. Hiding wires when actors and actresses move around. Unmatched colors and obvious touches of computer graphics are always visible, unlike in American or Korean ones."[71] The male respondent, KV28,[72] described rather specific technological aspects of offline Chinese media. When he pointed out the technological issues, other strongly represented global media—American—or local—Korean—media becomes a reference point. The global-ness or the local-ness of transnational audiences' local embedded consumption also emerged frequently with other interviewees.

Another respondent, KV66,[73] similarly pointed out misplaced computer graphics in Chinese television series and said, "China lacks content. Computer graphics are particularly *hujeop* (sloppy, lousy). In martial arts dramas, I could spot wires in the scene." Similar to what Junseo said, Hyunggyu shared these views in a short but powerful statement that, "Special effects and acting are somewhat missing."

While Korean male respondents commented on computer-mediated technologies, Korean women discussed technologies with a special focus on feminine issues. The feminine aspect was related to aspirations and beauty—the aesthetic capital.

Young Korean women, like Japanese women, satisfy a fantasy when they watch Korean dramas. They are also yearning for dreams and fantasies in their consumption of Korean dramas. A Korean woman in her late 20s who just finished her postgraduate studies, KV55, said, "For me, watching a drama should give me dreams, hopes, and a fantasy. When I watch Chinese dramas, I feel depressed. I wish they could produce dramas in a set. For that, I think they also need to have advanced technologies."[74] Television series should deliver entertaining and rosy images of life to her, yet Chinese offline television series do not match up with her expected level of technology, and do not inspire much motivation to keep consuming those products.

> Chinese drama styles are not good enough. They use reddish lighting. I really see this as problematic for achieving nice scenes. Put it shortly, they do not have a good sense [of aesthetic]. You know, if you look at how they divide the screen when they shot, what kinds of shots they use, how they do lighting, how they do the costumes, hair and make-up of actors and actresses. If you look at Korean dramas, they do it very well. Why can't the Chinese production team make better use of the resources that are available to them?[75]

For them, technologies are the underutilized tools for adding value to the Chinese stories that aspire to craft a rosy picture. The disappointment stems from two main aspects. First, under the pretense that China possesses material richness, the country has failed to produce products of a level equivalent to its economic resources. Given that the Chinese economy is growing, and China places increasing effort into further developing its cultural industry, it still falls short of Korean audiences' expectations. Second, "tastes" and "expectations" established through their consumption of other countries' dramas of higher quality may explain Korean audiences' expectations of a comparable level of technological advancement and style in Chinese dramas.[76] Korean audiences of Chinese dramas, who may also have watched Korean series, are likely expecting to see Chinese dramas of a similar or same level of quality. In other words, they will be disappointed with Chinese dramas if their expectations are not fulfilled.

> I found that the voices and the timing of the characters' talking were not matched?[77]

> First, I did not notice whether or not the voices and talking were happen simultaneously. But slowly I could learn more Chinese, and I watched the shape of mouth in order to imitate how Chinese people pronounce the language. Then, I slowly realized that it is not synchronized? (KV71 2012)[78]

When foreign television series are imported to another country, language often becomes an interesting vantage point. Depending on local practices in the importing country, and media practices on television stations, foreign languages are often dubbed into the language of the importing country. This linguistic element of Chinese television series is also related to technological capital, particularly for female Korean respondents in my study.

Particularly among female Chinese language learners, watching Chinese programs is an important way to learn and gain exposure to Chinese language and culture. Female Chinese language learners often notice and place importance on the media practices of dubbing, or post-synchronization. Arguably, this might be a way of mass producing media products in China, but it dramatically damages the quality of Chinese TV dramas. Some of the imported Chinese dramas are dubbed in Korean; in some or many instances, Korean audiences, who are not usually used to listening to dubbed programs, feel they are "awkward."

CONCLUSION

At the beginning of this chapter, I set a background for the recent development of inter-Asia media and cultural flows—emerging Chinese media—that have raised concerns for Korean media professionals in the Korean marketplace. Such sentiments were more prevalent in South Korea than in Japan, seeing that South Korea entered the flows and markets later than Japan. While cultural proximity is an important factor of constructing a geocultural market (Straubhaar 1991), factors like common language and values, shared experience, local identity and cultural proximity between countries (e.g., Iwabuchi 2002; La Pastina and Straubhaar 2005) reinforce the volume of cross-national flows of cultural products. These factors also shape audience preference for TV programs, which may reflect domestic tastes (Chang 2010). Against this backdrop, I asked how we make sense of China's televised soft power dilemma in South Korea and Japan, despite the relevant development of the field with sophisticated Chinese subfields of TV series on the ground. Delving into the process of how China's soft power dilemmas in South Korea and Japan are constructed, I showed the underdevelopments of different forms of capital in the imported Chinese televisual subfields that exist in a transnational soft power field in South Korea.

The notion of local embeddedness was employed to establish understanding of the limited consumption of Chinese TV in the two receiving countries, but especially to illuminate the reasons why Chinese TV programs are not extensively consumed or widely acknowledged by Korean and Japanese audiences. The intercountry comparison sheds light on similarities between responses and the creation of China's soft power paradoxes in quasi-Sinophone East Asian receiving countries. At the same time, locally embedded factors of these dilemmas in South Korea and Japan provides us nuanced stories and highlights differences between the two societal contexts.

Young Korean male and female informants point out factors that constituted Chinese programs as "domestically" problematic because highly historicized and politicized capital, and rarity of aesthetic and technological capital, are well documented. Aspects of Chinese dramas, such as content, genres, local peculiarities, context, and mode of production, continue to be critical selling points for dramas to be transnationally consumed by Koreans. Technological and aesthetic capital tied to the local embeddedness of Chinese TV series played an important part in the transnational consumption of Chinese dramas for both male and female Korean respondents. Young Korean men were interested in both general and specific technologies that are used in Chinese dramas. They commented that these technologies need improvement, in order to boost transnational consumption of the TV series. Young Korean women demonstrated their interests in make-up, costumes, and voice synchronization. In both cases, Korean dramas were often mentioned as reference points that the Chinese dramas should follow, or at least be at a similar level of quality with. This links to the structural positioning of Chinese dramas in South Korea. The local embeddedness of foreign dramas needs to be understood within the local context. Also, existing perceptions about China and Chinese products serve an important role in Korean audiences' embrace of, or resistance to, Chinese TV series.

Similar but different from their counterparts in South Korea, young Japanese male and female interviewees perceive highly historicized and politicized capital in Chinese television series, while China is cast as a rising superpower. In this spirit, they feel that the media and cultural scenes also replicate and reproduce the ways in which China is emerging. Successfully translating the cultural into the political is such an important factor and emerging point of contention that Japanese informants are reluctant to connect with the Chinese television series.

As young South Korean and Japanese people negotiate their choices to watch Chinese TV series, they oscillate between acceptance and resistance. For young Koreans, enjoying Chinese media not only challenges their intention to watch dramas for enjoyment and interest, but also simultaneously reduces their doubts about the domesticated factors of dramas, such as plots, technological differences and absences of capital and vitalized subfields. In this way, Chinese TV dramas have emerged as spaces for limited transnational influence, which creates predicaments for the making of Chinese soft power.

Notes

1. In Korean discourse, terms such as *Hwaryu* (华流, *hualiu*), *Hanryu* (汉流, *hanliu*) and *Jungryu* (中流, *zhongliu*) are used to refer to the Chinese Wave. These three terms are used interchangeably. In South Korea, the Chinese Wave (*Hualiu*) is often understood as the mixed popularity of cultural products with origins of mainland China, Hong Kong, and Taiwan. In Korean discourse, the term does not always specify which location the products originate from. It is particularly observable in the discussions of Korean audiences/consumers. Thus, according to the experiences and responses of our interviewees, mainland China is not separated from Hong Kong or Taiwan, but often grouped collectively as *Hualiu* sources.

2. This is also discussed in an interview with a Korean journalist who works for a Japanese magazine. She said, "Taiwanese dramas were popular in Japan around 2006. That time, *Karyū* was popularly discussed. But dramas from Taiwan have certain patterns and are childish. Thus, these characteristics did not allow them to last for long."

3. In South Korea, people were concerned about the loss of popularity for Korean cultural products, which is also collectively referred to as the Korean Wave (*Hallyu*). *Hallyu*, the Korean Wave, and *Hanryu* (or *Hallyu*), the Chinese Wave, have the same pronunciation in Korean.

4. In fact, "domestification" has other meanings and uses in academic literature beyond Ivy's definition that is used in this chapter. From the perspectives of scholars in sociology (of technology), and media and communication studies, it refers to how (media) technology is accepted, rejected, and used (Berker et al. 2006). Local embeddedness or domestication of media and cultural consumption in other contexts, see La Pastina and Straubhaar 2005; Martin-Barbero 2010; Straubhaar 2007; Otmazgin 2013.

5. KV85, interview with a South Korean respondent, February 24, 2013, Seoul, South Korea.

6. JV12, interview with a Japanese respondent, March 28, 2012, Tokyo, Japan.

7. KV43, interview with a South Korean respondent, December 24, 2011, Seoul, South Korea.

8. JV17, interview with a Japanese respondent, April 13, 2012, Tokyo, Japan.

9. There are key differences between American, Japanese, and Korean TV series. First, American series overall have a small number of episodes per a TV series or a season. However, these can typically have more than one seasons. Second, Japanese and Korean TV series do not usually have more than one season for a TV series. Third, Korean TV series that air on TV in the morning, which target a specific time and group of people of housewives or older people, have a large number of TV series.

10. KV67, interview with a South Korean respondent, June 9, 2011, Seoul, South Korea.

11. KV14, interview with a South Korean respondent, December 8, 2011, Seoul, South Korea. She, who learned Chinese as a non-degree student in Shanghai in 2003, has lived in China for eight years.
12. Ibid.
13. JV39, interview with a Japanese respondent, April 24, 2012, Tokyo, Japan.
14. JV32, interview with a Japanese respondent, April 21, 2012, Tokyo, Japan.
15. JV11, interview with a Japanese respondent, March 27, 2012, Tokyo, Japan.
16. This means "certainly" in Japanese.
17. KV71, interview with a South Korean respondent, June 28, 2012, Seoul, South Korea.
18. KV77, interview with a South Korean respondent, July 2, 2012, Seoul, South Korea.
19. KV82, interview with a South Korean respondent, July 10, 2012, Seoul, South Korea.
20. JV44, interview with a Japanese respondent, April 27, 2012, Tokyo, Japan.
21. KV44, Interview with a South Korean respondent, December 27, 2011, Yongin, Gyeonggi, South Korea. He has lived about eighteen months in China.
22. KV81, interview with a South Korean respondent, July 4, 2012, Seoul, South Korea.
23. KV21, interview with a South Korean respondent, December 11, 2011, Seoul, South Korea.
24. Its meaning is "After several attempts to … finally…"
25. It started being aired in May 2010 and consists of 95 episodes. This series is also available in Cantonese.
26. KM4, interview with a South Korean producer, January 19, 2012, Seoul, South Korea.
27. JV10, interview with a Japanese respondent, February 13, 2012, Tokyo, Japan.
28. JV12, interview with a Japanese respondent, March 28, 2012, Tokyo, Japan.
29. KV19, interview with a South Korean respondent, December 10, 2011, Seoul, South Korea.
30. KV67, interview with a South Korean respondent, June 26, 2012, Seoul, South Korea.
31. KV18, interview with a South Korean respondent, December 9, 2011, Seoul, South Korea.
32. KV43, interview with a South Korean respondent, December 24, 2011, Seoul, South Korea.
33. Lack of capital—cultural, aesthetic, and economic capital: "What's there" and "what they are looking for."
34. *Three Kingdoms, Huangbihong* and *Shuihuji* are examples.

35. Jin Yong's novels are very famous in South Korea.
36. KV39, interview with a South Korean respondent, December 21, 2011, Seoul, South Korea.
37. Ibid.
38. Baidu Baike. n.d.-d. "*Jiayou'ernv* (*The Modern Family of China*)." Retrieved March 13, 2013 (http://baike.baidu.com/view/246459.htm).
39. KV54, interview with a South Korean respondent, February 16, 2012, Seoul, South Korea.
40. Baidu Baike. n.d.-a. "Aiqinggongyu (IPartment) Season 1." Retrieved March 13, 2013 (http://baike.baidu.com/view/221103.htm#1).
41. Haishang Dianying. Retrieved April 2, 2013 (http://www.sfs-cn.com).
42. Baidu Baike. n.d.-b. "Aiqinggongyu (IPartment) Season 2." Retrieved March 13, 2013 (http://movie.douban.com/subject/4707205/).
43. Baidu Baike. n.d.-c. "Aiqinggongyu (IPartment) Season 3." Retrieved March 13, 2013 (http://movie.douban.com/subject/6312211/).
44. KV68, interview with a South Korean respondent, June 26, 2012, Seoul, South Korea.
45. Luo (2013)'s list in Douban and *Haishang dianying* (n.d.) are such examples.
46. KV40, interview with a South Korean respondent, December 21, 2011, Seoul, South Korea.
47. KV88, interview with a South Korean respondent, November 29, 2013, Seoul, South Korea.
48. KV40, interview with a South Korean respondent, December 21, 2011, Seoul, South Korea.
49. KV84, interview with a South Korean respondent, February 6, 2013, Seoul, South Korea.
50. KV86, interview with a South Korean respondent, March 18, 2013, Seoul, South Korea.
51. KV85, interview with a South Korean respondent, February 24, 2013, Seoul, South Korea.
52. KV46, Interview with a South Korean respondent, January 10, 2012, Seoul, South Korea.
53. KV36, interview with a South Korean respondent, December 19, 2011, Seoul, South Korea.
54. KV1, interview with a South Korean respondent. November 19, 2011, Seoul, South Korea.
55. KV18, interview with a South Korean respondent, December 9, 2011, Seoul, South Korea.
56. KV53, interview with a South Korean respondent, February 5, 2012, Seoul, South Korea.
57. KV52, interview with a South Korean respondent, February 5, 2012, Seoul, South Korea.

58. KV4, interview with a South Korean respondent, November 28, 2011, Seoul, South Korea.
59. FKV18, interview with a South Korean respondent, December 9, 2011, Seoul, South Korea.
60. KV65, interview with a South Korean respondent, June 7, 2012, Seoul, South Korea.
61. The Chinese word "shanzhai" literally means "small mountain village," but it is now used to describe products that have names similar to famous brands, or people who imitate celebrities. On this topic, see Yang (2015).
62. KV33, interview with a South Korean respondent, December 17, 2011, Seoul, South Korea.
63. JV12, interview with a Japanese respondent, March 28, 2012, Tokyo, Japan.
64. KV58, interview with a South Korean respondent, March 17, 2012, Seoul, South Korea.
65. KV49, interview with a South Korean male respondent, January 24, 2012, Seoul, South Korea.
66. KV85, interview with a South Korean respondent, February 24, 2013, Seoul, South Korea.
67. KV56, interview with a South Korean respondent, February 16, 2012, Seoul, South Korea.
68. KV86, interview with a South Korean respondent, March 18, 2013, Seoul, South Korea.
69. KV57, interview with a South Korean respondent, February 16, 2012, Seoul, South Korea.
70. KV44, Interview with a South Korean respondent, December 27, 2011, Yongin, Gyeonggi, South Korea. He has lived about eighteen months in China.
71. Ibid.
72. KV28, interview with a South Korean respondent, December 15, 2011, Yongin, Gyeonggi, South Korea.
73. KV66, interview with a South Korean respondent, June 9, 2012, Seoul, South Korea.
74. KV55, interview with a South Korean respondent, February 16, 2012, Seoul, South Korea.
75. KV63, interview with a South Korean respondent, June 7, 2012, Seoul, South Korea.
76. Korean audiences in general have experienced Korean, Japanese, and American programs.
77. KV69, interview with a South Korean respondent, June 26, 2012, Seoul, South Korea.
78. KV71, interview with a South Korean respondent, June 28, 2012, Seoul, South Korea.

REFERENCES

Baidu Baike. n.d.-a. *Aiqinggongyu* [IPartment] Season 1. Accessed March 13, 2013. http://baike.baidu.com/view/221103.htm#1.

———. n.d.-b. *Aiqinggongyu* [IPartment] Season 2. Accessed March 13, 2013. http://movie.douban.com/subject/4707205/.

———. n.d.-c. *Aiqinggongyu* [IPartment] Season 3. Accessed March 13, 2013. http://movie.douban.com/subject/6312211/.

———. n.d.-d. *Jiayou'ernv [The Modern Family of China]*. Accessed March 13, 2013. http://baike.baidu.com/view/246459.htm.

Berker, Thomas, Maren Hartmann, Yves Punie, and Katie J. Ward. 2006. Introduction. In *Domestification of Media and Technology*, ed. Thomas Berker, Maren Hartmann, Yves Punie, and Katie J. Ward, 1–16. Berkshire: Open University Press.

Bicket, Douglas. 2005. Reconsidering Geocultural Contraflow: Intercultural Information Flows Through Trends in Global Audiovisual Trade. *Global Media Journal* 4 (6): 1-16. Accessed November 16, 2015. http://www.globalmedia-journal.com/open-access/reconsidering-geocultural-contraflow-intercultural-information-flows-through-trends-in-global-audiovisual-trade.php?aid=35122.

Chang, Tsan-Kuo. 2010. Changing Global Media Landscape, Unchanging Theories? International Communication Research and Paradigm Testing. In *International Media Communication in a Global Age*, ed. Guy Golan, Thomas Johnson, and Wayne Wanta, 8–35. New York and Oxon: Routledge.

Haishang Dianying [Films on the Sea]. n.d. Accessed April 2, 2018. http://www.sfs-cn.com.

Ivy, Marilyn. 1995. *Discourses of the Vanishing: Modernity, Phantasm, Japan*. Chicago and London: University of Chicago Press.

Iwabuchi, Koichi. 2002. *Recentering Globalization: Popular Culture and Japanese Transnationalism*. Durham: Duke University Press.

Keane, Michael. 2007. *Created in China: The Great New Leap Forward*. Oxon and New York: Routledge.

Kim, Eunjin. 2006. Hwaryue jjogineun 'Hallyu Drama' … ilbon TV bangyeongje-olban 'dduk' ['Hallyu Drama' is Now Being Chased by the Chinese Wave … 'because of' Now Only Half of the Usual Broadcast in Japan]. *Sekye Ilbo*, March 8.

Kolker, Robert. 2009. *Media Studies: An Introduction*. Malden and Oxford: Wiley-Blackwell.

La Pastina, Antonio C. and Joseph D. Straubhaar. 2005. Multiple Proximities Between Television Genres and Audiences: The Schism Between Telenovelas' Global Distribution and Local Consumption. *Gazette: The International Journal for Communication Studies* 67 (3): 271–288.

Lee, Youngsup. 2006. Hallyuga jamdeunsai 'Hwaryu'ga ddenda ['Hwaryu' is Emerging while Hallyu is Sleeping in Japan]. *Hankook Ilbo*, April 4. Accessed May 20, 2013. http://hankookilbo.com/v/8fff204cf7354ed2bcebbc1832062ccd.

Liang, Samuel Y. 2010. Property-Driven Urban Change in Post-Socialist Shanghai: Reading the Television Series Woju. *Journal of Current Chinese Affairs* 39 (4): 3–28.

Luo, Gui. 2013. Douban gaofen dianshiju [Douban's Top Rated Television Series]. *Douban*, October 17. Accessed April 2, 2018. https://www.douban.com/doulist/3038463/.

Martin-Barbero, Jesus. 2010. The Cultural Mediations of Television Consumption. In *Consuming Audiences? Production and Reception in Media Research*, eds. Ingunn Hagen and Janet Wasko, 145–162. Cresskill: Hampton Press, Inc.

Otmazgin, Nissim Kadosh. 2013. *Regionalizing Culture: The Political Economy of Japanese Popular Culture in Asia*. Honolulu: University of Hawai'I Press.

SARFT. 2012. *Guanyu 2012 niandi yiji quanguo guochandianshiju faxing xukezheng banfa qingkuang tongji jieguo de tonggao* [Notice on the Statistical Information on the Authorized Domestic TV Series in the First Quarter of 2012]. Accessed February 14, 2013. http://www.chinasarft.gov.cn/articles/2012/05/08/20120508165936620990.html.

Straubhaar, Joseph D. 1991. Beyond Media Imperialism: Asymmetrical Interdependence and Cultural Proximity. *Critical Studies in Media Communication* 8 (1): 39–59.

———. 2007. *World Television: From Global to Local*. London and New York: Sage Publication.

The Economist. 1997. A World View. *The Economist*, 71, November 29.

Yang, Fan. 2015. *Faked in China: Faked in China: Nation Branding, Counterfeit Culture, and Globalization*. Bloomington: Indiana University Press.

Yoo, Heekyung. 2008. Hwaryu polppaljeok seongjang ... 'Hanguk gongseup' daebihaeya [The Explosive Growth of Hwaryu ... Is Getting Ready for 'Attacking Korea']. *Munhwailbo*, August 21. Accessed May 20, 2013. http://www.munhwa.com/news/view.html?no=2008082101031424100002.

Yu, Haiqing. 2011. Dwelling Narrowness: Chinese Media and Their Disingenuous Neoliberal Logic. *Continuum: Journal of Media & Cultural Studies* 25 (1): 33–46.

PART II

Dilemmas of (Outsourced) Soft Power and Futures with Digital Media

CHAPTER 5

The Conversion Paradox in Quasi-Sinophone East Asia

SHAPING INTEREST IN THE RISE OF CHINA: CONVERGENCE IN CONTEXT[1]

After a seminar in the heart of Seoul in May 2017, several graduate students and three Korean scholars who work on China, including myself, were discussing issues related to our research and the world over the dinner. At one point, sharing which foreign language we had studied in high school, a male and a female professor lamentably, but also with a degree of pride, shared that they had learned German and French, respectively. They continued to elaborate on their rationales for choosing these two languages, claiming, "At that time, we [students] and the [South Korean] government thought Germany and France were great powers, and it was useful to learn German and French. But honestly, I don't remember anything except for the very basic stuff. Much of our generation studied one of these languages in high school." The scholar who hailed from Taiwan nodded in strong agreement with them and chimed in, "I learned both, but at the university." She comically added, "I am the worst." We all laughed. She asked me what I had studied as a second language in school by presuming, "French? German?" I proudly replied, "No, I learned *Chinese*." The female Korean professor was surprised, then, as she assumed I also benefited from studying European languages, but the Korean male professor quipped that it must be "Because she's of the post-80s generation." They kept remarking how I was lucky to learn such a useful language.

© The Author(s) 2018
C. S. Lee, *Soft Power Made in China*,
https://doi.org/10.1007/978-3-319-93115-9_5

Of my generation, a substantial number of students were fortunate enough to learn Chinese language in high school, as their chosen foreign language. This evidently led me to become interested in studying China, and later choosing a research path in the sociology of China. Only a few years later in South Korea, for an even luckier post-90s generation, Chinese language education has expanded beyond high schools to primary and middle schools.

By inheriting the idea of teaching Chinese language and culture in a larger scope, which is the aim of the Confucius Institutes (Cheng 2009; Chey 2008; Gil 2008; Hartig 2010, 2016; Hughes 2014; Lee 2009; Paradise 2009; Starr 2009), and expanding the language "boom" to other related scholarship on China, two quasi-Sinophone East Asian countries have arguably evolved into major host countries of educational and research institutions devoted to Chinese Studies at the tertiary level. For instance, "There are more than 90 research institutes in South Korea that are conducting research on China," according to a current head of one of these Chinese Centers in South Korea (Sungkyun Institute of China Studies 2017). This is a significant number, as most Korean universities now have one of these Chinese institutes and offer a Chinese Studies major. This, in turn, means that there is a certain level of interest in learning Chinese at the tertiary level.

Joseph Nye's model of soft power, in this regard, offers a useful framework to unpack this phenomenon and offer a counterintuitive story. This model, the "conversion of soft power resources to behavior (outcomes)" (Nye 2011: 100), explicates the process by which resources are turned into policy tools, reach target audiences, and generate soft power. A modified model, used in this book to integrate different forms of capital and capital conversion, is documented in Fig. 5.1. It illustrates the implementation of soft power policies that relate directly to media or cultural products and are based on both traditional and contemporary cultural sources. In the current context of the rise of China, present and future phenomena as well as sources of capital conversion are important. Social phenomena shape and transform interest in and experiences of the country, potentially contributing to China's soft power reach. In the following figure, an interrelational model for this process is proposed as South Korea and Japan involuntarily, or unintentionally, act as the gatekeepers and intermediaries of Chinese soft power (see Fig. 5.1).

As Nye's model shows, if resources and platforms of soft power are effective sources for the configuration China's soft power into a transna-

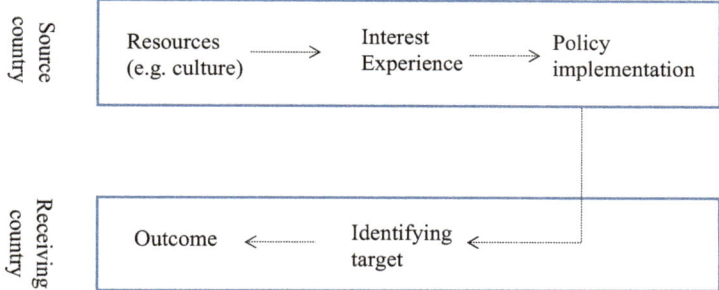

Fig. 5.1 Reception of soft power: from resources to reception. Source: Modified from Nye (2011: 100). Note: This is based on Nye's model of "conversion of soft power resources to behavior (outcomes)" (Nye 2011: 100)

tional soft power field, why do we still see weak conversions of such capital into Chinese soft power in both South Korea and Japan?

RISING GLOBAL CHINA AND ITS PARADOX

Media products contain language, content, context, and messages. In the action of consumption, the audience encounters the values and messages embedded in the media products and either identifies, absorbs, or rejects them. Before considering the audience's responses to any foreign media product, an often-neglected question needs to be taken into account: how and why do transnational audiences come to consume foreign media products? This question is particularly important regarding the consumption of China's media products and the paradox of Chinese soft power generation.

The continued rise of China is widely recognized in tropes that point to its massive economy, high export levels, and deep interconnectedness with other countries; in particular, this is well recognized by its two East Asian neighbors—South Korea and Japan.[2] China, transformed from a developing socialist country to a growing post-socialist *global* power in the twenty-first century, is symbolically and materially important to both South Korea and Japan across history. The growing political and economic influences of China beyond this sphere have allowed Chinese Studies to develop as a prominent field in many more countries, as well (Ngeow et al. 2014: 103). With the interconnected rise of China and emerging geopolitical shifts, the study of China has become particularly popular and important in East Asia.

Those who aspire to know and learn more about China face a rite of passage that is learning Chinese languages. To successfully interact with a new language, media, particularly television series, are arguably a useful medium for learning and facilitating a higher speed of learning about any language, culture or society. Conversely, learning a foreign language encourages a further investment of interest in studying, and even living in the society under study.[3]

Undoubtedly, the rise of global China has attracted more foreigners to learn Chinese, one of the most popular languages in the world, than ever before.[4] Especially in quasi-Sinophone East Asia, which has been sending the largest population of international students to China as presented in Chap. 1 (Lee 2013), there has been a fever/boom to learn Chinese, study China, and/or major in Chinese Studies, particularly since the 2000s (Gao 2011; Kim 2006). Against this backdrop that indicates a strong academic interest in China from South Korea and Japan, we cannot easily see the expected conversion from language studies/major to media consumption for Chinese soft power generation in both receiving countries where Chinese influence is still on the rise. Why does this happen and by what mechanisms does this occur?

In answering these twin questions, this chapter is devoted to two groups of people to illustrate a paradox of Chinese soft power: those who major(ed) in humanities-based and social science-based Chinese Studies, and those who have studied in China on a non-degree or degree program. By "humanities-based Chinese Studies," I refer to the academic programs of Chinese language, linguistics and literature, while "social science-based Chinese Studies" is defined as studies related to China from the perspectives and disciplinary boundaries of social sciences such as Economics, Political Science, and Sociology (Lee 2018). These two groups of informants often overlap, and I also pay special attention to interview data from my Korean and Japanese informants who have studied in China for a short-term or long-term program to offer an inherently comparative account. Given that the mobility of international students from these two quasi-Sinophone East Asian countries—South Korea and Japan—to China is greater than that of any other countries, as presented in Chap. 1, it is important to highlight this population in this chapter. Those who pursue area studies of unfamiliar subjects and aspire to carry out different, international career prospects juggle two balls at the same time: they wish to use the additional ability of speaking Chinese as a stepping stone for their career, while they succeed in their main task of studying. Those who decided to study in China basically share similar rationales with those who chose Chinese Studies as their major.

THE POWER OF INFLUENTIAL CHINA AND ITS (DIS)CONTENTS

China is influential. China becomes more and more influential. This line was prevalent in almost all of my interviews, as well as in my survey data on China.

On the one hand, some respondents highlighted China's massive influence on both South Korea and Japan. "There are big Chinese influences in South Korea. That's why many students, including me, decided to learn Chinese language,"[5] a Korean informant answered, regarding the question of China's influence on their own country. Another Korean interviewee opined, "[...] looking only at China's economic development, the Chinese economy will be much better than the Korean economy."[6] The economic rise of China is an important facet of its influence upon its neighboring countries. A Korean student who studies Chinese language not as an academic major requirement but for extra linguistic capital narrated her view that, "China is an emerging economic power. As a Korean, knowing China and learning Chinese language is a necessity, not a luxury. The proportion of trade with Chinese is the highest among our economic partners. China has become much more important to Korea."[7] The emergent importance of China to the Korean economy is also discussed.

Others shed light on geographical proximity as a factor that accords greater Chinese influence upon their countries. The statement "We are neighbors and we're located just next to each other" emerged in conversations with both Korean and Japanese people. A Korean male informant highlighted the regional impact of China and said, "we [South Korea and China] are both Asian countries. Our country is being strongly influenced by China in economic and political domains."[8] This view was also observed in interviews with Japanese participants.

These informants essentially agreed about China's influence on their own country and region, and its growing influence on the global stage. However, there are also conflicting views about this, particularly for some Korean informants. Some informants often highlighted that what they, as students and research experts on China, know of and feel about China is different from that of ordinary people. One such informant said, "If you go anywhere or turn on the TV or read newspapers, you often hear that 'China is rising.' However, it is and it isn't. Some people, who are not experts on China, do not often feel this way."[9]

A Korean informant, who spent two of his early school years in Beijing and is now enrolled at a university as a Chinese language major,[10] narrated a view similar to that of the previous informant: "The rise of China is real, but not all people agree with this." He alluded to a mixed perception of China, adding, "to Korea, China's economic influence is big, [but] culture, media and other influences are rather difficult to find."[11]

This shows an ambivalent view of China in South Korea, and perhaps in Japan, too, that links to the next section where I explain why the first stage of the soft power pathways—influential China as a source of linguistic capital—does not connect seamlessly to the later stage of the soft power pathways—media product consumption—in quasi-Sinophone East Asia.

The Limited Power of Linguistic Capital: Locating and Dislocating Soft Power in Linguistic Capital for Chinese Majors

What causes the issue of converting linguistic capital into a practical soft power in both South Korea and Japan?

Those who study China and Chinese language as university majors have a tendency to watch Chinese television series more frequently than others. JV58,[12] who started to learn Chinese in April 2012, said, "Being Japanese, I have a basic knowledge of Chinese characters, [so] I thought it was a good move to learn Chinese language. I also see an increasing number of Chinese people in Japan."

In the age of a rising China, the Chinese language is increasingly becoming a new lingua franca (Ding and Saunders 2006). By doing so, students of Chinese language and Chinese Studies who were mostly inspired to learn about China, including international students in China, accumulate and acquire globally relevant linguistic capital (Smits and Gündüz-Hoşgör 2003).

KV39, who studied in China at both her local high school and at a university in Qingdao before moving back to South Korea for postgraduate Chinese Studies, said, "I think watching Chinese television series is a way of remembering Chinese, as opposed to not forgetting the Chinese language that I had learned for years. As Chinese television series are not cutting-edge or very interesting, except for those who like China a lot, people do not watch them."[13] Here, an advanced Chinese speaker and graduate student in Chinese Studies highlighted the value of Chinese television series as a tool for maintaining linguistic capital, but not offering cultural capital.

Another Korean interviewee, as a previous major in Chinese language and literature, has a profile similar to that of the previous informant. She studied Chinese language in a non-degree language program in 2002, and spent another year from 2005 to 2006 in an advanced level non-degree Chinese program.[14] She delivered her opinion strongly, saying, "We, Korean people, usually think Chinese stuff lags behind. Things about and from China are underdeveloped compared to our own. This is why Chinese stuff is not easily popular in Korea. What we have to distinguish here is that exposure to Chinese language and the ability to speak the language has grown, but China-related things are not popularized." This informant's view overlaps with those of some of the Korean and Japanese respondents in Chaps. 4 and 6, who highlighted a lack of conversion from both Chinese influence to transnational audiences' consumption of Chinese television series, and from the capital of Chinese influence to actual soft power.

Other informants, who did not choose Chinese Studies as their major but instead learned Chinese as non-degree students in China, have slightly different views and behaviors from the previous participants in my study. According to KV45,[15] "when I was studying abroad for a Chinese language program, [most of the] [...] or (...) female students were majoring in Chinese Studies. Interestingly, half of the male students were also students in Chinese Studies. Another half were different majors, from economics to management, engineering, and other disciplines. At that time, I was in my early 20s. I did not know and was wondering why they came to China to learn Chinese language, although their majors were very different from Chinese Studies and they did not have to learn the language. Now looking back, I can understand this. They can add a linguistic ability to their major. Perhaps they're much better than me, who studied Chinese language for four years." Her rationalization of the decisions of her classmates in their non-degree Chinese language program in Beijing epitomizes how the second, non-major group of students in this chapter approaches Chinese language as a form of linguistic capital with a potential convertible value into economic capital. Simultaneously, they also show that these non-major students live outside of the influence created by a full pathway of Chinese soft power, as Fig. 6.1 represents, which shows the resources of soft power to be converted to actual soft power.

This point is also reinforced by KV10: "Unless Chinese Studies is your major, it is hardly the case that you are interested in Chinese culture, media, televisual products, or songs." In line with KV10's opinion, a male Chinese Studies major in his 20s shared a similar perspective: "Chinese pop culture is not popular. In Korea, people are interested in the language and the economy of China, but they are not interested in the culture, society, or media of China. In terms of cultural sphere, we—Koreans—have a tendency to believe that Korean culture is above Chinese culture."[16] Comparing two cultures and societies from a perspective of superiority comes from setting one's own culture as the standard. This links to his other point; he continued to elaborate that, "These two perceptions exist together: 'do not know much about Chinese culture or China,' and, at the same time, 'look down on China.'"[17] The "fever" for traditional cultural and linguistic capital, which is convertible to economic capital, is much more relevant to transnational audiences. The pathways of soft power conversion, from platforms/resources to capital, are beyond the reach of the sending country, and instead lie in the hands of audiences in the transnational, receiving country.

Neither the informants who enrolled in a short-term non-degree program for learning Chinese, nor those who majored in Chinese Studies and/ or studied abroad in China enthusiastically mentioned consuming Chinese television series or other types of media, except in involuntary cases such as homework. Paradoxically, the pathway from resources and platforms to soft power by linguistic capital is apparently an incomplete circuit.

Japanese respondents have also presented narratives similar to those of Korean participants. Nakamura, who started to learn Chinese about a decade ago for his work, clearly indicated, "I only learned the language, but I don't watch Chinese films or dramas." He continued to tell me, "An increasing number of Japanese people started to learn Chinese.[18] Nowadays, Chinese is the most popular language among the foreign languages offered at the university level; not French or German." This is similarly observed in South Korea, as presented at the opening narrative of this chapter, wherein learning Chinese has sparked a generational "fever" in South Korea. He continued on to say, "Not only universities, but also Japanese companies have increased business with China. English is important, but it is basic. Chinese is becoming more important than other foreign languages. Many people who learn Korean language do it as a hobby, not for economic reasons or to find jobs that require spoken fluency of the language." JV6[19] narrated a sharp contrast between Korean language learning and Chinese language learning, and how people value these two practices differently. Chinese language has more linguistic capital, which has greater potential to be turned into economic capital, while Korean language has cultural capital. Reasons behind learning these languages and how they function have divergent patterns. JV6[20] added, "But to most, like myself, language is language." He implied that the conversion of linguistic capital from Chinese language does not directly translate into creating a transnational Chinese soft power field in Japan.

It is interesting to note the nuances in relation to JV6's point vis-à-vis Korean language learning and the Korean Wave.[21] The way in which Korean media products are consumed by Japanese informants and shape their experiences of the Korean Wave are patently different from their consumption of Chinese media products. Thus, the lesson is that the effectiveness of Chinese soft power through its media products could be projected and consumed through the effort to engender a unique "China Wave." Two qualifications of a "China Wave" exist here: at one end, as mentioned in the beginning of Chap. 4, Korean media practitioners have preempted concerns about the potential rise of a "China Wave." At another end, a secondary "China Wave" that will be mentioned in Chap. 6, in the case of Japan, is created in Hong Kong and Taiwan out of outsourced Chinese soft power.

With the Korean Wave, learning the Korean language is a byproduct of its influence; thus, it is an outcome of Korean soft power expressed through the popularity of Korean media and pop culture. By contrast, this study shows that Chinese soft power, which is still weak and developing, might gain some momentum by attracting people to learn the Chinese language for study, business, future work, personal interest, or just plain enjoyment. In a nutshell, expected outcomes of soft power in quasi-Sinophone East Asian countries are seemingly similar—to win over foreign audiences—whereas the mechanism varies between the two case studies. In both cases, the pathways of soft power need to firmly join together.

Even though they are majoring in Chinese Studies, some students who were interviewed do not watch Chinese dramas. One insistently explained, "It is not interesting," and, "I am not interested in the culture or media of China, but [only] interested in the Chinese language. China is the neighbor of South Korea and has been important to the country, especially during this era of China's rise. That's why I learn Chinese and major in Chinese Studies. In the process of learning Chinese, there is no need to watch uninteresting programs." To them, China and the Chinese language are only means and tools for preparing for the future or securing a good job, while the programs of China are not enjoyable to them. This is fairly different from the case of American and Japanese dramas, which are commonly watched, even by students who do not major in English or Japanese, study the languages, or even take interest in their root cultures.

In connection, KV9[22] further elaborated, "Chinese majors, or people who already have an interest in China, are the only groups of people who consume [Chinese media]. I made a great effort to learn more about China, and conducted research out of interest in China. By doing this, I made considerable endeavors to encounter Chinese culture. But actually, if I or people like me do not deliberately devote ourselves to do so, I do not always feel like watching them [Chinese programs]. In South Korea, there is no such Chinese mania. We instead prefer to watch Korean programs." She pointed out that she made some effort to consume Chinese television series, and that she separates learning about China from consuming and being affected by Chinese culture and media. This is very problematic for China, in its quest to identify transnational soft power audiences. In fact, students of Chinese Studies are easy targets. To her earlier response, she also added, "Aside from someone who has lived in China and gained a stronger interest in China, most South Koreans' feelings towards China are negative." This is linked to politicized and antagonistic locally embedded sentiments, as presented in Chap. 4.

Many South Koreans and Japanese think that learning the Chinese language offers work and business opportunities; they consider China as an opportunity for their own career development. While studying the Chinese language and visiting the country can function as the starting point from which interest in China may begin, as byproducts they are simultaneously also the end in itself.

On the whole, in both Japanese and South Korean contexts, acquiring linguistic capital by learning Chinese language does not translate to other actions that are related to China's soft power configuration. The absence of outstanding Chinese televisual subfields, as I discussed in Chap. 4 and will revisit in Chap. 6, as well as a deficiency of covalence in the reverse media flow in East Asia are conducive to China's paradox of capital conversion to soft power.

CONCLUSION: THE LIMITS OF LINGUISTIC CAPITAL CONVERSION AND ITS SETBACKS

This chapter has examined the consumption and reception of Chinese soft power through media products as a vehicle of soft power in the two receiving countries of South Korea and Japan. It has investigated the variation in responses to soft power production via media consumption when different factors—culture, the boundaries of China, images, and perceptions—are managed among South Korean and Japanese audiences. Likewise, the soft power translation process takes place only when such products are consumed by the audience. This final section will revisit issues of interest and byproducts, cultural boundaries, and taste-making, which are embedded in the South Korean and Japanese consumption of Chinese media products and also serve as factors in constructing the soft power field that further shapes the transnational consumption and reception of soft power.

The ways in which interests evolve, and the byproducts that are generated in the course of making Chinese soft power in South Korea and Japan, are often entangled with each other. This also has to do with the rise of China. On the South Korean side, this entanglement is linked to potential economic gains. On the Japanese side, this has to do with antagonism over issues with China, which discourages further pursuit of knowledge about and exposure to the country. Nonetheless, many South Koreans and Japanese believe that learning the Chinese language offers work and business opportunities, and consider China an opportunity for their own career development. While studying the Chinese language and visiting the country can function as starting points for interest in China, as byproducts they are simultaneously also ends in themselves.

In the consumption of Chinese products, South Koreans and Japanese informants negotiate their choices and oscillate between an unwritten mechanism of acceptance and resistance. In South Korea, people with a background of majoring in Chinese language or Chinese Studies consume Chinese media products more actively than others, but their answers and degrees of commitment to transnational consumption still vary.

As argued earlier, many South Koreans do not clearly delineate the origins of the "Chinese" products, unlike politically boundaried Chinese societies. To them, it is not meaningful to make such distinctions about the origins of the products; rather, the themes, historical backgrounds, and locations featured in the products play a significant role. This leads to an ambivalence regarding Chinese soft power. In contrast with the South Korean response, fewer people in Japan consume Chinese media products or know about their existence in the domestic market. This is in part because the only Asian products that are prevalent in the Japanese media marketplace are South Korean; Japan's experience of PRC soft power products is eclipsed by the power of *Hallyu*. However, the South Korean and Japanese preference for Hong Kong and Taiwan's media products has helped China build upon Greater China relations as a means of cultural intermediation for audiences.

From the perspective of soft power maximization, it is problematic if only one particular group—Chinese Studies majors—emerges as the most likely "target audience." Under this circumstance, how could the Chinese government effectively expand its soft power reach to more audiences? This is a setback to the limits of linguistic capital conversion and its failure to transform into other forms of capital and, ultimately, influential soft power in South Korea and Japan. Looking ahead, it is an essential question for the industry in China. Relatedly, Chap. 6 explores how China might benefit from unintentionally tapping into Hong Kong and Taiwan as backup banks of outsourced soft power, as well as how this outsourced soft power might lead to a potential chain of problems that add to its dual soft power paradox.

Notes

1. Sections of this chapter are adapted from Lee (2018).
2. Sonoda and Hsiao (2016), in particular, Kim and Lee (2016) explore the changing dynamics and potential risks in socio-economic sectors in East Asia due to the rise of China.
3. The case of learning English and the conversion of Korean wave is opposite to the Chinese wave.
4. One of such examples is the objective and the number of Confucius Institutes in the world. See Cheng (2009), Chey (2008), Gil (2008), Hartig (2010, 2016), Hughes (2014), Lee (2009), Paradise (2009), Starr (2009).
5. KV13, Interview with a South Korean respondent, December 8, 2011, Seoul, South Korea.
6. KV14, Interview with a South Korean respondent, December 8, 2011, Seoul, South Korea.
7. KV11, Interview with a South Korean respondent, December 8, 2011, Seoul, South Korea.
8. KV16, Interview with a South Korean respondent, December 9, 2011, Seoul, South Korea.
9. KV9, Interview with a South Korean respondent, November 30, 2011, Seoul, South Korea.

10. KV25, Interview with a South Korean respondent, December 15, 2011, Seoul, South Korea.
11. KV25, Interview with a South Korean respondent, December 15, 2011, Seoul, South Korea.
12. JV58, Interview with a Japanese respondent, May 24, 2012, Seoul, South Korea.
13. KV39, Interview with a South Korean respondent, December 21, 2011, Seoul, South Korea.
14. KV45, Interview with a South Korean respondent, November 30, 2011, Seoul, South Korea.
15. KV45, Interview with a South Korean respondent, November 30, 2011, Seoul, South Korea.
16. KV16, Interview with a South Korean respondent, December 9, 2011, Seoul, South Korea.
17. Ibid.
18. JV59, Interview with a Japanese respondent, May 24, 2012, Seoul, South Korea.
19. JV6, Interview with a Japanese respondent, February 14, 2012, Tokyo, Japan.
20. JV6, Interview with a Japanese respondent, February 14, 2012, Tokyo, Japan.
21. On the Japanese media market, South Korean media products often function as a reference for the provision of Chinese programs. The Korean Wave in the Japanese media market reduces opportunities for alternative products from other places, such as the PRC.
22. KV9, Interview with a South Korean respondent, November 30, 2011, Seoul, South Korea.

REFERENCES

Cheng, Xu. 2009. Education: The Intellectual Base of China's Soft Power. In *Soft Power: China's Emerging Strategy in International Politics*, ed. Mingjiang Li, 103–124. Lanham, Boulder, New York, Toronto, and Plymouth: Lexington Books.

Chey, Jocelyn. 2008. Chinese 'Soft Power': Cultural Diplomacy and the Confucius Institutes. *The Sydney Papers* 20 (1): 32–46.

Ding, Sheng, and Robert A. Saunders. 2006. Talking Up China: An Analysis of China's Rising Cultural Power and Global Promotion of the Chinese Language. *East Asia* 23 (2): 3–33.

Gao, Hong. 2011. An Analysis of the Phenomenon of Global 'Mandarin Fever'. *Asian Social Science* 7 (12): 253–257.

Gil, Jeffrey. 2008. The Promotion of Chinese Language Learning and China's Soft Power. *Asian Social Science* 4 (10): 116–122.

Hartig, Falk. 2010. *Confusion About Confucius Institutes: Soft Power Push or Conspiracy? A Case Study of Confucius Institutes in Germany.* Paper presented at the 18th Biennial Conference of the Asian Studies Association of Australia in Adelaide, July 5–8.

———. 2016. *Chinese Public Diplomacy: The Rise of the Confucius Institute.* Oxon and New York: Routledge.

Hughes, Christopher R. 2014. Confucius Institutes and the University: Distinguishing the Political Mission from the Cultural. *Issues & Studies* 50 (4): 45–83.

Kim, Kye Hwan. 2006. Segyeneun Jigeum Junggukeo Baeugi Yeolpung [The World Is Now a Craze for Learning Chinese]. *The Hankyoreh*, January 12. Accessed March 21, 2018. http://www.hani.co.kr/arti/international/international_general/94702.html.

Kim, Yuntae, and Claire Seungeun Lee. 2016. Kankoku chūshōkigyō no chūgoku tekiō senryaku [Coping Strategies of Korean Small and Medium-Size Companies in China]. In *Chaina risuku to ika ni mukiau ka: Nikkantai no kigyō no chōsen [How to Cope with China Risk: The Challenges of Japanese, Korean, and Taiwanese Firms]*, ed. Shigeto Sonoda and Hsin-Huang Michael Hsiao, 111–147. Tokyo: University of Tokyo Press.

Lee, (Claire) Seungeun. 2009. China's Cultural Diplomacy in the Hu Jintao Era: The Geocultural Role of the Confucius Institute. *Yonsei Journal of International Studies* 1 (1): 44–59.

———. 2013. China's Leap Forward from 'Brain Drain' to 'Brain Gain': Its International Student Recruitment Strategy and the Decision-Making Process of Foreign Students. *Journal of Contemporary China Studies* 14 (2): 319–361.

———. 2018. Developing Social Science-Based Chinese Studies in East Asia: Geopolitics, Discipline, Knowledge. *International Journal of China Studies* 9 (2): 143–162.

Ngeow, Chow Bing, Tek Soon Ling, and Pik Shy Fan. 2014. Pursuing Chinese Studies Amidst Identity Politics in Malaysia. *East Asia* 31: 103–122.

Nye, Joseph S., Jr. 2011. *The Future of Power.* New York: Public Affairs.

Paradise, James F. 2009. China and International Harmony: The Role of Confucius Institutes in Bolstering Beijing's Soft Power. *Asian Survey* 49 (4): 647–669.

Smits, Jeroen, and Ayşe Gündüz-Hoşgör. 2003. Linguistic Capital: Language as a Socio-Economic Resource Among Kurdish and Arabic Women in Turkey. *Ethnic and Racial Studies* 26 (5): 829–853.

Sonoda, Shigeto, and Hsin-Huang Michael Hsiao, eds. 2016. *Chaina risuku to ika ni mukiau ka: Nikkantai no kigyō no chōsen [How to Cope with China Risk: The Challenges of Japanese, Korean, and Taiwanese Firms].* Tokyo: University of Tokyo Press.

Starr, Don. 2009. Chinese Language Education in Europe: The Confucius Institutes. *European Journal of Education* 44 (1): 65–82.

Sungkyun Institute of China Studies. 2017. *Policies Towards China in the New Administration.* Colloquium at Sungkyun Institute of China Studies, Seoul, South Korea. June 1.

CHAPTER 6

The Limits of Outsourced Soft Power

In this chapter, after focusing on quasi-Sinophone East Asian audiences, we redirect to Sinophone East Asia as the center that shapes a transnational soft power field in South Korea and Japan. I include Hong Kong and Taiwan to draw comparisons and state pertinent implications for China's soft power. These two localities, as sources of a reverse media flow in East Asia, are situated as export regions for the mediatization of "Chinese" televised soft power to South Korea and Japan. I will argue that Hong Kong and Taiwan's shared cultural capital—ethnic and linguistic—and shared celebrity capital projected through their television series will help the Chinese state minimize its soft power dilemma when it approaches foreign audiences.

Hong Kong and Taiwan as Targets of China's Soft Power

Ministry of Culture (2012) clearly identifies the principal targets of its soft power projection, beginning with Hong Kong and Taiwan (see Chap. 1). Along the PRC's "One China, Two Systems" policy, it is widely understood that Hong Kong and Taiwan are parts of China. However, in their trade of goods, services and cultural products, Hong Kong and Taiwan are largely separate from the PRC. This is expressed both from these stakeholders' perspective, as well as those of individuals in other countries. It is thus important to include Hong Kong and Taiwan in analyses of China's soft power targets.

© The Author(s) 2018
C. S. Lee, *Soft Power Made in China*,
https://doi.org/10.1007/978-3-319-93115-9_6

Along with other parts of Asia—namely South Korea, Japan, and Southeast Asia, Hong Kong and Taiwan have previously served as export sites for Chinese TV series, particularly in 2011. In line with China's soft power policy, it is documented that "Hong Kong, Taiwan, Japan, South Korea, and other Asian regions are still China's main export target at this moment, although the market has been expanding to Europe, the US, and some Middle East countries" (Italian Trade Commission 2011: 24). China thus intends to export Chinese TV series to both Sinophone and quasi-Sinophone East Asia.

From 2010 to 2014, China's television series were exported to Hong Kong and Taiwan, on average, in the amounts of 20 million RMB (with 1561 episodes) and 20.7 million RMB (with 1750 episodes), respectively (National Bureau of Statistics 2011, 2012, 2013, 2014, 2015). The amount of export revenue to these two sites is almost equal to China's television series export revenue in the entire Southeast Asian region. China's television series were also sold at an overall higher price to Hong Kong and Taiwan (12,300 RMB per episode) than to Southeast Asia (At 4541 RMB per episode). Likewise, in this view Hong Kong and Taiwan appear as targets of China's soft power and serve as important destinations for China to wield its televised soft power.

(Un)Making the Boundaries of China and Chinese Television Series

"Have you ever watched Chinese (*jungguk*) television dramas?" If I asked this question in South Korea in the late 1990s and early 2000s, my generation as well as many of my younger informants in the early 2010s would say, "Yes, I enjoy watching *My Fair Princess*." This was fairly true among Korean participants; in particular, female informants. Growing up with an unprecedentedly popular *Chinese* drama, I remember how my high school classmates talked enthusiastically about the drama's characters and shared in our consuming fandom. The show coincidently aired on TV around the time we elected to begin studying Chinese as a second foreign language. Some of my high school classmates, and those at my university, even decided to take their Chinese language studies further, largely due to the series. *My Fair Princess* sparked our interest in the language, and served to better prepare us as cosmopolitans in the age of rising China.

Yet, having said this, is *My Fair Princess* really a *Chinese* television drama? Unlike the word "Chinese" in English, which carries an ambivalent meaning that refers to things that belong to China and (ethnic) Chinese, the Korean word "jungguk" only carries a meaning equivalent to "belonging to China." When some Korean interviewees used "jungguk," it was along their understanding of what China "is"; at least when it comes to television series. Not only do these interviewees from the aforementioned cohorts cite *My Fair Princess* as being among their favorite Chinese dramas, but consensus also exists elsewhere across age, gender, and other demographics.

Along with these answers, some Korean informants reacted to my interview prompt, "When I think about *Chinese* dramas, the first thing that came to mind were Taiwanese dramas" (emphasis mine). Like other Koreans I interviewed, these participants could differentiate *jungguk* from *Chinese*, while others beyond this group do not.

While these informants' understanding of what "jungguk" is, and which "jungguk" television series are centered around this particular genre, another group of people have slightly different views on the same question.

Others generally cite programs in which Jackie Chan, Jet Li, or Stephen Chow appear as "Chinese" (jungguk). This is the most frequent answer I encountered when I asked who, among their peers, watched these dramas and whether they are popular. Although the question during my interview sessions was precisely phrased with the word "jungguk," which again refers to China,[1] what I immediately received back from these informants fell beyond this category. In other words, their immediate answers were always about programs produced in another Chinese society; not China. This is contrary to the fact that, unlike in English where "Chinese" refers to (1) the language of China, (2) a native or inhabitant of China, or a person of Chinese descent, (3) anything else relating to China or its culture, the words for "China/Chinese," "Hong Kong(ese)" and "Taiwan(ese)" are different in Korean and indicate different things. Taken together, for Korean audiences, Chinese dramas do not necessarily mean that they originated solely in China. Indeed, the way that South Koreans delineate the boundaries of what constitutes "China" and "Chinese dramas" do not necessarily correspond to each other.

In Japanese language, by contrast, the word for "China" (Chūgoku) is the exact same as the Chinese word (*Zhongguo*), as these two languages share Chinese characters. To the same question "Have you ever watched Chinese television dramas?" some Japanese respondents intriguingly began answering by drawing a boundary around what "China" is and what "China" is not. This politicized boundary-making was the first step for these Japanese participants to make sense of how and why they consume Chinese television series.

Japanese informants drew certain boundaries and shared strong feelings about Taiwan when it comes to the issue of sovereignty. This is a common practice in Japan to delineate the boundaries of China and Taiwan. Thinking of Taiwan as a foreign "country" that has an "intimate" relationship with Japan is largely reflected in an imagined collective identity that ties the two together.[2] Japan's former colonial relationship with Taiwan is evident here and frames Taiwan as a country; not a society adhering to China's "One Country, Two Systems." Interestingly, in contrast to disapproving of China's boundary-making of Taiwan as part of China, JV18[3] strongly argued to me, "Hong Kong belongs to China, but not Taiwan."

Other Japanese respondents indicate that Taiwan is special and personal to them. The informant JV58[4] said, "Taiwanese like Japanese people. I met a Taiwanese couple while trekking before. They told me that they want to visit Japan sometime, they like Japan so much, and are interested in Japan." These mutual favorable feelings generate different sentiments in how Japanese informants perceive Taiwan compared to the Chinese mainland. It also implies that this relationship with Taiwan impedes Japanese participants in my study from investing greater interest in China. She also added, "On a different note, we received the biggest donation after the 3.11 earthquake in 2011 from Taiwan." Similarly, JV23[5] said, "Japanese think that Taiwanese like us, while Chinese dislike us...." As such, both the responses of JV23[6] and JV58,[7] and the latent citations of "mutual likeness," implies this sentiment matters and is shared by not only the informants, but other Japanese respondents in general.

The two different sets of Japanese relationships, with Taiwan as favorable and with China as unfavorable, are also well-captured in Fig. 6.1 by the public opinion survey of the Ministry of Foreign Affairs in Japan. This annual survey of public opinion on international affairs and opinions about foreign countries has yearly data on China as far back as the Chinese economic reform of 1978. The 2016 data was collected nationwide from 1,804 Japanese nationals age 18 or above (original target sample size was 3,000, with a 60.1 percent response rate).

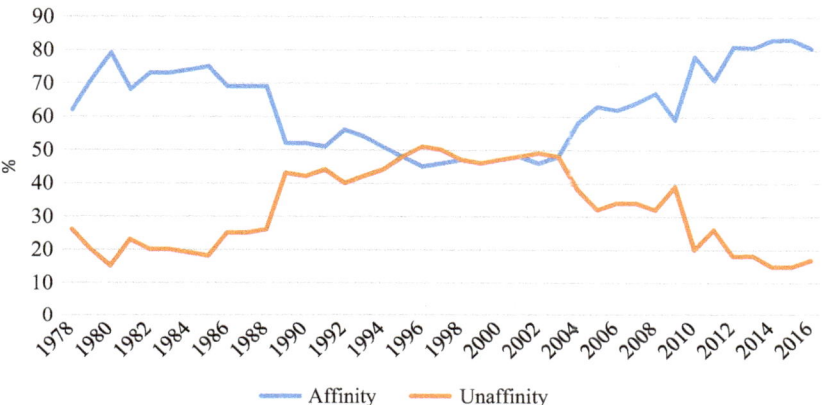

Fig. 6.1   Japan's affinity toward China. Source: Cabinet Office of the Government of Japan (2010, 2011, 2012, 2013, 2014, 2015, 2016, 2017). Notes: (1) The data of 2015 is not available. However, there are two records in 2016: One was collected in January 2016 and another collection was in November of the year. I, thus, treat January 2016 data as 2015 and November 2016 data as 2016. (2) All data is now without a decimal point

To the question "Do you feel an affinity towards China?" the Japanese respondents' views on China were friendly until the mid-1990s. In 1995, Japanese people noticeably began to view China in an unfriendly light. From 2004 on, the view was completely different from before, and in 2005 there was a history book controversy between Japan and China. Overall, since the mid-2000s, the regional and global rise of China has impacted and defined how Japanese people view China.

The increasingly and predominantly unfavorable views on China among Japanese people is also explained in Chaps. 4 and 5. The relationship between these two countries not only shapes Japanese society, but also influences its consumption and reception of China's foreign media and culture.

In what follows, I explain how these boundaries and opinions matter for how and why transnational audiences in quasi-Sinophone East Asia are inclined to consume television series from Hong Kong and Taiwan, but not PRC China. I also highlight why television dramas produced in Hong Kong and Taiwan are, ironically, still "Chinese" dramas to Japanese and Korean audiences, and how they function as outsourced soft power platforms for the PRC.

Japan: Partially Outsourced Soft Power of Hong Kong and Taiwan

Karyū[8] literally refers to the cultural flows from China, Taiwan and Hong Kong, but in reality it largely refers only to those of Taiwan and Hong Kong. JV39's[9] response was typical of Japanese informants: "Hong Kongese is different from Chinese; Taiwanese programs are different from Chinese, too." Notably, some Japanese respondents were not even aware of the term *karyū*, but understood the phenomenon. The following account articulates and defines the term from the viewpoint of a Japanese audience. JV33[10] said, "People who are now in their twenties or thirties tend to like the Korean Wave, but it seems that some people in their forties and fifties like Taiwanese culture and media (*karyū*) to some extent. Among them, there are quite a few who like Taiwanese idols or dramas. For example, the dance group F4, dramas, and singers." Apparently, *Karyū* may not be the most popular foreign cultural movement in Japan, yet there are some who still consume it (Kim 2006).[11] Still, it is observable that *Karyū* exists in concept as a "Taiwanese Wave," rather than a PRC one. Along this phenomenon, I argue in this section that Hong Kong and Taiwan's television series play a role in the incomplete transmission of outsourced PRC soft power to Japanese audiences.

Looking for a Distinctive Subfield

Consuming Hong Kong: Martial Arts/Kungfu Subfield
In one of the big Tsutaya stores in Shibuya, there is a section on Asian dramas and films. A few blocks from the store, you can find a "Jackie Chan Theater." When I asked Japanese interviewees for a list of Chinese television series they watched, they mostly replied that they watched those starring Jackie Chan. In response, I inquired about the origins of each production named by asking, "Is it Chinese?" They realized that each has Hong Kong origins.

Likewise, *kungfu*[12] is one of the most salient commodities of Chinese culture. Meanings of particular words (Chin 1996) and the interpretations of Chinese chivalrous novels (martial arts) (Pei 2010), particularly the novels of Chinese writer Jin Yong, have been spotlighted by scholars. Hamm (2005) explored the attraction of Jin Yong's *wuxia* novels and the culture of Hong Kong. Zhang (2003) linked Jin Yong's

Chinese martial arts novels to nationalism using *Ludingji* (*The Deer and the Cauldron*), one of the outstanding works of Jin Yong, as a case study (Zhang 2005). It is widely known among Japanese people that *kungfu* is the leading theme in the media products of Hong Kong and, thus, *kungfu* films and *wuxia* novels have received academic attention in Japan (Yamamoto 2007). Wu (2005) investigated how Jin Yong's martial arts novels are received in the context of Japan (Wu 2005). If Jin Yong is the best known Chinese novelist, as is frequently documented in Japanese academia, his counterpart in cinematic media is Jackie Chan. "Jackie Chan is famous in Japan" was one of the most frequent statements made by Japanese respondents. Besides Jackie Chan, no other name came up recurrently during my interviews with informants.

JV48,[13] who has been involved in translating subtitles and programs into Japanese, commented, "As far as I am concerned, oldies (gulao) are often shown on TV recently. Shaolin, *wudapian* (martial arts), the films and dramas of Cheng Long (Jackie Chan) and Liu Dehua (Andy Lau) are examples. I used to work as a translator of subtitles, for dubbing from Chinese to Japanese. Some of the aforementioned programs are my translation." Due to his rich experiences in media production, and crafting local tastes, he felt particularly drawn to Chinese dramas. Sharing his memories, he added, "There was another TV station that broadcast programs directly from Xianggang Meiya Dianshitai (Hong Kong Meiya Broadcasting Station) some time ago. It seems that it went bankrupt due to management reasons." This implies that it is rather difficult for Chinese media program providers to survive in Japan. The discontinuity and absence of such providers in the country allows us to reasonably speculate that there is only a limited number of fixed audiences because of the limited content, inaccessibility of the programs, and a general lack of recognition from the wider viewing public.

Acknowledging this situation, the following informant, JV42,[14] who studied in South Korea, has somewhat different experiences to those of other Japanese viewers in general: "The Chinese dramas that I have watched so far were all in South Korea when I was on an exchange program there for a year." He continued, "*Justice Pao* and *The Return of the Pearl Princess* were the ones that I watched in South Korea. In South Korea, there are some Chinese programs on TV, but I cannot get them in Japan." Although he was in South Korea in the late 2000s, decades after the dramas were produced, many South Korean cable TV channels re-run these famous and popular Chinese dramas. In virtue of this, the Japanese soft power experience of China can be mediated by and in another country, as was the case for JV42.[15] Yet, despite their limited import, JV23[16] conveyed her experience of intentionally consuming "PRC Chinese" products. She said, "Through watching dramas, movies or singing songs, I can learn some Chinese." For her as a student of Chinese, such consumption is for language learning. For the purpose of enhancing Chinese language ability, she deliberately chooses Chinese, not Taiwanese, products. Such scenario is also observed in South Korea.

Consuming Taiwan: Looking for a Contemporary Subfield
"Trendy" and "modern" Taiwanese dramas, like *Playful Kiss* and *The Meteor Garden*, were frequently mentioned by female viewers. As *The Meteor Garden* originated from a Japanese manga, many Japanese viewers were familiar with the story and thus felt the series was accessible and easy to understand.[17] All interviewees concluded that Taiwanese dramas can be characterized as modern, urban and trendy, in contrast with the backward, boring and unattractive PRC Chinese ones. JV9[18] said, "I have two purposes for watching media, generally. For enjoyment, Taiwanese dramas are the example. I watched some Taiwanese dramas that had teenage sentiments, although if I watch them now I don't feel like they fit my style. For learning language, I could be exposed to more Chinese by watching them."

JV39's[19] response was typical of Japanese informants who believe that the three societies are different from each other: "Hong Kongese is different from Chinese; Taiwanese programs are different from Chinese, too." JV23[20] provided an extensive account of her views on watching Taiwanese programs: "We—or I—like Taiwanese or overseas Chinese actors or singers. I cannot think of any 'Chinese' singers or actors … nor do I like them." She also added, "Taiwanese dramas are childish. I watched some, although they were for teenagers. I have never watched Chinese (PRC) dramas. Although PRC dramas are often shown on TV, Japanese people prefer to watch more Taiwanese dramas." Among the platforms for Taiwanese-produced products, "Tokyo Max has a corner and program to introduce Taiwanese films and drama." Also, "Nihon-TV usually has Taiwanese media, too. *Meteor Garden* was shown on Nihon-TV … BS has Taiwanese as well as (PRC) Chinese programs." The existence of Taiwanese programs in the Japanese media market impedes PRC Chinese programs from attaining success. In terms of the sources and channels for the latter, "There is neither special contact, nor information [on it]."

For Japanese audience members, as in the eyes of Korean respondents, PRC Chinese programs have no distinctive character, whereas Hong Kong and Taiwan programs have salient characteristics. JV39[21] said, "Hong Kongese programs are famous for action; in other words, they have some characteristics. I cannot think of a corresponding description for Chinese ones." Similarly, JV48[22] who lived in Harbin until age 10 due to family business, said, "For Chinese entertainment and dramas, Hong Kong and Taiwan, respectively, immediately came to mind. For PRC China, I would immediately think of history-related themes." The clear division of themes, which is consistent in the case of South Korea, shows that there is a possible limit to Japanese consumer exposure to Chinese programs. He said, "At home, I have a subscription to Sky Perfect TV (Sky Perfect TV n.d.). Sky Perfect TV is not a free channel. This channel has quite a few PRC Chinese dramas, and occasionally Taiwan and Hong Kong-made dramas and movies." He is one of the few devoted Japanese audience members of "Chinese" media. His stay in China for several years when he was young contributed to the maintenance of his interest in China and the Chinese language. He holds a very positive view of China and Chinese, saying, "Many Japanese people think 'I don't like China' or 'I don't like Chinese.' I do not carry such a strong sentiment. China has its own way of life. Of course, it is different from Japan's way of living. It's less clean than Japan, for sure. After some time living there, I could adapt to the way of life in China. I felt comfortable being there." The general antagonistic perception among Japanese people toward China that he alluded to is very frequently observed in the case of Japan, as well as in South Korea.

Yet, as we've seen, personal motives can indeed outweigh political sentiments. JV23[23] chooses only Taiwanese media products, not PRC Chinese products, when she wants to watch TV for entertainment. But for the purpose of enhancing her Chinese language ability she chooses PRC Chinese products rather than Taiwanese ones. This is also a common response among Koreans who are learning Chinese. These compartmentalized choices of products from different production locales show one way in which Chinese cultural commodities are consumed. Thus, China's soft power in Japan may be thought of as experiencing reconstruction.

Contested and Politicized Boundaries of "China" for Japan and for Configuring Its Chinese Soft Power Field

This section will focus on how boundaries and relations shape the Chinese soft power field in Japan while noting that Taiwan, Hong Kong, and the PRC remain as individual countries in the Japanese mindscape. A wide variety of views exist on these three locales. JV40,[24] an avid viewer of

"Chinese" media products and a frequent visitor to Taiwan, commented, "There is no good image about China. China ignores Taiwan, China prevents Taiwan from gaining de facto independence. There is an ongoing territorial issue. China, Taiwan, and Hong Kong are different." What is consequential is that this is not just a personal view limited to JV40. JV48[25] revealed a personal belief that, "The Chinese and Taiwanese are not good in relationships—this might mean they are not good at making friends [...] Hong Kong people and Chinese are different. Hong Kong people dislike Chinese. They don't want to be Chinese." On Hong Kong and China, JV45[26] also commented, "PRC Chinese people have a desire to become Hong Kongese. Hong Kong is different from China, but it is getting closer and even becoming similar to China after its return to China." On cultural similarities, JV23[27] commented, "Taiwan and Hong Kong are culturally close. China is different from them." On the political position of these three societies, she also mentioned, "The three are politically different entities." These boundaries do not simply end with the Japanese informants' perceptions and political views about these Chinese societies; they shape their transnational consumption of media products.

JV51[28] said, "What I like about China. Well, I and we—Japanese people—like Chinese food, movies … but Chinese people argue so strongly." I asked why she seems to have a problem with their argumentation style and whether she has experienced it before. She said, "I don't have Chinese colleagues or friends. But, I heard that from many people. If you look at Chinese students in Japan now, they don't speak Japanese or mingle with our culture." No matter whether what she has heard or observed is true, it is unquestionably a shared view among Japanese.

Reciprocity, connection, and interaction also matter in constructing images of China. JV35[29] shared her views on China's cultural influence in Japan: "Clothing, fashion: [influenced by] the United States, Europe. TV, drama, music: Korea (in recent years). Why is there no influence of Chinese culture on entertainment? The Japanese think that culture is equal to entertainment." Furthermore, "We never hear that there are people who like Japan in China from the news or media of Japan (whereas in China, Japanese products are popularly imported). We don't know much about the situation in China. On the other hand, I heard that in South Korea there are some people who like the Japanese boy bands Arashi, SMAP, or their songs, or that they have hosted performances there. From this, I know that Japanese culture is popular in South Korea." She further elaborated, "Chinese culture and Japanese culture are similar, in my opinion."

Despite such cultural similarities, this Japanese informant still claims to know nothing of China. She selectively and consistently refuses to embrace China by all means because of her predetermined perception of China.

In East Asia, history and geopolitics still matter and play not only an important role in themselves but also have a chain reaction effect into other seemingly irrelevant domains. JV33[30] reflected, "Recently the *Diaoyu/Senkaku* island issue was one of the hot topics, but not many people knew about it or were interested in it [...] I don't talk about it with my girlfriend—[who is] Chinese." He added, "The *Dokdo/Takeshima* issue was also the same. I knew that because I had a Korean friend; before, I had no interest in it at all." He further commented, "Koreans have *naembi geunsong*—easy to be stirred and easy to remember—while the Japanese do not act (*kanjouteki*).[31] We don't have any interest in other things and other people. In this regard, the Chinese reaction seems similar to that of the Koreans." He expressed that the Japanese indifference to sensitive historical issues is unequivocal: "I don't have an interest and many Japanese feel the same."

As a whole, there are several obstacles to embracing Chinese media in Japan. On the one hand, there is the Japanese perception of China and Chinese media, as argued earlier, and on the other hand, there is the Japanese media structure, as explained in Chap. 3. Both are constraints on the import of Chinese media products to the Japanese media market. This resulted from general perceptions in Japanese mindsets of Japanese culture as "superior," the continuous strength of Hong Kongese and Taiwanese products, and the role of Korean content in hindering China from entering and competing in the Japanese market in a way that may reshape soft power in the region. As Korean media products perform well in China, Japan and other Asian countries, China feels the pressure as a latecomer that wants to further develop its export market. This is well-captured in the discussion about the popularity of the Korean drama *My Love from the Star* that took place in the People's Congress of China in early 2014, and led to an inquiry as to why China could not make such successful programs (Long and Lee 2014).

This section has highlighted the roles of the cultural, political, and national boundaries of "China" in Japanese consumers' decisions to consume Chinese media products. The reciprocity and connection between Japan and Taiwan, in particular, dispose the Japanese to be more inclined toward Taiwan and its products, rather than those of PRC China. Furthermore, the historical and geopolitical relationships between China and Japan, and those between Taiwan and Japan, are influential in affect-ing the degree to which the Japanese consume the respective media prod-ucts of both locales.

SOUTH KOREA: UNINTENDED OUTSOURCING OF CHINA'S SOFT POWER FROM HONG KONG AND TAIWAN

Outsourced Soft Power from Distinctive Subfields

Korean audiences who seek new subfields of Chinese dramas often watch those that fall within either the contemporary/trendy subfield or the mar-tial arts subfield, no matter how they define "jungguk."

Historical and Contemporary Subfields as Sources of Distinct Outsourced Soft Power from Taiwan

Of the available Chinese media products, those belonging to the historical and martial arts subfields are widely available and well-known, as I docu-mented in Chaps. 3 and 4. However, unlike the cases were mentioned in Chap. 4, there are some television series that look "Chinese" to South Korean respondents but were actually directly from Hong Kong or Taiwan, or were co-produced with them.

In particular, *Justice Pao* (*Pocheongcheon*) and *My Fair Princess* (*Huanzhugege*)[32] were very much in fashion in the early and late 1990s, as well as the 2000s, in South Korea (Jeon 2008). Both dramas were based on novels by Taiwanese writers. Demographically speaking, there is a slight divide between the cohorts who watched these two popular pro-grams. An earlier cohort, born between 1976 and 1980,[33] watched *Pocheongcheon* during their secondary school years, possibly on Fridays with family members. The next cohort, born between 1981 and 1985, watched *The Return of the Pearl Princess* while in (junior) high school. Each cohort experienced different levels of familiarity and fandom with each of the programs. *Pocheongcheon* was phenomenally popular with South Koreans, regardless of age and gender, in the early 1990s. It was produced in Taiwan in 1990 and aired on KBS2 in 1993 with a 20 percent average audience rating. Watching it brought family members together, and turned the word "cheora" ("Chop!"), which appeared in the pro-gram, into a popular catchphrase. KV4[34] noted, "I happened to tune in to *Pocheongcheon* on TV while I was flipping through the channels when I was in the fifth grade, in primary school. I really liked Jeonjo, the main character. It was the first time I ever liked any actor, and he made me think about marrying him. The drama's theme song was in Chinese. I liked it although I did not know the language back then. A classmate who liked me gifted me with a figurine of Jeonjo. That's because he knew that I liked the drama and the character very much, and it was the most popular foreign TV drama at the time."

The Return of the Pearl Princess (or, *The Return of My Fair Princess*), on the other hand, was first broadcast on iTV (Incheon TV), a private regional TV channel in the Seoul metropolitan area. The first two seasons were originally broadcast in the late 1990s and early 2000s, and then repeatedly broadcasted throughout the 2000s (Jeon 2008). It had a 6 to 7 percent audience rate on average, which is remarkable for a "Chinese" (Taiwanese) drama (Shim and Min 2011). It was produced by E TV in Hunan Province, with two PRC castings and two Taiwanese castings. The two main characters, Ziwei and Prince Wu, were performed by Taiwanese actors with their voices dubbed. Perhaps this dubbing explains why it was difficult for even Chinese-speaking (or Chinese-learning) Koreans to tell that the actors were Taiwanese. Due to increasing co-production and co-starring of Chinese celebrities in Greater China (Lee 2018), "Chinese" media products nowadays are highly mobile and intertwined with Greater China. It is thus rather difficult to precisely demarcate their country or place of origin. Deciphering who is from mainland China, or not, may not be important for media professionals and audiences in Sinophone Asia. However, this in fact plays a significant role not only for media practitioners, in choosing what to import into their media market circuits, but, more importantly, for audiences to decide on what to consume.

The third season, *The Return of the Pearl Princess*, was broadcast in 2011. Some of the views expressed by interviewees about the change in cast in the third season included, "I think Seasons 1 and 2 were the best. I liked the cast, song and story. After the cast changed in the newer version, I lost interest in watching it."[35] KV41[36] said, "I watched dramas on Junghwa TV with my mom. She watched *The Return of the Pearl Princess* before and has a good impression of Lin Xinru (Ruby Lin), the main character. She also likes to watch *Meirenxinji* (*Schemes of a Beauty*)."

The unexpected success of *The Return of the Pearl Princess* prompted iTV to broadcast a series of Chinese dramas, such as *Shin Pocheongcheon* (*Xin Baoqingtian, New Justice Pao*), *Hoeokgongju* (*Huaiyu Gongzhu, Princess Huaiyu*), *Nohbangyuhui* (*Laofang youxi, Old House Has a Joy*) and *Angaebiyeonga* (*Qingshenshen yumengmeng, Romance in the Rain*). Some of them are historical, others can be categorized as premodern (1911–1948) (see Chap. 4). These were well-received in South Korea, as informants' accounts capture. KV46[37] said, "I watched *Angaebiyeonga* (*Romance in the Rain*), *Hoeokgongju* (*Princess Huaiyu*) and *Nohbangyuhui* (*Laofang youxi*). Lin Xinru (Ruby Lin) and Zhao Wei, the main actresses in *The Return of the Pearl Princess*, also appeared in these programs. That was why I became interested in the programs in the first place." Such a response was also expressed by KV40,[38] KV41,[39] KV43[40] and KV45.[41] As argued earlier, besides content and storyline, celebrities are also an important selling point for consumers of Chinese products.

Others, who like trendier and more contemporary subfields of television, like KV38,[42] pointed to other products. She elaborated, "Dramas I watched, among Chinese (*jungguk*) dramas? I think of something like *Liuxing Huayuan* (*The Meteor Garden*). It becomes very interesting after watching a few episodes." While she studied a China-related subject as an undergraduate student, as a result of her interest in the Chinese language like many consumers and audiences, she did not selectively consume mainland Chinese media content. Rather, she sought out an alternative to meet her consumer standards. When asked about their primary reason for watching Taiwanese instead of Chinese dramas, some of my informants said that the Chinese media products lack celebrity appeal. They could not think of any Chinese actors or actresses they liked.

In this vein, some of my informants felt that Chinese media products lack celebrities. This view overlaps with the ways in which media professionals, both in South Korea and Japan, similarly lament a lack of celebrity capital in PRC-produced television series. Some informants found that they were enticed to watch select "Chinese" dramas by the celebrities in the series. They also could not think of other Chinese actors or actresses they liked. On the other hand, KV1 shared, "I like Joseph Cheng. I started to watch all media products that he took part in. *Playful Kiss* is like *The Meteor Garden*, it is for teenagers.[43] It is funny and it often does not make any sense."

Views expressed by interviewees on the 2011 cast change in the third season of *New Return of the Pearl Princess* (*New My Fair Princess*) included, "I liked the cast, song and story of Season 1. I think it was the best among all seasons of this television series."[44] KV41[45] said, "I watched dramas on Junghwa TV with my mom. She watched *The Return of the Pearl Princess* before and has a good impression of Lin Xinru (Ruby Lin), the main character. She also likes to watch *Meirenxinji* (*Schemes of a Beauty*)." In fact, Ruby Lin is a Taiwanese actress, but she appears very frequently in dramas produced by the PRC and in those co-produced with Taiwan. This production arrangement masks the separation of "Chinese" dramas from Taiwanese dramas for Korean audiences. In turn, this ambivalent nature of "Chinese" dramas gives rise to the opportunity for Taiwanese dramas to involuntarily contribute to the influence of China's televised soft power, as a source of outsourced power.

Finally, respondents tend to agree that the Mandarin spoken by Taiwanese people speak may not be the most "authentic" Chinese language. This is in line with the mainland point of view, as the following interview with KV51[46] illustrates: "The Chinese language that Taiwanese people speak is not authentic; I also feel the same way. I don't want to learn that Chinese, but Taiwanese dramas are easy to watch, easy to understand and funny. I don't need to think a lot when I watch them." She also had this to say: "I went to Ha'erbin to learn Chinese. People say the Chinese sound there is clean and *haoting* (pleasant to listen to). I am inclined to the accent."

It might be suggested by some Korean Chinese language learners that one should visit China, rather than Taiwan, to learn Chinese. It is usually perceived that the PRC Chinese is the only authentic language. However, for them, "Chinese" dramas do not necessarily originate exclusively from China. Indeed, the way that South Koreans delineate the boundaries of what constitutes "China" and "Chinese dramas" does not make the two mutually exclusive.

The complex nature of seeking an "authentic" Chinese language is a paradox in itself. At one end, there is a relative absence of Korean and Japanese dubbing from Mandarin, as it is only available for aired programs that television stations have bought broadcasting rights for. This makes sense when considering the market size; either Korean or Japanese dubbing from Chinese series may not always be an attractive term for Chinese industries. Some products are dubbed, but most of them are subtitled to air on the Korean and Japanese "televisionscapes." In sharp contrast with this, "Within this 'Pop Culture China,' Japanese and Korean films and TV programs are usually dubbed as a means of 'domesticating' the foreign" (Chua and Iwabuchi 2008: 8). The Sinophone world, or "Pop Culture China," is big enough to generate and self-consume dubbed programs in the region. At another end, dubbed programs in Mandarin might make those co-produced with Taiwan or Hong Kong less consumable, due to their accents or dialects. By maintaining the original accents in the programs from Hong Kong and Taiwan, China might have benefited from freeriding on the soft power of these two Chinese localities, and perhaps had opportunities to transform them more fully into producers of outsourced soft power. Along these practices, China's influence encounters a predicament even with the help of outsourced soft power.

Martial Arts Subfield as Distinct, Outsourced Soft Power from Hong Kong

In the early modern era, one of the more popular drama genres was martial arts; *kungfu* in Chinese, or *muhyeop* in Korean (for consistency, I use "martial arts" hereafter). Most of the South Korean academic literature on media focuses on martial arts novels and movies,[47] such as the structure of Hong Kong martial arts films (Yeom 1997), Zhang Yimou's martial arts films (Yu 2007; Yun 2008), mainland China's *muhyeop* blockbusters from the 2000s (Mun 2011), and Chinese *kungfu* movies produced in Hollywood (Jai 2006). However, martial arts subfield dramas have yet to be examined. Although *muhyeop* dramas hail from both China and Hong Kong, many South Koreans believe that *muhyeop* is exclusively a product of Hong Kong. This is due to the recognizable success and characteristics of Hong Kong martial arts films. KV4[48] said, "I don't like historical dramas. It does not mean I never watch them. I watch dramas with historical themes when they have a lot of action scenes. The main characters can fly, hang onto cliffs, draw and use swords." Her interpretation of the attraction of these products demonstrates that she finds the visual effects, embodied actions, and techniques enjoyable.

Martial arts dramas and films that were made in Hong Kong were much more popular in South Korea in the 1980s than now, as explained earlier. The so-called "Bruce Lee generation"[49] is another interesting example (see Ahn 2016; Yoo 1995). A female respondent, KV5[50] had a favorite "Chinese" actor. She said, "I have an elder brother. He was an extremely big fan of him. Because of my brother, I had to strike poses seen in the dramas and movies with him, and practice *Chwigwon* (*Drunken Master*). Yeah, it might sound crazy, though I actually liked to do it with him. This sums up my childhood. I think that's why I used to listen to Hong Kong songs, and later develop further my interest in the Chinese language." Obviously, dramas and other media products can play an important role in shaping a person's thoughts and interest in the Chinese language, or even in the country more generally.

Remaking and Unmaking Boundaries of "China" in South Korea

Furthermore, the interviewees were very conscious of the political differences between Taiwan, Hong Kong, and China. KV37[51] said, "I am very angry when I hear Chinese people argue that Taiwan is part of China. Even Korea seems to be a territory of China to them,"[52] and, "Isn't Taiwan just Taiwan? I never had a chance to visit Taiwan, but the people seem so different from mainland Chinese. The language sounds different to me."

Another informant KV33[53] shared the same opinion as KV37[54] on this matter and reflected: "I know Hong Kong was returned to China, officially, but to me Hong Kong and China are still so different. They cannot be one country, in my perspective. Hong Kong, to me, is the 'hometown' of Leslie Cheung. But China is unordered and has a wide range of disparities within the country." Obviously, these South Koreans perceive Taiwan and Hong Kong as individual countries. In terms of culture and media, Taiwan/Hong Kong is one group and China is another; some viewers do not support the political stance of the Chinese government in relation to Taiwan and Hong Kong. The "disparity" in their responses showed that they do not equate "China" with dramas from China.

In line with this perspective, a small debate over the boundaries of China, Hong Kong, and Taiwan that emerged in a South Korean internet community named *Muhyeop Jungguk* (Martial Arts China), gives us a good illustration. This started with the question "What is *Jungguk*?" posed by a netizen under the user ID *1peaceyo*, and evolved into a thread called "Making boundaries of China/Hong Kong/Taiwan," published on November 5, 2011. There were 31 replies to the post on the same day. Most of the responses elaborated that Taiwan is not part of China. One reply by *Qianhao* indicates that Taiwan and Hong Kong are not countries; they are, respectively, an island and a city that are part of China. Interestingly, a subsequent reply to this particular comment asks: "Are you Chinese (*Junggukin*)?" *Qianhao* responded, "Differentiating between the dramas and movies of Taiwan, China and Hong Kong is quite easy. Hong Kongese dramas and films are produced in Cantonese; products of China and Taiwan are mostly in Mandarin." No matter the factual accuracy of the responses here, the thread shows the broad scope of debate over the boundary issue as it exists in a Korean public sphere.

In significant contrast, for Korean media practitioners "China" only refers to the PRC. "In the Department of Global Business in our company, there are sub-divisions of China, Taiwan, and Hong Kong," said

KM7.[55] She distinguishes China from the other two Chinese societies in her department and business. Alternatively, some stations do not organize departments according to country, but only according to region. They see China, Taiwan, and Hong Kong as part of Greater China, but they perceive the three differently. The differences between the viewers' perceptions and those of media practitioners can be explained by the boundaries that are drawn between a professional and a layperson.

Some Korean informants could distinguish between "PRC Chinese" and other Chinese television series. KV73 is one such informant and said[56]:

> Chinese content is limited. Unlike dramas with origins in Korea or Taiwan, they are not [politically] free. When I watch Chinese dramas, I somehow feel something is not explicitly discussed, or is even censored. Background music is 'old.' Backgrounds in each scene are not well managed. There are many things that do not go over well with our perceptions.

Oftentimes some informants, like KV73, found mainland Chinese dramas to be different from Taiwanese dramas. In addition, they noted that Chinese dramas were not interesting enough, or were cheesy. In particular, underestimations about Chinese dramas originated from perceived shoddiness of quality and childishness; mainly issues with the storyline.

In nine out of ten cases, my informants said, "That we watch them does not necessarily mean they are popular, but rather they are unpopular." This rather contradictory response shows that Chinese culture and media products have gained the attention of students who major in Chinese studies, and not because they are popular. KV1[57] said, "Most people who have an interest in trendy Taiwanese dramas (*ouxiangju*) are learning Chinese. Otherwise, ordinary people have no interest in Chinese culture. There is a prevalent view that they [the dramas] are of bad quality."

When asked about Chinese shows, people generally think of programs in which Jackie Chan, Jet Li, or Stephen Chow appear as "Chinese" (*Jungguk*). This is the most frequent answer that I encountered when I asked who (among their peers) watched them and whether they are popular. However, from the interview data, I feel that this attitude is largely confined to specific groups of people with knowledge of Chinese. To put it differently, Chinese media products are only widely accessible to those who majored in Chinese.

There are some viewers who are considered Chinese media "maniacs."[58] Yet, these people are not big fans of Chinese—PRC—programs, but rather Hong Kong programs. Compared to those who love foreign cultures and frequently consume their media commodities, the number of people who are into Chinese dramas (i.e. Chinese drama mania) tends to be small. Hong Kong programs were undoubtedly popular among some South Koreans who were young in the 1980s and 1990s. Hong Kong celebrities were their ultimate superstars and idols, and their adoration is very much reflected in their definition of "popular." KV8[59] said, "Back then, some people even wore the so-called 'Chow Yun-Fat style,' which is a combination of a white shirt, black suit and trench coat. It was fashionable at that time. Yun-Fat Chow and Jackie Chan movies, for example *Drunken Master*,[60] were popular." However, attitudes toward them have changed. Some informants reflected on Hong Kongese programs in terms of teenage nostalgia. KV7[61] said "In the past, Hong Kong's programs were popular in South Korea. A lot of my friends like Leslie Cheung. However, the situation has somewhat reversed now. If I watch Chinese programs, I feel the background and setting in these products lag behind. I feel that actors only read scripts, instead of acting well. Their performance is limited. The content is even copied from somewhere else. Of course, some of our programs also copied Japanese ones, but in the case of China it is worse. When I watch them, I feel that they are full of cut-and-pastes from this drama and that drama. As a consequence of this, they do not well fit into the whole drama." Some media products are faked in China, with or without acknowledging the fact of having done so. As a result, transnational South Korean audiences keep a distance from faked Chinese television series, as they not only evoke Korea's past participation in such practices that it does not want remembered, but it also makes it difficult for the Korean industry to keep up with the influx of faked Chinese series.

With a feeling of nostalgia, this brings us to another point. In the East Asian televisionsphere, some Korean viewers were aware of Hong Kong's strength for popular TV series and films. However, the development of the Korean media industries has also produced popular TV dramas and increased their import to markets across Asia, including those of China, Hong Kong, and Taiwan. KV6[62] commented, "In the old days, Hong Kongese movies were well developed, which got people to watch them very often. Nowadays, we are better than China and, in other words, China is below us." From what the informants conveyed, the loss of popularity of "Hong Kong" programs occurred in only a narrow, individual-level sense, while the reduced importation of good "Chinese" programs by Korean media happened in a broader sense (more institutional) and was significant for the exclusive group of potential consumers.

The change in attitude obviously has much to do with the phenomenon of the Korean Wave. KV9[63] also shared her view that, "The Korean Wave is popular in China. The cultural flow in the old days from Hong Kong to South Korea is now reversed. Now, the South Korean cultural level is high," and, "the meaning of 'popular,' to transnational audiences, is having famous celebrities that the PRC is currently lacking. In South Korea, there is no point in differentiating PRC Chinese dramas or Taiwanese dramas; this is because neither of them is that popular and they do not have to be classified into different categories. Interestingly, some 'Chinese' celebrities have developed fan communities: Joseph Cheng, Jay Chou, and Mike Ha...." The response of KV9 is intriguing in that her classification of dramas is rather contradictory to her aforementioned views about the Chinese. In particular, she turned these three actors into "Chinese" (*Jungguk*) celebrities, not Taiwanese ones. Although she consciously tries to separate China from Taiwan, and vice versa, it is difficult for her to completely make sense of the boundaries between China and Taiwan in terms of their cultural commodities.

Apparently, South Korean viewers and non-viewers feel that the Chinese are inferior to them, technologically and culturally. The quality of Chinese programs and a shortage of celebrities diminish their attraction to and consumption of Chinese cultural commodities. Perceptions about China influence South Koreans not to watch Chinese programs. KV6[64]'s comment is interesting: "Mainland Chinese movies that are shown in movie theaters tend not to be very popular. They either earn no profit or fail to gather enough moviegoers. South Korea's perceptions towards China are generally not good. The prevalent view is that China is a backward country; as a consequence of this line of thinking, we do not want to know or learn about Chinese culture." Under these circumstances, Chinese efforts at generating soft power among these Koreans must be said to have failed.

As shown earlier, "Chinese" media in South Korea is not a latecomer but was instead one of the existing foreign players. While it may not be the most predominant of foreign media products in South Korea, it could suggest the possibility of a different Chinese Wave. Since Hong Kong's return to China in 1997, the pattern of producing Chinese dramas has changed. Hong Kong's culture and cultural products have diminished while those of China have grown. As discussed in the previous chapter, a number of cable stations carry Chinese programs on a regular basis. More importantly, unlike other foreign programs, there are cable stations committed to delivering only Chinese programs, and this extends the reach of such programs in new directions.

I have examined Chinese media product consumption in Korea, and how South Korean viewer responses vary depending on their level of personal engagement with China and the Chinese language. Although ambivalent attitudes about PRC Chinese, Hong Kongese, and Taiwanese may not be the intended outcome of the Chinese government's "going global" strategy, it is evident in Korean viewers' perceptions, which may be based on the political relations between the three. The "complicated" relationship positions South Korean viewers to see the boundaries of these Chinese societies differently. As with Taiwan, there was also popular resistance to the "One Country, Two Systems" policy in the case of Hong Kong.

In summary, it is worth revisiting the reactions of both the South Korean media practitioners and viewers to Chinese media products. For the media professionals, the Chinese media-export-as-soft-power strategy had not influenced their decision; instead, their company practices played the most important role in importing overseas programs. The reasons why Chinese programs are visible in South Korea are as follows: availability, reasonable price, and the fact that the programs tend to run longer. The media professionals' practices are also significantly shaped by the local market. Such invisibility of power relations between local and foreign products, in turn, shape the consumption patterns of South Koreans and their inclination toward South Korean products. Inevitably, there is a tug-of-war contest between the local and the foreign. It intertwines with the processes of import and consumption, and is critical in the media-making marketplaces.

From viewer responses, we find two main patterns. First, there are diverse motivations behind viewers' decisions to watch Chinese dramas, including possessing lived experience, such as studying and traveling to China, or enjoying other facets of China, such as culture and history. These viewers became interested in Chinese media because of their non-media interests. Second, the experiences of Korean viewers with Chinese dramas, and constructing boundaries for China, Hong Kong and Taiwan, largely depend upon their interpretations. Transferring Chinese values, which are at the core of such media programs, to a culturally proximate but ideologically different group, is not easy to do and makes it difficult to expand the market for Chinese media in South Korea. This is especially so, since South Korea's own products prevail domestically and in other countries, thereby giving South Korean media practitioners confidence in their products.

Lastly, for non-viewers China may only represent a means of future job stability; not a country with cultural power or a globalized culture. Non-viewers of PRC Chinese dramas also tend to prefer to watch programs from other parts of Greater China, namely Taiwan and Hong Kong. Overall, the global media strategy of the Chinese government is only partially successful. From the Chinese government's point of view, Hong Kong and Taiwan are inherently part of China, so it sees these two societies as falling within the category of Chinese media. In this light, the Chinese government is unintentionally successful to a degree, with the help of cultural products of Hong Kong and Taiwan. This is especially true for reaching South Korean consumers.

CONCLUSION

This chapter comparatively shows how Hong Kong and Taiwan's television series are involuntarily shaping China's transnational soft power field, as it extends to South Korea and Japan. South Korean and Japanese audiences recognize China's missing toolkits, such as diverse subfields and celebrity capital, that may lead to a successful transmission of its televised soft power in other "Chinese"—Hong Kong and Taiwanese—series.

In delineating the boundaries of "China," most South Koreans see Hong Kong, Taiwan, and China along distinct political terms. However, as individual consumers of media and cultural products, they do not necessarily differentiate between the boundaries of China, Taiwan, and Hong Kong. In other words, South Korean consumers do not know or distinguish the origin of their products within the boundaries of "China" without having them explicitly differentiated from one another. Interestingly, in contrast with South Koreans, Japanese tend to treat these two societies—China and Taiwan—as individual countries. This is particularly prevalent when it comes to Taiwan's independence, or political boundaries. Most Japanese respondents also show their strong support and emotional engagement with Taiwan by upholding it as a separate country; hence, Taiwanese products are the ones they are most likely to consume.

How did this contested boundary-making impact the ways in which (co)produced television series hailing from Hong Kong and Taiwan outsource Chinese soft power? Similar yet divergent patterns emerged in South Korea and Japan. In South Korea, most Korean audiences do not necessarily differentiate between the origins of products, namely those of the PRC from those made in Hong Kong and Taiwan. To them, it is not meaningful to make such distinctions; the PRC dramas on Korean TV or internet platforms are often dubbed in Mandarin Chinese, even if the dramas are co-produced by Hong Kong and Taiwan and feature celebrities from those communities. Thus, the television series of Hong Kong and Taiwan cover the settings of the real origins of the dramas, as well as feature their celebrities. This helps to build China's transnational soft power field, and these two locations serve as resources of outsourced soft power for the PRC. Along a similar vein in Japan, Hong Kong, and Taiwan's television series are recognized as *Karyū* products and have gained popularity in recent decades. Due to the lingering colonial connection between Japan and Taiwan, however, Japanese audiences are more likely to identify television series as "Taiwanese" than Korean audiences are. When this mask is lifted, Hong Kong and Taiwan's television series function as *incomplete* and *partially* outsourced forms of PRC soft power to Japanese audiences.

In both South Korea and Japan, television series imported from Hong Kong, mostly of the martial arts subfield, are easily recognizable for both Korean and Japanese audiences due to their strongly distinctive subfields and celebrity capital. The South Korean and Japanese preference for Hong Kong and Taiwan's media products have helped China build upon Greater China relations, as a means of cultural intermediation for audiences. In turn, a tug-of-war between China's media and other "Chinese" products transforms into a problematic long-term dilemma for the PRC.

NOTES

1. In order to avoid creating biased implications or confusion among the informants, and to be faithful to the aim of this study, I consciously use "China" instead of "Taiwan" or "Hong Kong," unless the respondents' answers contained certain elements of the other two Chinese societies. It is important to note that when it comes to culture and cultural/media products, these three Chinese societies—China, Hong Kong, and Taiwan—have different developmental stages and histories. Hence, my usage of these terms or boundaries reflect their development, rather than deliver my political stance on how to draw boundaries between them. On a different note, in Korean "China/Chinese," "Hong Kong(ese)" and "Taiwan(ese)" are different words, unlike when they are contextualized in English; "Chinese" often then does not convey "China" per se, but what is "Chinese" in the adjectival sense.

2. In fact, this is a mutual sentiment. This is not only the case in how Japanese people feel about Taiwan, it is also the case in how Taiwanese people feel about Japan. The 2008 Taiwanese film *Cape No. 7* (*Haijiao qihao*) by Taiwanese film director Te-sheng Wei captures a love story which also touches upon Taiwanese notions of nostalgia toward Japan.
3. JV18, interview with a Japanese respondent, April 13, 2012, Tokyo, Japan.
4. JV58, interview with a Japanese respondent, May 24, 2012, Tokyo, Japan.
5. JV23, interview with a Japanese respondent, April 17, 2012, Tokyo, Japan.
6. Ibid.
7. JV58, interview with a Japanese respondent, May 24, 2012, Tokyo, Japan.
8. There is only limited documentation of this. Yet, there are records of news media discussions on the Chinese Wave in the South Korean Integrated Newspaper Database System (KINDS). The discussions, which concentrate on the rise of Taiwanese and PRC Chinese media products, go back as early as 2006. See E. Kim (2006). This discourse indicates fears about the decline of the Korean Wave as the prevailing force not only in South Korea but in countries such as Japan and China. Discussions from 2007 to 2008 are focused on PRC Chinese media products, as well as traditional culture by acknowledging China's strategy of going global. It is interesting that such discussions have not been visible in South Korean newspapers since 2008, after which China has pushed such strategy forward even further.
9. JV39, interview with a Japanese respondent, April 24, 2012, Tokyo, Japan.
10. JV33, interview with a Japanese respondent, April 22, 2012, Tokyo, Japan.
11. See Kim, Eunjin. 2006. "Hwaryue jjogineun 'Hallyu Drama' … ilbon TV bangyeong jeolban 'dduk'" ["'Hallyu Drama', Now Only 'Half' of the Usual Broadcast, is Run After the Chinese Wave."] *SekyeIlbo*, March 8. Retrieved May 20, 2013.
12. In English writing, "kung fu" is almost always separated into two words as a function of Anglicization. However, I will consistently use "kungfu" for this book (see Appendix A). Kungfu has been discussed in the context of films, for more details see Hunt (2003), Li (2001).
13. JV48, interview with a Japanese respondent, May 7, 2012, Tokyo, Japan.
14. JV42, interview with a Japanese respondent, April 25, 2012, Tokyo, Japan.
15. Ibid.
16. JV23, interview with a Japanese respondent, April 17, 2012, Tokyo, Japan.
17. There is a Taiwanese version as well as a mainland version.
18. JV9, Interview with a Japanese respondent, February 14, 2012, Tokyo, Japan.
19. JV39, interview with a Japanese respondent, April 24, 2012, Tokyo, Japan.

20. JV23, interview with a Japanese respondent, April 17, 2012, Tokyo, Japan. JV23 is a Ph.D. candidate in Chinese Studies at Tokyo University.
21. JV39, interview with a Japanese respondent, April 24, 2012, Tokyo, Japan.
22. JV48, interview with a Japanese respondent, May 7, 2012, Tokyo, Japan.
23. JV23, interview with a Japanese respondent, April 17, 2012, Tokyo, Japan.
24. JV40, interview with a Japanese respondent, April 24, 2012, Tokyo, Japan.
25. JV48, interview with a Japanese respondent, May 7, 2012, Tokyo, Japan.
26. JV45, interview with a Japanese respondent, April 27, 2012, Tokyo, Japan.
27. JV23, interview with a Japanese respondent, April 17, 2012, Tokyo, Japan.
28. JV51, interview with a Japanese respondent, May 13, 2012, Tokyo, Japan.
29. JV35, interview with a Japanese respondent, April 23, 2012, Tokyo, Japan.
30. JV33, interview with a Japanese respondent, April 22, 2012, Tokyo, Japan.
31. The Japanese word translates to "easily sentimental/stirred."
32. The title is also translated as *The Return of the Pearl Princess*. They are two most famous, well-received and popular Chinese TV series in South Korea.
33. For this cohort, they might have had a chance to watch *The Return of the Pearl Princess* when they were in college.
34. KV4, interview with a South Korean respondent, November 28, 2011, Seoul, South Korea.
35. Such views were also found interviews with KV2, KV3, KV4, KV5, KV7, KV9, K39, K41, K43, and K45.
36. KV41, interview with a South Korean respondent, December 21, 2011, Seoul, South Korea.
37. KV46, interview with a South Korean respondent, January 10, 2012, Seoul, South Korea.
38. KV40, interview with a South Korean respondent, December 21, 2011, Seoul, South Korea.
39. KV41, interview with a South Korean respondent, December 21, 2011, Seoul, South Korea.
40. KV43, interview with a South Korean respondent, December 24, 2011, Seoul, South Korea.
41. KV45, interview with a South Korean respondent, January 2, 2012, Seoul, South Korea.
42. KV38, interview with a South Korean respondent, December 21, 2011, Seoul, South Korea.
43. These are Taiwanese dramas that are based on Japanese manga or novels. Both have also been reproduced by South Korean production companies into Korean-language versions.
44. Such views were also found interviews with KV2, KV3, KV4, KV5, KV7, KV9, K39, K41, K43, and K45.

45. KV41, interview with a South Korean respondent, December 21, 2011, Seoul, South Korea.
46. KV51, interview with a South Korean respondent, February 4, 2012, Seoul, South Korea.
47. It is important to note that South Korean novels also have a *muhyeop* genre, which is largely influenced by Chinese *muhyeop* novels, including those by Jin Yong.
48. KV4, interview with a South Korean respondent, November 28, 2011, Seoul, South Korea.
49. This is included in a book title by Yoo (1995). The author is a South Korean poet and film director.
50. KV5, interview with a South Korean respondent, November 29, 2011, Seoul, South Korea.
51. KV37, interview with a South Korean respondent, December 20, 2011, Seoul, South Korea.
52. This is in line with a comment I received in my presentation on South Koreans in Singapore, which was held in Beijing on August 2, 2013. A Chinese audience member shared his opinion on what the Chinese think of Singapore, stating that, "We, Chinese people, think that Singapore is part of China (*Xinjiapo shi Zhongguode*)."
53. KV33, interview with a South Korean respondent, December 17, 2011, Seoul, South Korea.
54. KV37, interview with a South Korean respondent, December 20, 2011, Seoul, South Korea.
55. KM5, interview with a South Korean media professional, January 25, 2012, Ilsan, South Korea.
56. KV73, interview with a South Korean respondent, June 29, 2012, Seoul, South Korea.
57. KV1, interview with a South Korean respondent, November 19, 2011, Seoul, South Korea.
58. *Jungd(rama) pein* describes Chinese drama mania in Korean.
59. KV8, interview with a South Korean respondent, November 29, 2011, Seoul, South Korea.
60. The Korean title of this movie is *Chwigwon*.
61. KV7, interview with a South Korean respondent, November 29, 2011, Seoul, South Korea.
62. KV6, interview with a South Korean respondent, November 29, 2011, Seoul, South Korea.
63. KV9, interview with a South Korean respondent, November 30, 2011, Seoul, South Korea.
64. KV6, interview with a South Korean respondent, November 29, 2011, Seoul, South Korea.

REFERENCES

Ahn, Young Yeun. 2016. Bruce Lee Myth is Not Over. *Journal of Modern Chinese Literature* 78: 159–195.

Cabinet Office of the Government of Japan. 2010. Chōsa Kekka No Gaiyō [Outline of Survey Results]. *Gaikōni Kansuru Seronchōsa [Overview of the Public Opinion Survey on Diplomacy]*. Accessed October 9, 2013. https://survey.gov-online.go.jp/h22/h22-gaiko/2-1.html.

———. 2011. Chōsa Kekka No Gaiyō [Outline of Survey Results]. *Gaikōni Kansuru Seronchōsa [Overview of the Public Opinion Survey on Diplomacy]*. Accessed October 9, 2013. https://survey.gov-online.go.jp/h23/h23-gaiko/2-1.html.

———. 2012. Chōsa Kekka No Gaiyō [Outline of Survey Results]. *Gaikōni Kansuru Seronchōsa [Overview of the Public Opinion Survey on Diplomacy]*. Accessed November 15, 2015. https://survey.gov-online.go.jp/h24/h24-gaiko/2-1.html.

———. 2013. Chōsa Kekka No Gaiyō [Outline of Survey Results]. *Gaikōni Kansuru Seronchōsa [Overview of the Public Opinion Survey on Diplomacy]*. Accessed November 15, 2015. https://survey.gov-online.go.jp/h25/h25-gaiko/2-1.html.

———. 2014. Chōsa Kekka No Gaiyō [Outline of Survey Results]. *Gaikōni Kansuru Seronchōsa [Overview of the Public Opinion Survey on Diplomacy]*. Accessed November 15, 2015. https://survey.gov-online.go.jp/h26/h26-gaiko/2-1.html.

———. 2015. Chōsa Kekka No Gaiyō [Outline of Survey Results]. *Gaikōni Kansuru Seronchōsa [Overview of the Public Opinion Survey on Diplomacy]*. Accessed February 23, 2018. https://survey.gov-online.go.jp/h27/h27-gaiko/2-1.html.

———. 2016. Chōsa Kekka No Gaiyō [Outline of Survey Results]. *Gaikōni Kansuru Seronchōsa [Overview of the Public Opinion Survey on Diplomacy]*. Accessed February 23, 2018. https://survey.gov-online.go.jp/h28/h28-gaiko/2-1.html.

———. 2017. Chōsa Kekka No Gaiyō [Outline of Survey Results]. *Gaikōni Kansuru Seronchōsa [Overview of the Public Opinion Survey on Diplomacy]*. Accessed February 23, 2018. https://survey.gov-online.go.jp/h29/h29-gaiko/2-1.html.

Chin, Pinyuan. 1996. The Implications of 'Sword' in Chinese. *Foreign Languages and Literature Series* 23: 182–193.

Chua, Beng Huat, and Koichi Iwabuchi, eds. 2008. *East Asian Pop Culture: Analysing the Korean Wave.* Hong Kong: Hong Kong University Press.

Hamm, John Christopher. 2005. *Paper Swordsmen: Jin Yong and the Modern Chinese Martial Arts Novel.* Honolulu: University of Hawai'I Press.

Hunt, Leon. 2003. *Kung Fu Cult Masters.* London and New York: Wallflower Press.

Italian Trade Commission [Istituto nazionale per il Commercio Estero]. 2011. *China Television Industry Market Report*. June 3. Shanghai: Italian Trade Commission. Accessed November 30, 2013. http://www.ice.it/paesi/asia/cina/upload/174/CHINA%20TELEVISION%20INDUSTRY%20MARKET%20REPORT%20 2011.pdf.

Jai, Lei Lei. 2006. Jungguk Muhyeop action yeonghwa oe gukjehwa jinjeon [Internatlization of Chinese Muhyeop Action Movies]. *Hanguk Yeonghwa Hakhoe Proceedings [Korea Cinema Association Conference Proceedings]*: 44–45.

Jeon, Changhoon. 2008. Jungguk choego ingidrama 'hwangjeoe ddal' jaebangyeong [Best Chinese TV Drama 'The Pearl Princess (My Fair Princess)' Will Be Broadcasted]. *Busan Ilbo*, November 29. Accessed January 2, 2013. http://news20.busan.com/controller/newsController.jsp?newsId=20081129000035.

Kim, Eunjin. 2006. Hwaryue jjogineun 'Hallyu Drama' … ilbon TV bangyeongjeolban 'dduk' ['Hallyu Drama' is Now Being Chased by the Chinese Wave … 'because of' Now Only Half of the Usual Broadcast in Japan]. Sekye Ilbo, March 8.

Lee, Claire Seungeun. 2018. Experiencing "Internationalized Precarity" in Inter-Asian Film Production: A Case Study of *Seediq Bale*. *Poetics* 66: 42–53.

Li, Siu Leung. 2001. Kung Fu: Negotiating Nationalism and Modernity. *Cultural Studies* 15 (3–4): 515–542.

Long, Yun, and Claire Seungeun Lee. 2014. 2014 Hanguo chuanmeichanye fazhan baogao [Report on the Development of Media Industry in South Korea 2014]. In *Quanqiu chuanmeichanye lanpishu (2014) [Annual Report on the Development of Global Media (2014)]*, ed. Zhengrong Hu, Jidong Li, and Xiaofen Tang, 88–100. Beijing: Shehuikexue wenxian chubanshe.

Ministry of Culture. 2012. *'Shi'erwu' shiqi wenhuachanye beizeng jihua [Plan to Make Cultural Industries Double During the '12th Five-Year' Period]*. Beijing: Ministry of Culture.

Mun, Hyunsun. 2011. Jungguk daeryuk muhyeop blockbosterrul gwantonghaneul yesuljeok areumdaumoe jeonsiseonge daehan bunseok [An Analysis of Representation of Artistic Beauty: Mainland China's Muhyeop Blockbuster]. *Cineforum* 13: 97–137.

National Bureau of Statistics. 2011. *Quanguo dianshijiemu jinchukou qingkuang (2010)* [Basic Statistics on Imported and Exported TV Programs (2010)]. In *2009 Zhongguo wenhua ji xiangguan chanye tongji nianjian [China Statistical Yearbook on Culture and Related Industries-2010]*, 942. Beijing: China Statistics Press [*Zhongguo tongji chubanshe*].

———. 2012. *Quanguo dianshijiemu jinchukou qingkuang (2011)* [Basic Statistics on Imported and Exported TV Programs (2011)]. In *2009 Zhongguo wenhua ji xiangguan chanye tongji nianjian [China Statistical Yearbook on Culture and*

Related Industries-2011], 937. Beijing: China Statistics Press [*Zhongguo tongji chubanshe*].

———. 2013. *Quanguo dianshijiemu jinchukou qingkuang* (2012) [Basic Statistics on Imported and Exported TV Programs (2012)]. In *2009 Zhongguo wenhua ji xiangguan chanye tongji nianjian [China Statistical Yearbook on Culture and Related Industries-2012]*, 848. Beijing: China Statistics Press [*Zhongguo tongji chubanshe*].

———. 2014. *Quanguo dianshijiemu jinchukou qingkuang* (2009) [Basic Statistics on Imported and Exported TV Programs (2013)]. In *2013 Zhongguo wenhua ji xiangguan chanye tongji nianjian [China Statistical Yearbook on Culture and Related Industries-2013]*, 784. Beijing: China Statistics Press [*Zhongguo tongji chubanshe*].

———. 2015. *Quanguo dianshijiemu jinchukou qingkuang* (2014) [Basic Statistics on Imported and Exported TV Programs (2014)]. In *2014 Zhongguo wenhua ji xiangguan chanye tongji nianjian [China Statistical Yearbook on Culture and Related Industries-2014]*, 182–183. Beijing: China Statistics Press [*Zhongguo tongji chubanshe*].

Pei, Fengxue. 2010. Reinterpretations Concerning 'Jianghu' in Chinese Chivalrous Novels. *Studies on Humanities and Social Sciences of Chiba University* 21: 337–349.

Shim, Doobo, and In-cheol Min. 2011. Popular Culture Formations in Asia and the Context of Taiwanese Drama Consumption in South Korea. *Journal of Asiatic Studies* 52 (2): 155–183.

Sky Perfect TV. n.d. Accessed May 7, 2012. http://www.skyperfectv.co.jp/.

Wu, Weiming. 2005. The Adaptation of Jin Yong's Martial Arts Novels in Japan. *Japan-China Journal of Sociological Studies* 12: 27–43.

Yamamoto, Noriko. 2007. The Tide of Wuxia Novel: Think About the Film and Literature in Perspective. *The Humanities* 25: 245–259.

Yeom, Chan-hee. 1997. Hong Kong Muhyeop yeonghwa gujo bunseok: Jeulgeoum and Ideology [Analyzing Hong Kong Muhyeop Films' Structure: Enjoyment and Ideology]. *Hyeonsang gwa Insik [The Korean Journal of Humanities and the Social Sciences]* 20: 31–45.

Yoo, Ha. 1995. *Dedicate to the Bruce Lee Generation [Lee Soryong sedae egye bachinda]*. Seoul: Munhakdongnae.

Yu, Kyungchul. 2007. Zhong Yimou's Muhyeop Yeonghwa, Muhyeop genre [Zhang Yimou's Muhyeop Films and Dangaerous Attempts to the Genre]. *Jungguk Hyeondae Munhak [Chinese Contemporary Literature]* 42: 141–168.

Yun, Sung-eun. 2008. Hyeondae Jungguk Yeonghwa oe Nationalism: Zhang Yimou's Muhyeop Series [Contempoary Chinese Movie's Nationalism: Zhang Yimou]. *Hyeondae Yeonghwa Yeongu [Contemporary Film Research]* 5: 129–152.

Zhang, Wenqing. 2003. Kin Yō bukyō shōsetsu to nashonarizumu [Jin Yong's Martial Arts Novel and Nationalism]. *Chūgoku bungaku kenkyū [Journal of Waseda University Society of Chinese Literature]* 29: 18–35.

———. 2005. Diasupora to shite no shujinkō—Kin Yō no bukyō shōsetsu 'kateiki' kara miru bunka-teki ekkyō [The Main Character as Diaspora: The Cultural Transcendence from Jin Yong's Martial Arts Theory]. *Chūgoku bungaku kenkyū [Journal of Waseda University Society of Chinese Literature]* 31: 48–65.

CHAPTER 7

Seeking Virtual Capital Through Online Media in the Digital Age

Living in the Digital Age with Virtual Capital

"We are living in a new/digital media era." A media professional I interviewed in Hong Kong in December of 2013 mentioned, "We are moving almost completely to a digital media platform."[1] China is without exception an active player in an exponentially multiplying digital media market. In 2006, China had 137 million netizens with a 10.5 penetration rate; at the end of December 2016, it reached 731 million online users with a penetration rate of 53.2 of the entire country (China Internet Network Information Center (CNNIC) 2017; CNIDP 2017).[2] In other words, the number of Chinese netizens amounts to the total population of Asia (CNNIC 2017).

Until now, *Soft Power Made in China* has primarily focused upon the paradox of Chinese soft power expansion via traditional media platforms. But as new media and digital platforms are increasingly emerging, these forms of consumption have eminence not only in the media industry but also in locating and dislocating China's soft power in the global and transnational soft power fields. How do digital media and its platforms contribute to China's soft power, and help to outsource Chinese soft power to both Koreans and Japanese audiences?

The purpose of this chapter is to explore the digital media and other platforms of China's outsourced soft power across transnational audiences in quasi-Sinophone East Asia. I will explain the relevance of different digital media platforms, in particular, online streaming websites and mobile

© The Author(s) 2018
C. S. Lee, *Soft Power Made in China*,
https://doi.org/10.1007/978-3-319-93115-9_7

155

applications that are available in China and elsewhere. On the one hand, these platforms aid in the presentation and interpretation of how Chinese new media shapes its outsourced soft power and subscribes to these emergent forms. On the other hand, the recent development of regulations and policies around China's digital media are some ways in which the government manages and censors the outward flow of media. I also argue that such management, which seemingly intends to build soft power as the end goal, in turn unintentionally contributes to China's soft power paradox by diminishing its outsourced soft power by the time it reaches transnational audiences.

In this chapter, I define *virtual capital* as a type of capital that exists within a virtual, digital platform and has the potential to turn economic and cultural value. Virtual capital is further defined as the manner in which Chinese television series are consumed via online methods through cyberspace. Platforms, including online streaming websites, smartphone applications and websites as well as digital media, are spaces for cultivating virtual capital. These platforms, which have provided us easy access to media without the restrictions of physical boundaries, are fast-growing. Young people, who better utilize and foster such connectivity, understand strong virtual capital to mean high access at low cost. In the transnational soft power fields of China, these seemingly value-free platforms are oftentimes operated and influenced by the Chinese authorities, as are the platforms and digital media hosts where people can access Chinese television series. In this regard, the value of digital access to Chinese television series may not always be highly realized, making it difficult for these televisual products to convert to virtual capital.

The Development of Digital Platforms

Over-the-Top (OTT) Content, a newly established type of content, includes portal services, mobile IPTVs, and streaming and mobile services and platforms (see also Lee 2013; the Ministry of Science, ICT and Future Planning and Korea Commissions Committee 2016). In China, these three distinct types of OTT content are intertwined and, ultimately, integrate into digital streaming service platforms. Referencing this framework, I explain the online streaming market.

Since the launch of peer-to-peer (P2P) websites in 1999, the online streaming market has been skyrocketing. This development has created a culture of downloading audio-visual products and software from their

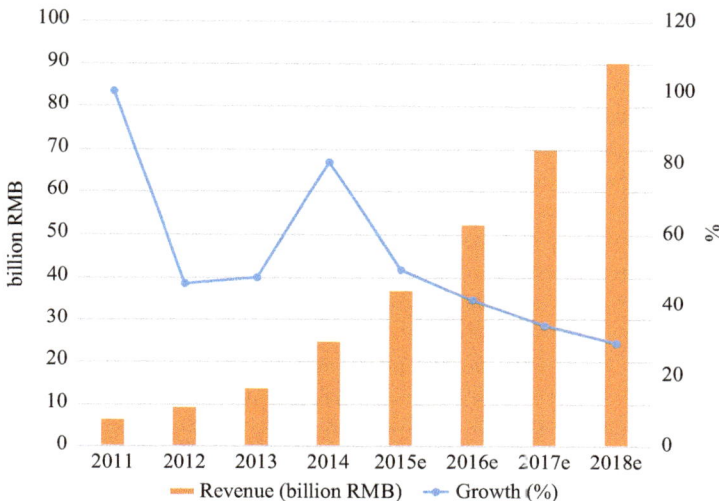

Fig. 7.1 The online streaming market (2011–2018e). Source: iResearch Consulting Group (2015)

host websites. Industry revenue in 2011 amounted to 6.3 billion RMB, and saw an average annual growth rate of about 47 percent from 2011 to 2017. In 2018, it is expected to generate about 90 billion RMB in revenue, which is 14 times its earnings from seven years ago (see Fig. 7.1).

China's OTT market, which offers both TV and video content, is the second largest in the world. The world's largest OTT market is held by the US, worth 8.24 billion USD in 2015 with an expected value of over 22 billion USD in 2021 (Digital TV Research 2016). China's market for OTT is expected to develop the volume and revenue and potentially exceed the current US market share in the near future (Digital TV Research 2016).

The big three Chinese ICT companies—Baidu, Alibaba, and Tencent, known collectively as BAT—with 1998-established Internet portal site, Sohu, are the leading figures in China's market and intrinsically shape trends, and the market itself. As one of the four pioneers of the OTT market, the Alibaba Group has been able to acquire Youku and Tudou, two of the first established players in the digital media market for foreign-created content. To achieve similar access to foreign media, Baidu enhances its ability to create its own content through iQiyi. Tencent imports a large amount of American content, while also creating own content. Sohu (via tv.sohu.com) hosts the largest platform for Korean television series and is increasingly becoming a U.S.-oriented platform (Moon et al. 2016).

The involvement of these ICT companies in this market has created a new value chain (Kim 2015). In a traditional media market, content is produced by a production company and distributed from a single network by multiple distribution companies, which are often the television and/or broadcasting stations for televisual products. Through the gatekeeping and intermediary roles of media market players in this traditional marketplace, consumers access screen-ready content that was directly managed by these media professionals. In the digital market, on the other hand, the media circuit is more complicated but often because it is more diversified and open than the traditional media market. Figure 7.2, which is modified from the Korean Film Council (KOFIC), presents this new circuit of media in the digital market. In this new circuit, streaming sites as well as new media platforms intervene at each step in the usual circuit of media—production, distribution, and reception, as also described in Chap. 3. These new players and platforms not only engage in creating content and circulating it within multiple channels, but they also interactively create ways to reach potential audiences and consumers.

Streaming and mobile services and platforms can be identified along four types, which are detailed in Table 7.1. First, television station-based platforms: Chinese television stations correspond to four administrative

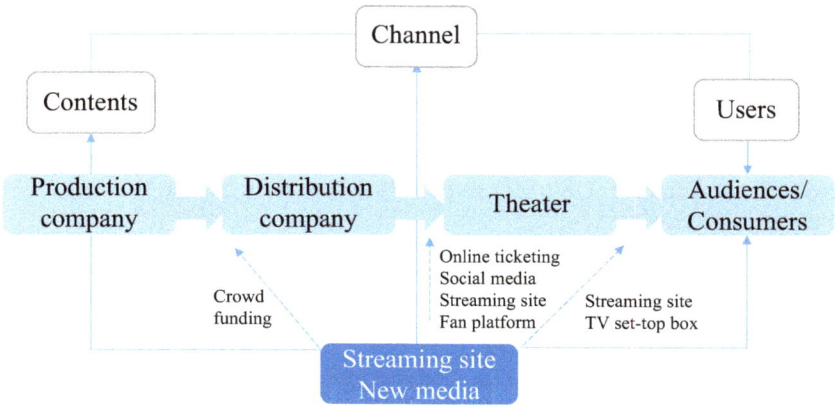

Fig. 7.2 A new circuit of media in the digital market. Source: Modified from the Korean Film Council (KOFIC) and KDB Daewoo Securities Research Center

Table 7.1 Type of platforms

Type of platform	Key examples	Type of capital
TV station-based	CNTV, Hunan Mango TV	State-owned capital
Portal site-based	Tencent (Tengxun) Video (*shipin*), Sohu Video (*shipin*)	Private capital
Internet TV-based	PPTV, PPS	Private capital
Online streaming distributer-based	Youku, Tudou, Ku6, LeTV	Private capital

Source: Guo (2011: 8)

levels in China—central, provincial, municipal, county—as a unique characteristic of Chinese televisual markets is that they are funded by state-owned capital. For example, CNTV is an online television platform of China Central Television (CCTV), and Hunan Satellite TV has its online version in Hunan Mango TV (Mango TV n.d.). Unlike this first, state-sponsored type, the other three types of platforms are privately funded. The second type, portal site-based platforms, are developed by Internet portal site companies that have expanded to other related businesses; Sohu Video (*shipin*)[3] and Tencent (*Tengxun*) Video (*shipin*) are examples. Third are Internet TV-based platforms, such as PPTV and PPS. The fourth, online streaming distributer-based platforms offer streaming services in interactive and video formats; Youku, Tudou, Ku6, and LeTV are examples (Chen 2014; Fo 2016; Lin 2015; Zhang 2012).

As mentioned earlier in this chapter, the market is predominantly owned by the five big platform players—Youku, Tudou, iQiyi, Sohu, and Tencent—accounting for about 70 percent of the entire market share (Lin 2015). Baidu, LeTV, PPTV, and IPTV are relative latecomers to the platform market; however, these four Chinese ICT companies are also principal players for online streaming service platforms. As the leader among ten key players, Youku has a 63 percent penetration rate and the highest level of subscribed members, at 10.7 percent (Table 7.2).

On the app market, Baidu iQiyi, Tencent Video (*shipin*) and Youku Video (*shipin*) are the three dominant players. iQiyi draws 15.8 percent of total active users per week, and a weekly average of 25.2 usages per app user. Tencent hosts 14.8 percent of total active users weekly, with 23.4 usages per week on average (*Zhongguo Shipinwangzhanfazhan Yanjiu Ketizu* (China Video Website Development Research Group) 2014).

Table 7.2   Top ten online streaming service platforms in China

Company	Parent company*	Brand penetration rate (%)	Ratio of royal customers (%)	Ratio of subscribed members (%)
Youku	Alibaba	63.0	40.4	10.7
iQiyi	Baidu	56.6	22.2	6.6
Tencent shipin	Tencent	54.2	22.3	5.1
Baidu shipin	Baidu	48.8	10.5	2.5
Tudou	Alibaba	47.3	16.1	4.0
Sohu shipin	Sohu	46.4	13.8	4.7
LeTV		39.5	7.4	1.9
PPS yingyin		39.0	5.4	0.8
PPTV Internet (*Wangluo*) TV		37.0	6.7	1.2
Xunlei Kankan		32.9	7.6	2.4

Source: Modified (*) from http://www.wokeji.com/guojipindao/tjxw/201508/t20150806_1524241.shtml; Park and Lee (2016)

These platforms are inherently interwoven with virtual capital, which will be presented in the next section.

CONSUMING MEDIA ON THE NET

Digital platforms shape the Chinese market and develop the mediasphere at an exceptional speed. While research has yet to discover how transnational audiences and media practitioners perceive and experience Chinese online media, there is a growing body of research on China's emerging online video industry, with commentary from Chinese audiences and professionals (Hu 2014; Liu et al. 2016; Wang et al. 2017; Zhao 2017; Zhao and Keane 2013).[4] Inevitably, this emerging phenomenon is simultaneously taking a place in other countries, particularly where there is high potential to generate Chinese soft power; both media practitioners and audiences whom I interacted with for my research observed this trend.

A media professional from South Korea who has worked extensively in China for more than 10 years mentioned, "What we need to pay attention to are the emerging platforms. How we use this is the key to success."[5] While he highlighted that Chinese media platforms are emerging, the ways in which transnational audiences in quasi-Sinophone East Asia connect with Chinese media are also changing accordingly.

In this light, Sara, who first began studying Chinese language as a high school student and now majors in Chinese Studies, expressed, "I watch some famous Chinese television series that are recommend by Baidu or by my Chinese friends."[6] Another informant also pointed out to me that, "There are many online streaming services where you can watch Chinese media, too."[7] In fact, Korean netizens share such information with those who are interested in inquiring about this, online. For example, an informal inquiry about "any free Chinese television series websites?" was posted on Daum T!P, one of the biggest portal sites of Korea, on February 4, 2017. On the same date, an answer was posted with a QR code for iQiyi, along with, "I would recommend iQiyi to you." Another reply, posted on February 27, 2017, was more informative than the first: "I recommend you an application, 'Shift Up.' You can find pretty much all Chinese television series there, and even find those of other countries too" (Kingkong62 2017).

There are other platforms for sharing information about what to watch, and even how to watch the selected media in a more lively, collective manner. MJBox,[8] the biggest Chinese television series café within NAVER, the largest Korean portal site, opened on April 8, 2005, and has 152,118 members as of August 2017. This digital café hosts seven main forum sections: (1) Synopsis, (2) Information sharing, (3) Fan club, (4) Drama, (5) Clubbox Data, (6) Subtitle data and (7) Related weblinks. Another big online community was established four years after MJBox's opening. Since its birth on May 5, 2009, CDZM BOX,[9] within NAVER has accumulated 66,609 members, as of August 2017. The main contents of this online community are divided into seven parts: (1) "Subtitle," (2) "Members' playground," (3) "Star (celebrity) Room," (4) "Novel room," (5) "Special recommendations," (6) "Video and music data," and (7) "Drama." In these two communities, members not only share information about appealing television series and their related details, such as featured celebrities and cultural and media products, but they also share and create subtitles for the television series content.

KM39[10] said, "I watched some dramas via an online streaming service that was recommended by an online community. One of my favorite programs was *The Return of the Pearl Princess*." The streaming service becomes popular among young people due to its accessibility—it is versatile in efficiency and portability, and is used at little or no cost.

Some informants from the Internet generation, that started using the Internet as teenagers if not earlier, have experience with a variety of smartphones and portable devices for connected viewing, which is a new way of consuming media in this digital age. With this connected viewing, consumers not only watch media on different devices and platforms, they can share and sell media content in online space (Holt and Sanson 2014). Likewise, they not only consume the Chinese media with these devices, but they also watch Chinese television series while they are on the move.

A Japanese informant, JV14,[11] introduced me to this notion: "I am watching Chinese television series on a PPS application. Initially, my Chinese friend recommended this to me. You can watch many interesting programs on this app, wherever you are." Her satisfaction with the PPS application is largely due to its ubiquitous characteristics and the wide selection of media choices. By sharing this, she also alluded as to how Japanese media plays a gatekeeper role to run the system on traditional media platforms. With mobile devices and platforms, all choices are offered and decisions can be made by consumers without the bottleneck screening of professionals in the process.

In a similar vein, JV58[12] explained how she watches Chinese television series online: "Watching online basically happens two ways. Watching with/out payment, or going through dark and illegal downloading sites to get to audiovisual products. I believe that many of my Japanese friends usually go with the first option, as I do. I subscribed to a streaming service, and put whatever I want to watch in my shopping cart and can access it anytime, anywhere. I like it that way." These online services enable some informants to consume series efficiently.

KV67[13] told me, "I learnt about the latest version of *Three Kingdoms* through an online club where you can share information about Chinese dramas and media products. I looked for this version of *Three Kingdoms* on one of the P2P sites and downloaded several episodes. I started to watch them, but there were 95 episodes."

Unlike the Japanese preference for a paid online subscription, quite a substantial number of Korean informants who encounter Chinese television series on cyberspace would rather go to the second, free route: "You can get at least some Chinese television series on any P2P site or Torrent. It's a matter of whether or not you are lucky enough to get a good subtitle-embedded version," Korean informant KV88[14] said. She continued, "We don't buy Microsoft packages or things like that in Korea. I learned for the first time that you should actually be paying for it when I bought a new computer abroad. You can get these basic computer programs for free, so who would pay for this? It's the same. If you have chance to get free television series online, why would I spend money on this?" Heeju framed her actions as guilt-free efficiency. According to her, everyone would do the same—at least in South Korea. Even in this way, the reach of Chinese television series spreads online.

Other informants, however, lamented upon their experiences of being caught in the firewall, even outside of China. A Korean interviewee[15] said, "when I was in China, I watched some programs on Tudou and Youku. In Korea, it's not always available. I would often get that message, 'it is not available where you are.' Then I was disappointed by this and did not consider watching them [again]." Like her narrative tells, many Korean interviewees' experiences of facing the "Great Firewall" and having streaming services blocked are not pleasant. As such, the expanded regulatory mechanism of the Great Firewall is hampering overseas streaming services and their influence.

KM39[16] said, "I watched some dramas on cable TV and online. One of my favorite programs was *The Return of the Pearl Princess*." The unexpected success of *The Return of the Pearl Princess* prompted iTV to broadcast a series of Chinese dramas, such as *Shin Pocheongcheon* (*New Justice Pao*), *Hoeokgongju* (*Huaiyu Gongzhu, Princess Huaiyu*), *Nohbangyuhui* (*Laofang youxi, Old House Has a Joy*) and *Angaebiyeonga* (*Romance in the Rain, Qingshenshen yumengmeng*). Some of them are historical, while others can be categorized as premodern (1911–1948) (see Chap. 2). These were well-received in South Korea, as captured in some informants' accounts. KV46[17] said, "I watched *Angaebiyeonga* (*Romance in the Rain*), *Hoeokgongju* (*Princess Huaiyu*) and *Nohbangyuhui* (*Laofang youxi*). Lin Xinru (Ruby Lin) and Zhao Wei, the main actresses in *The Return of the Pearl Princess*, also appeared in these programs. That was why I became interested in the programs in the first place." Such a response was also expressed by KV40,[18] KV41,[19] KV43[20] and KV45.[21] As argued earlier, aside from content and storylines, the role of celebrities and level of celebrity capital are also important for consumer decisions.

Censorship and Its Discontents

Chinese streaming services are, in theory, effective tools for facilitating the expansion of China's soft power and communicating to bigger, overseas audiences. Unlike traditional TV programs on a TV set, apps on smartphones or websites on computers provide easier access for foreign audiences/consumers. Ubiquitous access to TV programs on these gadgets creates opportunities for foreigners to gain exposure to new TV programs and, potentially, become wielded by China's soft power. Yet, in reality, the situation is much more complicated than this.

Some recent developments on the Chinese side have made the situation far more complicated and create discontent for potential audiences in both South Korea and Japan.

On the one hand, the exponential development of Information and Communications Technologies (ICTs) and the widespread use of mobile devices, particularly smartphones and the IPTV, have achieved rapid growth over the past few years. This trend not only creates a new market for companies and consumers, but it also announces that the IPTV could play an imperative role in spurring opportunities for China to restore and revise its soft power paradox. However, these advances have also become a double-edged sword.

In spite of these high hopes of generating soft power more effectively and better communicating with wider audiences, China instead plays a different game. What has emerged from this scene is the manufacturing of "soft power" through censorship. This was observed not only when I conducted my major fieldwork in 2011–2013, but it also became more salient recently. A comment from KV88,[22] a Korean interviewee, is worth mentioning on this connection. She said, "Due to the strong censorship, the content circulated via online platforms is still limited. You know, I wanted to consume Chinese content online, but I can't help [instead] consuming Korean content via Chinese online platforms. I don't need Korean subtitles for Korean content, but it's freely available as digitized media in Chinese cyberspace." This is truly an intended outcome, facilitated by both the industries and governments of China and Korea. Yet ironically, Chinese digital platforms, which are expected to serve as the foundation for a Chinese soft power build-up, instead function as effective generators of Korean soft power.

Regulations for the IPTV and digitized televisual products in China have also been strengthened, which in turn affects the behavior of transnational audiences. A Korean informant[23] said, "I thought I could access any Chinese television series that I could watch on China's online media platforms, even when I came back to Korea. I often find the platforms inaccessible. It made me disappointed in continuing to watch Chinese television series online." Likewise, transnational audiences expect more freedom to consume products online. In fact, this can turn out to be an illusion, and turns interest into dissatisfaction.

The regulations governing the platforms are more institutionalized than audiences might imagine. With the newly established regulatory regime, foreigners who play or broadcast any Chinese media or cultural content should request authorization to do so in advance. A Korean media professional said, "All these arrangements are dangerous for my company, as well as the whole Korean industry."[24] What he delivers here is that the ripple effect of this new regulation might engender restrictions on the appearance of Korean celebrities and cut Korean media products. Unfortunately, this concern is not imaginary; leading newspaper Chosun Ilbo in 2016 reported:

> A Seoul Broadcasting System (SBS) drama, *Saimdang*, which was set for simultaneous broadcasting between South Korea and China next month, has been postponed to air on TV next January, due to the Chinese Government's sudden deliberation regarding its approval. "Good products find ways, even out of dead ends. Amidst a fear of China's regulation of Korean content after THAAD," a high-level executive of a broadcasting company said, "political conflicts cannot come between culture and business." [...] There are some changes to move from the China-oriented export market of the Korean Wave. Last October, Korean Broadcasting System (KBS) already set an agreement to make a Hollywood version of a KBS drama with an American production company, U2K. [...] The KBS drama, *Uncontrollably Fond*, which is now aired on China's largest streaming website, Youku, exceeds 35 billion clicks. This is a new record for Korean drama clicks. People in the industry said, "We should turn this crisis into another strength/opportunity (Jung 2016)."

> "With the decision to deploy THAAD came the expected difficulty of entering the Chinese market. Korean companies have strategies for using *Wang hong* (an internet celebrity), a Chinese version of power bloggers. [...] Wang Hong's activities are not dependent on the political situation. Wang Hong will be the new way of pioneering the market, in order for Korean companies to enter the Chinese market." "The areas that Wang Hong has introduced so far are focused on fashion and beauty, and will expand to games, home appliances, and furniture, among others." "Korean companies should pay attention to China's new consumer culture and actively utilize the power of *Wanghong* (Internet celebrity)," said Chosun Ilbo in another article published in 2016. (Lee 2016)

Success stories of Korean celebrities, as well as potential ways of politically salvaging the THAAD crisis are framed as sources of economic opportunity. Reports claim that the crisis could actually provide Korea with beneficial momentum for a new type of success to continue the national Korean Wave project (Kim 2013; Lee 2012).

These two news reports in 2016 that illustrate a Korean media professional's narrative in detail reveal that the recently agitated relationship between China and South Korea, tied to Seoul's decision to deploy THAAD, does not stop at the military and diplomatic levels, but goes far beyond and reaches into the cultural and social realms.

China also possesses sophisticated mechanisms of censorship and surveillance (Hassid 2016; MacKinnon 2011; Yang 2013). Affecting domestic users, the *Administrative Provisions on Internet Audio-Visual Program Service* was created by the State Administration of Radio, Film and Television as early as 2007 and took effect in January 2008. An earlier name of this branch was SARPPFT, under the Ministry of Information Industry of the People's Republic of China.[25] The document also announced a Permit for Spreading Audio-Visual Programs via Information Networks (*xinxi wangluo chuanbo shiting jiemu xukezheng*), which is required for the online sharing, streaming, and circulation of audio-visual programs. Perhaps the market was predominantly occupied by local players back then, but there have since been new players in the online media market who either engage with foreign media, or essentially are foreign themselves.

New guidelines appeared recently to tighten control of the content and its flow. The Chinese Central Government enacted a "guideline of managing Internet broadcasting service (*hulianwang zhibo fuwu guanli guiding*)" on December 1, 2016 (Seo 2017: 4). It defines the boundaries of Internet broadcasting services, and who can perform the services. In line with this strengthening of cyberspace management, shortly after the last guideline was enacted in June 2017, streaming services on *Weibo* and other similar social networking services began to come under the control of the Chinese government. A high level of censorship, and control of the flow of programs and information, engender a further absence of virtual capital in the online media platform economy.

Conclusion

Various methods of gaining closer access to Chinese television series are available to consumers in both South Korea and Japan, in the forms of online media and via online platforms through portal services, mobile IPTV, and streaming services. The recent rapid development of digital media and the globalization of platforms in China have seemingly sparked a glimmer of hope not only for the promising industry, but also to create a mode and space for Chinese soft power expansion. The growth of the industry and its platforms is certainly on the rise; however, as this chapter has shown, the conversion of platforms into virtual capital for fostering a transnational soft power field is remarkably underdeveloped.

In this chapter, I highlighted the chain effect of China's soft power paradox along digitized platforms. While Korean and Japanese consumers seek "free" virtual capital in China's digital media, with expectations of low levels of cost and censorship, they often instead experience Chinese televisual virtual capital in their countries that is censored and manufactured; physically remote to China, yet virtually connected to China. Censored Chinese digital media apparently does not convert into other types of capital, such as cultural or economic capital, which are essential to generate Chinese soft power among transnational audiences.

On the one hand, I framed China's emerging media platforms as a new source of outsourced televised soft power in a virtually transnational soft power field with virtual capital. On the other hand, digital platforms are simultaneously utilized by the Chinese government as a tool for governing transnational audiences. This has impacted the feelings South Korean and Japanese consumers actively express about the state's censorship and how it is wielding its soft power. Through this perplexed situation, China's digital media is inherently lacking virtual capital.

Cyberspace is the new medium for China's soft power expansion; however, the ways in which cyberspace may contribute to configuring Chinese soft power are not much different from those of traditional Chinese soft power products, as presented in previous chapters. The paradox China's soft power faces continues regardless of the types of platforms or media utilized—at least to local audiences in both South Korea and Japan.

Along this emerging mode of generating soft power via digital platforms, one thing is clear: the rupture between prepared platforms and unconverted potential capital—generating and converting virtual capital to other forms of capital—will perpetuate the struggles and paradoxes that China faces in developing its soft power in the near future.

NOTES

1. CM29, interview with a Chinese media practitioner, June 16, 2012, Hong Kong; CM37, interview with a Singaporean media practitioner, October 10, 2014, Singapore.
2. In June 2014, China had 632 million netizens with a 46.9 percent penetration rate (CNNIC 2014). Within two years, the country's Internet penetration rate increased to 50 percent.

3. http://tv.sohu.com/.
4. For the *danmaku* system, please see Liu et al. (2016).
5. KM1, interview with a South Korean media practitioner, December 20, 2011, Seoul, South Korea; April 2, 2017, Seoul, South Korea.
6. KV20, interview with a South Korean respondent, December 11, 2011, Seoul, South Korea. Her second foreign language during her high school years was Chinese language.
7. KV13, interview with a South Korean respondent, December 8, 2011, Seoul, South Korea.
8. MJBox (n.d.). http://cafe.naver.com/mjbox/497218 (Accessed August 1, 2017).
9. CDZM Box (n.d.). http://cafe.naver.com/cdzm (Accessed August 1, 2017).
10. KV38, interview with a South Korean respondent, December 21, 2011, Seoul, South Korea.
11. JV14, interview with a Japanese respondent, April 8, 2012, Tokyo, Japan.
12. JV58, interview with a South Korean respondent, May 24, 2012, Tokyo, Japan.
13. KV67, interview with a South Korean respondent, June 9, 2012, Seoul, South Korea.
14. KV88, interview with a South Korean respondent, November 29, 2013, Seoul, South Korea.
15. KV63, interview with a South Korean respondent, June 7, 2012, Seoul, South Korea.
16. KV39, interview with a South Korean respondent, December 21, 2011, Seoul, South Korea.
17. KV46, interview with a South Korean respondent, January 10, 2012, Seoul, South Korea.
18. KV40, interview with a South Korean respondent, December 21, 2011, Seoul, South Korea.
19. KV41, interview with a South Korean respondent, December 21, 2011, Seoul, South Korea.
20. KV43, interview with a South Korean respondent, December 24, 2011, Seoul, South Korea.
21. KV45, interview with a South Korean respondent, January 2, 2012, Seoul, South Korea.
22. KV88, interview with a South Korean respondent, November 29, 2013, Seoul, South Korea.
23. KV71, Interview with a South Korean respondent, June 28, 2012, Seoul, South Korea.
24. KV74, Interview with a South Korean respondent, June 29, 2012, Seoul, South Korea.

25. The Ministry's name has changed to the Ministry of Industry and Information Technology [*Zhonghuarenmingongheguo gongye he xinxihuabu*]. The website is http://www.miit.gov.cn/.

REFERENCES

CDZM Box. n.d. Accessed August 1, 2017. http://cafe.naver.com/cdzm.

Chen, Ziyan. 2014. *Shipinwangzhan de Shangyemoshi Yanjiu [Research on Business Model of Video Websites]*. Master's Thesis. Changsha: Hunan Normal University.

China Internet Network Information Center [CNNIC, *Zhongguo Hulianwang Xinxi zhongxin*]. 2014. *Gao Shuang: Wangmin zengzhang fangman: Feiwangmin zhuanhua jindu tuxian, gongneng jibuanjichao jiejinweisheng [Gao Shuang: Netizen's Growth Slows Down: The Difficulty of Turning Netizens into Non-Internet Users Becomes More Prominent, and the Change in Functions is Nearing Competition]*. July 22. Accessed July 13, 2017. http://www.cnnic. cn/hlwfzyj/fxszl/fxswz/201407/t20140722_47452.htm.

CNIDP. 2017. Wangmin Shuliang [Netizens' Number]. *Jichu Shuju* [Basic Data]. Accessed July 12, 2017. http://www.cnidp.cn/.

CNNIC. 2017. *Zhongguo Hulianwangluo fazhan zhuangkuang tongji baogao [China Statistical Report on Internet Development]*. January. Beijing: China Internet Network Information Center.

Digital TV Research. 2016. *Global OTT TV & Video Forecasts*. July. Accessed July 13, 2017. https://www.digitaltvresearch.com/ugc/Global%20OTT%20 2016%20TOC_toc_149.pdf.

Fo, Ran. 2016. *Zhongguo Shipinwangzhanchanpinde Yingxiaocelveyanjiu [Research on Marketing Strategies of China's Internet Video Products]*. College of Broadcasting, Film and TV Arts. Changsha: Hunan University.

Guo, Qing. 2011. *Zhongguo shipin wangzhan xianzhuang tantao [Discussing the Current Trend of China's Internet Website]*. Master's Thesis. Shanghai: Shanghai Jiaotong University.

Hassid, Jonathan. 2016. *China's Unruly Journalists: How Committed Professionals Are Changing the People's Republic*. New York and London: Routledge.

Holt, Jennifer, and Kevin Sanson, eds. 2014. *Connected Viewing: Selling, Streaming and Sharing Media in the Digital Era*. London: Routledge.

Hu, Kelly. 2014. Competition and Collaboration: Chinese Video Websites, Subtitle Groups, State Regulation and Market. *International Journal of Cultural Studies* 17 (5): 437–451.

iResearch Consulting Group. 2015. *2015nian Zhongguo Zaixianshipinhangye Nianbao Jiancebaogao [China's Online Video Industry: Annual Monitoring Report 2015]*. Beijing: iResearch Consulting Group.

Jung, Sanghyuk. 2016. Junggukui Gyeonjeleul Gihoelo… Segye Anbangeulo Nuneul Neolbhida [China's Containment as an Opportunity … Expanding Horizons to the World]. *Chosun Ilbo*, September 30. Accessed December 1, 2016. http:// news.chosun.com/site/data/html_dir/2016/09/30/2016093000300.html.

Kim, Youna, ed. 2013. *The Korean Wave: Korean Media Go Global*. London and New York: Routledge.

Kim, Young-Ju. 2015. OTT Seobisu Hwagsani Kontencheu Saengsan, Yutong, Sobie Michin Yeonghyangeui Gwanhan Yeongu [Impact of OTT Service on the Content Creation, Distribution and Consumption]. *Studies of Broadcasting Culture* 27 (1): 75–102.

Kingkong62. 2017. Any Chinese Television Series Free Website. *Daum T!P*, February 4. Accessed August 2, 2017. http://tip.daum.net/question/ 92432674.

Lee, Eunmin. 2013. Juyo Inteones Dongyeongsang Seobiseuui Choegeun Donghyang [The Current Trends of Major Internet Streaming Services]. *ICT & Media Policy* 25 (7): 57–66.

Lee, Jaeeun. 2016. Hangug Gieob, Sadeulo Maghin Jung Sijang Jung Gugpan Pawobeullogeo 'Wanghong' eulo Gaecheoghaeya [Korean Companies Should Open Up the Chinese Market, Which Is Blocked by THAAD, with China's Power Blogger 'Wanghong']. *Chosun Ilbo*, October 6. Accessed December 1, 2016. http://news.chosun.com/site/data/html_dir/2016/10/06/2016100602321. html.

Lee, Jung-yup. 2012. Managing the Transnational, Governing the National: Cultural Policy and the Politics of 'Culture Archetype' Project in South Korea. In *Popular Culture and the State in East and Southeast Asia*, ed. Nissim Otmazgin and Eyal Ben-Ari, 123–144. London and New York: Routledge.

Lin, Jinjin. 2015. Zhongguo Shipinwangzhanpinpaihua Fazhan Fenxi [Analysis on the Development of Brands of China's Internet Video Websites]. *Dianying Wenxue [Movie Literature]* 6: 36–38.

Liu, Lili, Ayoung Suh, and Christian Wagner. 2016. Watching Online Videos Interactively: The Impact of Media Capabilities in Chinese Danmaku Video Sites. *Chinese Journal of Communication* 9 (3): 283–303.

MacKinnon, Rebecca. 2011. China's 'Networked Authoritarianism'. *Journal of Democracy* 22 (2): 32–46.

Mango TV. n.d. Accessed August 1, 2017. http://www.mgtv.com/tv/.

Ministry of Industry and Information Technology [*Zhonghuarenmingongheguo gongye he xinxihuabu*]. n.d. Accessed August 2, 2017. http://www.miit.gov.cn/.

Ministry of Science, ICT and Future Planning and Korea Communications Commission *[Bangsong Tongshin Wiewonhoe]*. 2016. *2016 nyeon Bangsong Siltae Sanoepjosa Bogoseo [A Report of Broadcasting Industry of 2016]*. Seoul: Korea Communications Commission.

MJBox. n.d. Accessed August 1, 2017. http://cafe.naver.com/mjbox/497218.

Moon, Jihyun, Hongmei Cui, and Nuri Ha. 2016. *China Next Player*. Seoul: KDB Daewoo Security Research Center.

Park, Sung-eun, and Gun-Woong Lee. 2016. Research on Online Video Content Distributors in China. *The Journal of the Korea Contents Association* 16 (5): 137–147. https://doi.org/10.5392/JKCA.2016.16.05.137.

Seo, Uktae. 2017. *Jungguk Munhwasanup hyunhwang mit sisajeom [The Current Status of and Implications for China's Cultural Industry].* Seoul: Korea International Trade Association [KITA].

Sohu TV. n.d. Accessed August 1, 2017. http://tv.sohu.com/.

Wang, Wei-Ching, Shule Cao, and Jia Dai. 2017. Copyright Regulations as Political and Economic Leverage: The Case of the Online Video Industry of China. *Chinese Journal of Communication* 10 (2): 175–191.

Yang, Guobin. 2013. Social Dynamics in the Evolution of China's Internet Content Control Regime. In *The Routledge Handbook of Media Law*, ed. Libby Morgan, Monroe Price, and Stefaan Verhulst, 285–302. London and New York: Routledge.

Zhang, Yudong. 2012. Zhongguo Wangluoshipinhangyefazhan Shitan [An Analysis of China's Internet Video Industry Development]. *Dianshi Yanjiu [TV Research]* 11: 39–42.

Zhao, Elaine Jing. 2017. The Bumpy Road Towards Network Convergence in China: The Case of Over-the-Top Streaming Services. *Global Media and China* 2 (1): 28–42.

Zhao, Elaine Jing, and Michael Keane. 2013. Between Formal and Informal: The Shakeout in China's Online Video Industry. *Media, Culture and Society* 35 (6): 724–741.

Zhongguo Shipinwangzhanfazhan Yanjiu Ketizu [China Video Website Development Research Group]. 2014. Zhongguo Shipinwangzhanfazhan Yanjiubaogao [Research Report on China's Video Website Development]. *Chuanmei [Media]*, March: 7–13.

PART III

Conclusions and Postscript

CHAPTER 8

Conclusions

Just as the tale of the Chinese soft power dilemma is unexpected, yet real, most of the existing literature on China's soft power does not highlight the relative absence of Chinese soft power from virtually all domains, and virtually all mediums, in an explicitly and empirically ground manner. Considering how soft power projection is transnational in essence, this is rather surprising.

Against this backdrop, this study of a soft power of transitional and global China was motivated by a seemingly simple question: "How does China's soft power actually reach transnational audiences, in response to Chinese policies and ample discussion by scholars of soft power?" Yet, this question is not as simple as it sounds, and led unexpectedly to a different story by shedding light on a different aspect of China's soft power. While the Chinese government pronounced its soft power strategy at a powerful moment in the midst of China's global rise, what we find is that the seemingly closest and easiest targets of its policy—quasi-Sinophone East Asian countries—are simply almost unaffected. The research behind this book not only discovered that China's soft power contains paradoxes, in that it is not successfully meeting its standards through current efforts to connect with transnational audiences, but also that there is a dualistic nature to this soft power dilemma.

This book journeyed into the predicaments of transnational soft power—a nation-state's attempts to create attraction by reaching out to

© The Author(s) 2018
C. S. Lee, *Soft Power Made in China*,
https://doi.org/10.1007/978-3-319-93115-9_8

transnational audiences via mediums in its pathway—by specifically locating the pursuit of soft power in the complicated relations between sending and receiving states. In the process, this book presents a discrepancy between an imagined transnational soft power projection and its reality. In particular, the book traces the interplay between Chinese governmental policies that aim to reinforce its soft power build-up—the idea that China should reach transnational audiences with its globalized media—and the resultant dual dilemmas of being unable to move beyond national boundaries to create prominent televisual subfields, and being caught in the circuits of media with outsourcing from Hong Kong and Taiwan.

Transborder soft power-building is inherently transnational, relational, and political. At the institutional level, this generation occurs in both sending and receiving nation-states. An intermediary level reveals both international and interstate media circuit systems, and media professionals in the circuits that shape soft power projection. Sufficiently appealing televisual subfields are not prominently available, while historicized and politicized factors impact decisions about what, why, and how to consume this media (or not). Due to the ambiguous boundary of "Chinese" in minds of the foreign audiences, unintentionally outsourced soft power from Taiwan and Hong Kong has sparked a new attraction in products that expand China's soft power. However, without further development of these subfields and pathways in the long run, the future of China's soft power will be jeopardized. Emerging digital media platforms have also introduced a potentially powerful tool for expanding soft power; but in reality, unexpected censorship of the content and the flow of online media shape consumer interests, and create different textures of Chinese soft power in quasi-Sinophone East Asia.

The following sections will highlight each of these arguments, juxtaposing industrial and individual responses against the broader literature on markets, media, and globalization. As this book depicts China's soft power dilemma, successful cases of soft power expansion for other countries are likely to be beneficial for China's future planning. How the cases of other states can be applied to China, in order to enhance its long-term efficacy and capability to wield its transnational soft power, are discussed. The section outlines a future research agenda that is derived from and motivated by the conclusions of this book. In its closing, this book provides implications for China's future in the political, economic, and social realms.

SOFT POWER ENDEAVORS

Taking Nye's now renowned concept of "soft power" as its starting point, the theoretical argument of this book has been empirically substantiated and lead to the assertion of the following two positions. First, according to Nye (2004, 2011: xiv), "All power depends on context—who relates to whom under what circumstances—but soft power depends more than hard power upon the existence of willing interpreters and receivers." The translation of soft power is effective to the extent that the source country has a capacity to develop and project its soft power, as well as pertinent policy to realize its potential influence. Furthermore, and more importantly, the way in which China's projection of its soft power relates to institutional arrangements and mediators (interpreters and receivers) in the target countries operates under the direct and indirect influence of the cultural and foreign policies of the receiving countries. In other words, the receiving country's contextual and institutional environments create the soft power field that facilitates and generates soft power for the source country. Institutions, such as media systems and markets, play a critical role in regulating the flow and ability of the exporting country's soft power instruments, which reach potential consumers in the importing countries.

Second, Nye contends that "attraction often has a diffuse effect, creating general influence rather than producing an easily observable specific political capital to be drawn on in future circumstances" (Nye 2004: 16). On this understanding, China's projection of its soft power can be understood as a strategic shaping of an international stage to reduce not only other nation-states' anxieties over perceived threats from China, but also those among Chinese citizens about the country's stability. For example, as mentioned in Chap. 1, President Xi Jinping's blueprint of the "China Dream" underscores and resonates with the internal dynamics of its development and the state's core relations with local people and the outside world.

Third, reflecting upon these two characteristics of soft power, a country's achievement of soft power influence is thought to be the outcome of interactive co-production between the exporting and importing countries. Regarding the two cases considered in this study, South Korean and Japanese audiences, the media circuit from production to consumption plays an important role in the making of Chinese soft power in these countries. The media market structures, official and unofficial regulatory regimes, market demands, and local customers' preferences spur media institutions and practitioners in the importing country to operate concertedly to control the exporting country's level of transnational soft power influence. The Korean and Japanese cases featured in this book exemplify how media practitioners contribute significantly to restricting China's capacity to promulgate its soft power abroad via media products. Indeed, it has faced difficulties reaching foreign audiences in these realms due to the intervention of market structures and interests, as well due to the attractiveness of its media products to these audiences. Thus, soft power projection is shaped both by China's external cultural policy and the receiving country's location within the soft power field.

Pathways to a Transnational Soft Power Dilemma: Linking Macro, Meso, and Micro

Media products, which have potential soft power influence, are reflections of the source country's culture and society. PRC Chinese commercial media products have a tendency to emphasize its rich culture through the historical subfield. While Taiwanese dramas choose a different path by featuring depictions of modern lifestyles, Hong Kong dramas are known for stressing the martial arts subfield. These compartmentalized TV subfields give the Chinese government a broader scope to consider how to draw upon or reject such genre-based media products for constructing and projecting its soft power. As shown in Chaps. 4 and 5, both media professionals and audiences in Korea and Japan find PRC Chinese media products specifically less compelling and attractive than those from Hong Kong and Taiwan. This leads China to another soft power dilemma in that the outsourced, and out-of-reach, soft power produced by Hong Kong and Taiwan is ultimately going to backfire on PRC influence in the future. With China's strong central government and state organizations, including the Ministry of Culture and SARPPFT, advancing the idea of soft power in coordination, limited autonomy and opportunities for participation are offered to other stakeholders in construction its soft power. As shown by this study, China may encounter difficulties in projecting its soft power as a centralized sole stakeholder. More active engagement of different stakeholders, such as those from non-state institutions and the public, may be beneficial to China in projecting its soft power.

In this book, "a pathway to (or a circuit of) a soft power dilemma" refers to the process by which the Chinese state has experienced its soft power projection as a chain of instrumentalized dilemmas, between its aspiration to project soft power and its reality. The ways in which the intertwined dual dilemmas of institutionalized soft power arise are explained.

On the one hand, these paradoxes are embedded in a circuit of media. Chinese media products are managed by the Chinese authorities, but also by transnational media professionals who serve as gatekeepers by circulating only certain hand-picked products. The media practitioners in South Korea and Japan have the power to decide what is put on their local markets by oscillating between personal and company preferences and market practices. Imagined values of economic capital from cultural, historical, celebrity, and technological capitals are driving forces behind such decisions.

These institutionally and politically governed export media products are, in fact, still perceived by transnational audiences as highly historicized and politicized. Thus, nationally specific factors can be hard for foreign audiences to accommodate. The dilemmas and byproducts that are generated in the course of making Chinese soft power in South Korea and Japan are often entangled with each other. This entanglement, on the South Korean side, is linked to potential economic capital. On the Japanese side, it has to do with politicized antagonism over historical issues with China. This hinders the pursuit of further knowledge about and exposure to the country.

In particular, many of my Korean informants failed to distinguish between the different Chinese societies that produce "Chinese" media. Surprisingly, South Koreans who were exposed to Chinese language and had knowledge about China were equally as confused as those who were not when asked to differentiate between Chinese societies and to identify the origins of various Chinese media products. For the Japanese, close and friendly Japan-Taiwan relations alluded that Taiwanese products are viewed more positively in Japan than Chinese products. Hong Kong's media products again perform exceptionally well in Japan because the Japanese are very familiar with movie stars Jet Li and Jackie Chan. Existing perceptions about and images of China in these two receiving countries contribute to the absence of transnational soft power fields by ineffectively turning problematic but potential-filled capital into failed soft power.

The boundaries and images of China, as constructed by South Koreans and Japanese, reflect their cultural proximity, traditions, and management of the cultural, political, and commoditized spheres. A multi-faceted "China" and other Chinese societies are well-captured in the images and perceptions of transnational audiences in South Korea and Japan.

On the other hand, double paradoxes are entangled with media and platforms. Co-ethnicity and shared languages between the PRC and the two Chinese societies it co-produces media with—Hong Kong and Taiwan, whose shows are embedded into "Chinese" television programs—are often sources of ample, involuntarily outsourced soft power. In the long term, this accidently outsourced Chinese soft power will require more work and strategic consideration from the PRC. The ways in which resources, policies, and industrial development are co-evolving to shape China's soft power via media should be revised by generating more salient televisual subfields with stronger forms of capital and more reliable capital conversion.

In addition, with the high convergence of offline and online media, media digitalization in the new media landscape is important for offsetting China's soft power dilemma and configuring China's soft power projection. However, in the current stages of the market and online media development, censorship is still heavily exercised by the Chinese government for not only contents, services, and platforms, but also their flow between China and its import countries. In turn, the government's management of the digital landscape functions as a form of digital gatekeeping against its problematic domestication of the foreign and, ironically, its problematic domestication of the local. This paradox is detrimental to China's future soft power projection and transnational soft power field expansion.

In Search of Typologies of Soft Power Projection

Based upon these theoretical grounds, this study has aimed to offer a modified conception of soft power with the intention of understanding how Chinese soft power negotiated through mass media encounters a series of dilemmas in the contexts of South Korea and Japan. It is important to be cognizant of the particularities of these two receiving countries of Chinese soft power when considering China's potential for building transnational soft power fields in them. Empirical findings reveal that mass media, particularly commercialized TV products as instruments for the projection of Chinese soft power, has so far encountered dilemmas in

South Korea and Japan, unlike its Korean Wave and Japanese pop culture counterparts in China. What are the possible reasons for this dilemma and relative failure?

First, one of the major reasons for such limited penetration of China's soft power into South Korea and Japan can be explained by referencing the differences between the dynamics of Chinese soft power, as presented in this study, and those of the Korean Wave and Japanese pop culture for transnational audiences.

As has been emphasized in this study, Chinese media consumption takes place by and large because it is considered a useful and entertaining way to learn the Chinese language. Unlike the successful cases of the Korean Wave in China and Japan (citing some of my Japanese informants) or the consumption of Hong Kong and Taiwanese media products in South Korea and Japan, there is a relative shortcoming of China's projection of its soft power into South Korea and Japan via its media products. This can be explained in many ways, such as the stardom of featured celebrities, program content, and interest in the culture and language to reinforce the mechanism of soft power.

Furthermore, as presented in Fig. 8.1, the interplay between interest in the country (including its culture, history, language, and other aspects), and the collective images and boundaries of China and "Chinese" plays an important role in ensuring Chinese soft power successfully reaches foreign audiences. As seen in Chaps. 5 and 6, the reception of Chinese soft power

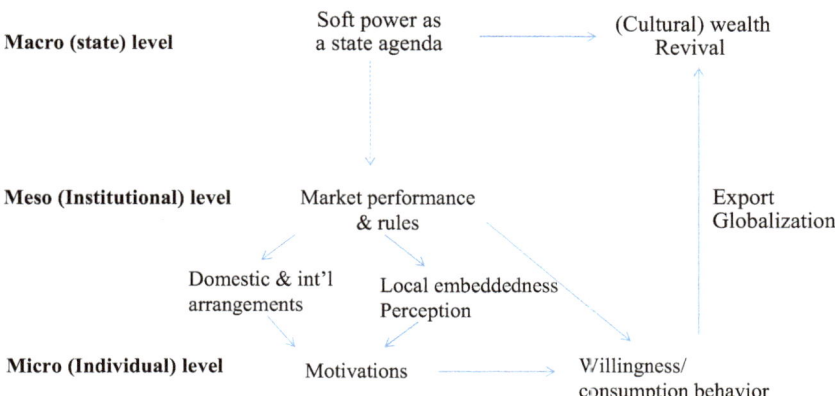

Fig. 8.1 Pathways of the "co-construction" of China's soft power. Source: Compiled by the Author

among South Korean and Japanese audiences varies considerably, to the extent that it can be concluded that the effectiveness of Chinese soft power is unreliable and perhaps unstable at this moment.

Third, at the macro level, the interplay between state, market, and business is important for China in further developing its soft power. Reflecting on the soft power model presented in Table 8.1, the Chinese government-led strategy does not necessarily translate well on the ground, so to speak, in other countries. Market-oriented models or multiple engagements between state, market, non-state actors, and business are likely to perform better.

Normatively speaking, if the Chinese state were to take into account the above-mentioned factors, the realization of their soft power ambitions vis-à-vis the expectations of South Korean and Japanese audiences might be in greater harmony than they are at present.

Based on the above theoretical characterization of soft power, the major findings of this research can be summarized as follows. First, given that the soft power mechanism is relational and interactive, a cooperative co-construction of the Chinese soft power configuration can be illustrated, as in Fig. 8.1.

As can be seen, the three, hierarchically ordered macro (state), meso (market), and micro (individual) levels correlate to the Chinese state's agenda of reviving cultural wealth (see Bandelj and Wherry 2011; Wherry 2012), the market performance of China's globally exported media products, and the behavior of the consumer audiences in the target countries, respectively. More specifically, the state level focuses on the Chinese government's soft power policy and its projection to foreign countries along its cultural globalization strategy. The media market level explores how embedded market structures and the practices of the target countries manage the importation of Chinese media products. The market is the place where domestic institutional structures and cultural intermediaries play an important role in the selection of products conveyed through the media circuit. This is exemplified by the role of market players in South Korea and Japan in regulating the flow of foreign and Chinese commodities into their own markets. Ironically, as soft power regulators, or "filters," they also inadvertently become soft power generators and facilitators. By selectively importing media products, media professionals operate as gatekeepers and cultural intermediaries who determine what is perceived as "foreign culture." The individual level consists of individual audiences and their selective consumption of the media products as entertainment or "cultural" products, which have potential to generate soft power influence for the projecting country.

Table 8.1   The variety of soft power mechanisms and different paths of soft power development

Types	(1) Centralized (pure state)	(2) Profit-oriented (pure market)	(3) Multiple engagements (mixed)
Objectives	State	Commercial gains	Promoting the country and possible byproducts
Stakeholders	Producing soft power, marketized soft power	Business people	State, non-state
Intended consequences	A limited level of achieving soft power, byproducts as less preference over the country is generated	Gaining profits, cultural products as economic powerhouses	Producing soft power, marketized soft power
Unintended consequences	Neoliberalism	Soft power as byproducts	A limited level of achieving soft power, byproducts as less preference over the country is generated
Driving forces	Core culture that the country thinks	Market-oriented Neoliberalism	Nationalism-based (cultural) wealth Neoliberalism
Core/basic elements of soft power	Soft power as a reflection of the government's logic	Purely commodified culture	Core culture that the country thinks
Effects	Nationalism, protectionism, a kind of development leads another kind of development	Soft power as commercialized	Soft power as semi-commercialized
Internal factors	Changing power dynamics	Economic-determinism, profit-oriented	State policy, local institutions, nationalism, protectionism
External factors	As a highly regulated and institutionalized place	Exports	Foreign institutions, markets
Marketplace		A place of commodities	As a promoter and intermediaries, as a highly regulated and institutionalized place
Example	China	Japan	South Korea, United States E.g. 1: A developmental state E.g. 2: A highly neoliberalized state

Source: Compiled by the Author

In sum, the projection of one country's soft power policy through the export of media products to importing countries is contingent upon local institutional arrangements, as well as the local audience's perceptions, and reception, in the target country. The interplay between sender and receiver at all three levels needs, therefore, to be analyzed in order to better understand the workings of soft power. The present research has illustrated this by examining China's projection of its soft power through the export of its media cultural products to the neighboring countries of South Korea and Japan.

In order for media products to be translated into soft power, they clearly must possess the potential to reach an audience. Undoubtedly, as this study shows, there is a discrepancy between the Chinese state's intentions and the responses of Korean and Japanese audiences, as they resist Chinese programs; in part due to quality of the products, and in part due to the importation process. Media professionals and institutions in these countries are also resisting, in large part to the selling strategies of Chinese producers, and because they are following their established prescriptions for drawing viewership. In addition, China's configuration of soft power is obviously subject to the sense of cultural security and local market protections that exist in its target countries. Together, the exporting and importing countries work together in the construction of Chinese soft power and its dilemma.

Following from the main findings of the study, further theoretical claims can be drawn regarding the typologies of soft power mechanisms, as well as the cultural wealth of China. There is a debate over the classification of "strong states" and "weak states" in political sociology and political science (Kohli 2004; Midgal 1988, 2001). The variety of soft power models, presented in this Conclusion, are based on this line of literature. Delineations between "strong" and "weak" states are generally drawn along the characteristics of state centrality, state capacity, and intervention. "Strong" states, like China, tend to employ dual-faceted attitudes when dealing with social change and external power dynamics. To cite the example of South Korea, as a small but "strong" state, this nation has implemented state regulations and quotas on foreign products, while strongly encouraging the export of its products. This results from the South Korean media industry's export-driven structure, illustrated by the successful Korean Wave. On the other hand, the "weaker" state of Japan does not have a written regulatory regime nor, did it actively promote the export of its media cultural products until recently. Revisiting the typology of soft power models proposed in section "In Search of Typologies of Soft Power Projection," China's model is classified as "state-centralized," South Korea as a "multiple actor soft power" model, and Japan as a "profit-oriented" model of soft power.

As this book has focused on the configuration of China's soft power, the variety of models for projecting soft power in other contexts is denied attention. In proposing three models, this research extends the discussion to the broader research areas of soft power and cultural globalization in cultural and economic sociology. The active participant(s) in each model, which are derived from both the modes of implementation and the levels to which the state's economic development have been achieved, vary. The first type is centralized soft power as a state agenda (state-geared); hence, the state is the only active participant, with the help of sub-state organizations. The second type is a commercially oriented soft power model, and the third type is a public-and-private sector engagement in soft power development (e.g. cooperation between state and non-state actors) (see Table 8.1).

While soft power policies can vary from model to model, the way in which soft power is translated from its base medium is similar across all models. In other words, a source country's soft power can be projected through co-production with the state, institutions, and/or receivers. Projecting soft power and a national image to the world agrees with the prevalent global logic that a country's image can be exported through a conduit of soft power. Products, ideas, and images, in particular, are easily mobilized and intertwine with each other. The way in which nation-states utilize soft power is reflected in such logic. Ultimately, both the visible and hidden soft power aspirations of nation-states can lead them to acquire cultural wealth. China strives for the accumulation of soft power, but more specifically the conversion of cultural capital into economic wealth. Similar processes and aims of the projection of soft power can be observed in cases of Hollywood and South Korea. Such instances of the creative influence cultural industries have can be drivers of further economic development, as well as grounds for enhancing a country's image.

IMPLICATIONS: THE CONSEQUENCES OF DUAL PARADOXES

Whether offline or online media, Chinese soft power faces momentous impediments to branding appeal among transnational audiences. Sociologists Janssen and Verboord eloquently describe the significance of globalization and media:

> How increased globalization and the emergence of transnational cultural
> fields transform the role and practices of cultural mediators, and how this
> plays out, at the local and transnational level, for agents from different coun-
> tries and places across the globe. (Janssen and Verboord 2015)

In the era of globalization, a globally expanding and powerful China
wanted to transform its hard power and economic capital into different
forms of capital in a transnational soft power field. This book has discussed
the expected emergence of transnational soft power fields, imagined from
the Chinese perspective. But this book also conversely reveals the simulta-
neous dilemma China is faced with. With the development of digital technologies and other cultural tastes, we hope to see such dilemmas evolve
into opportunities for China to wield its soft power in innovative and
compelling ways in the near future.

This study takes a closer look at the dilemma of China's soft power via
media in quasi-Sinophone countries in East Asia, particularly South Korea
and Japan (Shih et al. 2013). These two countries, as receiving targets of
China's mediated soft power, were selected for examination not only
based on the current research gap, but also for empirically and theoretically grounded reasons.

Most of the current scholarship on China's soft power, particularly the
role of media, and Chinese media flow do not actively engage foreign
audience (see Wang 2011a, b, 2013). This book modestly contributes to
the gaps raised by J. Wang (2011a, b, 2013), in the current stage of
China's soft power development.

Empirically, this book has leveraged more than 160 original interviews
across China, Hong Kong, Taiwan, South Korea, and Japan, with media
professionals and audience members (see Appendix A). Theoretically, as
quasi-Sinophone countries in East Asia, South Korea and Japan are important to China as an export country seeking to expand its soft power reach.
First, these countries already possess strong soft power media flows into
China, and from a theoretical perspective, the reverse media flows from
China to South Korea and Japan are worth examining. Furthermore, the
"South-South" media flow is growing, but often receives less attention.
Second, as case studies vis-à-vis China's mediated soft power, the narratives
collected in South Korea and Japan shed light on the importance of linguis-
tic capital in media products when China communicates its soft power.

Empirically speaking, as my data shows, media products from Hong
Kong and Taiwan often trick Korean and Japanese audiences into mistakenly

delineating the media product boundaries between the PRC and Hong Kong/Taiwan. To a certain extent, this data demonstrates how Hong Kong and Taiwan play significant roles in unintentionally coproducing China's soft power; at least for audiences in South Korea and Japan. Thus, Hong Kong and Taiwan are qualitatively different from non-Sinophone East Asian countries, not only in China's projection of its soft power, but also in addressing China's soft power dilemma.

With that said, Hong Kong and Taiwan—belonging to Sinophone East Asia—are arguably the two regions where China's soft power might be most effective and has the highest impact. Given that Hong Kong and Taiwan predominantly host ethnically Han Chinese and Mandarin-speaking populations, and are rarely acknowledged as politically independent states, they were deemed unsuitable for investigating the reasons behind and the conditions for the relative underdevelopment of China's international communication and public diplomacy through the media.

Nonetheless, China's soft power projection is seemingly targeted at Hong Kong and Taiwan, as well as other Chinese diasporic communities that are embedded within predominantly non-Chinese populations. These two groups of populations in Hong Kong and Taiwan are qualitatively different from the quasi-Sinophone East Asian states of South Korea and Japan—the focuses of this study. Even between these two locales, differences exist. Both host an overseas Chinese population (*hwagyo* in Korean, *gakyo* in Japanese), but considering the population dynamics of overseas Chinese, the sizes of these two countries' Chinese populations are rather small. Their consumption of China's media is better understood along the notion of diasporic media consumption. This concept—traditional and digital media consumption by diasporic communities—is an interesting area to explore, as well as a potential diaspora-grown transnational field for Chinese soft power generation overseas, as will be discussed in the following section with other future research agendas.

LOOKING FORWARD: PROSPECTS FOR FUTURE RESEARCH

There is much potential for future research, building upon this study and the work of other scholars, as well as within interrelated fields of study.

Methodologically, future research could pursue cross-national comparative studies using mixed methods of comparative historical, qualitative, and quantitative studies, to give rise to more nuanced explanations of typified soft power mechanisms. It would be important to interview informants before and after their exposure to the various soft power mediums, to capture how different channels of soft power and their mechanisms affect audience perceptions. Conceptually and analytically, the typologies could be further codified as cogent and relevant models with greater empirical evidence.

Substantively, the key findings about Chinese soft power paradoxes in South Korea and Japan invite scrutiny. In general, any country's soft power can be studied under a similar framework of incorporating and situating the interactive dual processes of the projector and its potential transnational audiences. In other words, the model of soft power developed in this book can be applied to other countries, as well as their cultural and media industries. Future studies on soft power via other soft power mediums at the local, trans-local, and global levels can be further investigated.

More broadly, there is need to examine how media digitalization in a new media landscape shapes China on one end, and its soft power and relations with other societies at the other end. The emergence and convergence of interactions between traditional and digital media are important steps, not only for media and industrial development, but also for soft power projection. The ways in which transnational audiences consume media through "connected viewing" (see Holt and Sanson 2014), in this regard, merit attention.

Consequences for the influx of the digital media in Sinophone and non-Sinophone cyberspaces are key to understanding diasporic communities in Asia and elsewhere, as emerging actors and the targets of Chinese soft power projection illustrate the "local embeddedness of the foreign" paradigm in a foreign nation-state. The proliferation of virtual communities for short and long-term foreign (im)migrants in Chinese cyberspaces have also presented a new actor that is engaging with and consuming the OTT market. Traditional media professionals and established circuits of media are not noticeably transformed, by comparison.

Manufacturing censorship in a networked authoritarian society is another inherent form of political stability, and cultural and national security. Along this line, there is much work to be done to unpack the facades and un/intended consequences of networked authoritarianism. In digital China, social networking services, social media, and microblogs, such as QQ, WeChat, and Weibo, play roles as online streaming platforms for traditional offline televisual products, as discussed in Chap. 7. They provide the space for potential information-sharing, and misinformation, while the Chinese government and public and private sectors concertedly leverage censorship for their own purposes. In doing so, China co-constructs "market development and regulatory approaches" (Zhao 2017). The tug-of-war between netizens and the Chinese state may also foment a dilemma for soft power fields at the transnational level. It is equally important to explore how the birth of "big data"—a new way of manufacturing information and content by size, speed, and type that is partially reinforced by China's Internet Plus policies—shapes new byproducts and forms of "misconduct" in Chinese cyberspace. Such phenomena steer the further economic development of China, yet have significant implications for the socio-cultural domains, and the paradoxes of China's soft power expansion.

Future research will need to address the increasing interconnectedness between offline and online media; traditional and digital platforms; local Chinese and Chinese diasporic communities; "China" and "foreign"; and local and global forces.

REFERENCES

Bandelj, Nina, and Frederick F. Wherry. 2011. *The Cultural Wealth of Nations*. Stanford: Stanford University Press.

Holt, Jennifer, and Kevin Sanson, eds. 2014. *Connected Viewing: Selling, Streaming and Sharing Media in the Digital Era*. London: Routledge.

Janssen, Susanne, and Marc Verboord. 2015. Cultural Mediators and Gatekeepers. In *International Encyclopedia of the Social & Behavioral Sciences*, ed. James D. Wright, 2nd ed., 440–446. Oxford: Elsevier.

Kohli, Atul. 2004. *State-Directed Development: Political Power and Industrialization in the Global Periphery*. Cambridge: Cambridge University Press.

Midgal, Joel S. 1988. *Strong Societies and Weak States: State-Society Relations and State Capabilities in the Third World*. Princeton: Princeton University Press.

———. 2001. *State in Society: Studying How States and Societies Transform and Constitute One Another*. Cambridge: Cambridge University Press.

Nye, Joseph S., Jr. 2004. *Soft Power: The Means to Success in World Politics*. New York: Public Affairs.

———. 2011. *The Future of Power*. New York: Public Affairs.

Shih, Shu-mei, Chien-hsin Tsai, and Brain Bernands, eds. 2013. *Sinophone Studies: A Critical Reader*. New York: Columbia University Press.

Wang, Jian. 2011a. *Soft Power in China: Public Diplomacy Through Communication*. New York: Palgrave Macmillan.

———. 2011b. Introduction: China's Search of Soft Power. In *Soft Power in China: Public Diplomacy Through Communication*, Palgrave Macmillan Series in Global Public Diplomacy, ed. Jian Wang, 1–18. New York: Palgrave Macmillan.

————. 2013. *Shaping China's Global Imagination: Branding Nations at the World Expo*. New York: Palgrave Macmillan.

Wherry, Frederick F. 2012. *The Culture of Markets*. Cambridge and Malden: Polity Press.

Zhao, Elaine Jing. 2017. The Bumpy Road Towards Network Convergence in China: The Case of Over-the-Top Streaming Services. *Global Media and China* 2 (1): 28–42.

CHAPTER 9

Postscript: Envisioning the Future of China's Soft Power

> Until now, I was fortunate not to be directly attacked by the Terminal High Altitude Area Defense (THAAD) and kept holding on. This week, one project has just been blown away. And *Hallyu* in China is being destroyed because of a Korean ajumma's greed... (November 28, 2016, *Facebook*, a Korean user)[1]

In July 2016, when I was in Shenzhen and Hong Kong doing additional fieldwork, the PRC's Minister of Foreign Affairs announced that, "South Korea abandoned our longtime relationship." This was a direct result of the Korean government's announcement that it will deploy Terminal High Altitude Area Defense, as known as THAAD, on the Korean peninsula. Nobody expects consequences to follow for South Korea. Nobody expects this conflict is going to be so long and difficult to resolve at all.

The above quote, from a Facebook message published by a South Korean film director in China, epitomizes the way in which THAAD has affected his project, and, more generally, sparked anti-Korean sentiment. He highlights how the military implications of THAAD not only affect geopolitics, but also influence media, cultural flows, and society in general: it illustrates an example of cultural politics in Asia. This brief comment reflects the continuous influence of THAAD on his film projects, and implies that other projects have already been impacted by THAAD. It also expresses his anger at the destruction of potential success, the effect of THAAD upon the Korean Wave as a whole, and the negative feelings he attributes to South Korea's then-President.

© The Author(s) 2018   191
C. S. Lee, *Soft Power Made in China*,
https://doi.org/10.1007/978-3-319-93115-9_9

Complicating matters further, the Chinese Minister's earlier statement about China-South Korea relations was not simply rhetoric. In early August of that year, I returned to Seoul to renew my Chinese visa. Although I was fortunate enough to acquire a one-year multiple entry visa, the Chinese government announced around this time that the visa regulation would be more stringently managed than before. Since then, the one-year multiple entry visa, which was conveniently accessible for Koreans, has been temporarily suspended. From that August, many Korean politicians and scholars' official visits to China were canceled. There was even a rumor circulating that the Chinese government asked Chinese citizens not to travel to South Korea.[2]

In the soft power realm, the concerts and fan meetings of some Korean celebrities and K-pop groups were even canceled. Korean and Chinese dramas starring Korean celebrities were either banned from both the television sphere and cyberspace, or about to be pulled from these platforms. The following title of one newspaper article, among similar others, illustrates these unintended consequences for South Korea: "China bans Korean dramas, movies, and variety shows 'in retaliation against THAAD deployment'" (Bhattacharjya 2016).[3]

This epitomizes the intimate connection between international and domestic politics. Conflicts of politics and international relations at the inter-state level translate into predicaments for diplomatic and scholarly exchanges, as well as many aspects of everyday life, including trade, people-to-people interaction, culture, and entertainment.

What's more and ironically notable is the Chinese state's actions in recent years. The PRC desperately seeks to develop and project its soft power across East Asia and other parts of the world. In political terms, this signals a hypocritical return to the recurring frame of "China as a Threat," rather than an "opportunity" or a "peacefully rising country."

How do we then understand this predicament? Unlike the unintended pathways to dilemmas captured in this book, this diplomatic dilemma is qualitatively different from that created by the Chinese state itself. An emerging global power under an authoritarian regime has been provoked to push another stakeholder—South Korea—in a "vengeful" act. From another angle, China's attempt to limit the reach of the "Korean Wave" in turn secures more space for Chinese soft power in other countries, and perhaps at home, as well. In recent years, Korea and its media have predominantly occupied creative spaces and captured audiences in China, Japan, Southeast Asia, and beyond. Perhaps China is clandestinely preparing to inherit this position.

NOTES

1. The Facebook user is one of my informants (CM37, Beijing, a South Korean media practitioner in Beijing) and he agreed to give me a consent of his Facebook message that can be used in this book.
2. Although the Foreign Ministry of the People's Republic of China did not publish an official statement on this matter, Chinese tourists through China's travel agencies were not recruited or visit South Korea less. According to a Chinese national who works for Incheon airport, group tourists from China were hardly seen at the airport in this post-THAAD era, but Chinese individual tourists are consistently coming to South Korea (CH1, Interview, October 26, 2017, Incheon). This is in line with many newspaper reports and tourism statistics by Korea Tourism Organization (see Korea Herald 2017).
3. Please see Appendix C (Table C.1) for a detailed list of programs and celebrities were influenced by the recurring incident.

REFERENCES

Bhattacharjya, Samhati. 2016. China Bans Korean Drama, Movies, and Variety Shows 'in Retaliation Against THAAD Deployment.' *International Business Times*, November 21. Accessed November 22, 2016. http://www.ibtimes.sg/china-bans-korean-drama-movies-variety-shows-retaliation-against-thaad-deployment-4868.

Korea Herald. 2017. Chinese Visitors Number Drops for 6th Straight Month Amid THAAD Row. September 22. Accessed October 22, 2017. http://www.koreaherald.com/view.php?ud=20170922000626&ACE_SEARCH=1.

GLOSSARY OF FOREIGN TERMS

CHINESE TERMS

In Chinese	Pinyin	English translation
部	*bu*	Season
产业化	*chanyehua*	Industrialization
春节联欢会	*Chunjie lianhuanwanhui*	(CCTV program) New Year's Gala (Spring Festival Gala)
传播力量	*chuanbo liliang*	Communication capacity
传播能力	*chuanbo nengli*	Communication capacity
传记*	*chuanji*	Biography
传奇*	*chuanqi*	Legendary
创新能力	*chuangxin nengli*	Innovative and communicative influence/capacity
创造力	*chuangzaoli*	Creativity
当代*	*dangdai*	Contemporary
电视剧	*dianshiju*	TV series/drama
电影	*dianying*	Films
都市*	*dushi*	Urban
改革开放	*gaige kaifang*	Open reform
革命*	*geming*	Revolution
公共外交	*gonggongwaijiao*	Public diplomacy
宫廷*	*gongting*	Palace
古代*	*gudai*	Before 1911
古典小说	*gudian xiaoshuo*	Traditional Chinese novels

(continued)

© The Author(s) 2018   195
C. S. Lee, *Soft Power Made in China*,
https://doi.org/10.1007/978-3-319-93115-9

(continued)

In Chinese	Pinyin	English translation
古装*	*guzhuang*	Costume
国际影响力	*guoji yingxiangli*	International influence (of China)
和平崛起	*heping jueqi*	Peaceful rise
华人	*huaren*	(Ethnic) Chinese
集	*ji*	Episode
近代*	*Jindai*	1911–1949
禁区	*jinqu*	Forbidden areas
功夫	*gongfu*	Martial arts, Kungfu or Kung Fu
军旅*	*junlv*	Military
科幻*	*kehuan*	Science fiction
历史*	*lishi*	History
民族	*minzu*	Ethnic group
民族复兴	*minzu fuxing*	Revival of the Chinese people
农村*	*nongcun*	Village
偶像剧	*ouxiangju*	(Taiwanese) trendy dramas
软实力	*ruanshili*	Soft power
商业化	*shangyehua*	Commercialization
商业片	*shangyepian*	Commercialized products or blockbusters
涉案*	*shean*	Law
社会主义文化强国	*Shehuizhuyi wenhua qiangguo*	A "socialist" cultural power; cultural superpower status with socialism
试点	*shidian*	A "testing point", a pilot/experiment project
其他*	*qita*	Other
青少*	*qingshao*	Youth
网络文化	*wangluo wenhua*	Internet culture
文化安全	*wenhua anquan*	Cultural security
文化创意产业	*wenhua chuangyichanye*	Cultural creative industries
文化力	*wenhuali*	Cultural power
文化经济	*wenhua jingji*	Cultural economy
文化控制	*wenhua kongzhi*	Cultural control
文化强国	*wenhua qiangguo*	Cultural superpower
文化软实力	*wenhua ruanshili*	Cultural soft power
文化市场	*wenhua shichang*	Cultural market
文化外交	*wenhua waijiao*	Cultural diplomacy
文化影响力	*wenhua yingxiangli*	Cultural influence
文化综合国力	*wenhua zongheguoli*	Cultural comprehensive power
武打*	*wuda*	Martial arts
武侠	*wuxia*	*Kungfu*, martial arts
武侠小说	*wuxia xiaoshuo*	Martial arts novels
现代*	*xiandai*	Modern
辛亥革命	*Xinhai geming*	*Xinhai* Revolution
小康社会	*xiaokang shehui*	A well-off society
演出	*yanchu*	Choreography

(*continued*)

(continued)

In Chinese	Pinyin	English translation
引进来	yinjinlai	Bringing in; inward flow
影像	yingxiang	Audio-visual products
影响力	yingxiangli	Influence
艺术品	yishupin	Artifacts
娱乐	yule	Entertainment
战争*	zhanzheng	War
制片	zhipian	Producer
重大*	zhongda	Important
中华民族	Zhonghua minzu	Chinese (people)
中华文化	Zhonghua wenhua	Chinese culture
中共中央办公室	Zhonggong zhongyang bangongshi	The General Office of the Communist Party of China
中国梦	Zhongguomeng	Chinese dream
中国模式	Zhongguo moshi	Chinese economic developmental model; China model
走出去	zouchuqu	Going global/out; outward flow
走向市场	zouxiang shichang	Go to the market; marketization
综合国力	zongheguoli	Comprehensive national power

Note: Terms with an * (asterisk) indicate that they appear in the SAPPRFT's guideline regarding Chinese TV series. Thus, they are customized to such setting

Japanese Terms

In Japanese	Romanization	English translation
BS	Broadcasting Satellite (BS)	
武侠ドラマ	Bukyō dorama	Martial arts (Kungfu) drama
CS	Communications Satellite (CS)	
放送	Hōsō	Broadcasting
放送大学	Hōsō daigaku	Broadcasting University
放送権	Hōsōken	Broadcasting rights
ジャッキー・チェン劇場	Jakkī Chen gekijō	Jackie Chan Theater
感情的	Kanjouteki	Being easily sentimental/emotionally stirred
関東	Kantō	Honshu area of Japan
華流	Karyū	Chinese wave
日本放送協会	Nippon Hōsō Kyōkai	NHK

(continued)

(continued)

In Japanese	Romanization	English translation
日中韓歴史ドラマ・映画	Nitchūkan rekishi dorama・eiga	Japan-China-Korea Historical Drama・Film
新聞	*shimbun*	Newspaper
朱元璋	Shu Genshō	Zhu Yuanzhang
失われた20年	wushinarareta 20 nen	The two lost decades

Korean Terms

In Korean	Romanization	English translation
냄비근성	*naembi geunsong*	Easily stirred and easy to forget
단오절	*danoje*	Duan Wu festival
대체재	*dachaejae*	Replacement; substitute
무협	*Muhyeop*	Martial arts
방송	*bangsong*	Broadcasting
방송채널사업자	*Bangsong chaeneol saeopja*	Program Providers
삼고초려	*samgochoryeo*	After several attempts to … finally…
설날특선영화	*seolnal tekseon yeonghwa*	Special movies for holidays
소장가치	*sojang gachi*	Goods of value
위성방송	*Wiseong bangsong*	Satellite TV
제작피디	*jejak pidi*	Production producers
주말명화	*jumal myeonghwa*	Weekly movies
중개인	*junggaein*	An agent; a broker
중국	*jungguk*	China; Chinese
중국인	*Junggukin*	Chinese people
중류	*Jungryu* (中流, *zhongliu*)	Chinese wave
지상파	*Jisangpa*	Terrestrial TV
지상파 계열 PP 채널	*Jisangpa gyeyeol pp chaeneol*	PP channels affiliated with terrestrial TV
추석	*chuseok*	Thanksgiving day
판권	*pangwon*	Copyrights
한류	*Hallyu* (韩流)	Korean wave
한류	*Hanryu* (汉流)	Chinese wave
해외판권팀	*haeoe pangwon team*	Overseas copyright teams
화류	*Hwaryu* (华流)	Chinese wave (*Karyū* in Japanese)

APPENDICES

APPENDIX A: INTERVIEWS CONDUCTED DURING THE FIELD RESEARCH (BY FIELD SITE)

Table A.1   China: interviewees

Code	Place	Date	Type
CM1	Beijing	December 5, 2011; June 15, 2012	Film production company
CM2	Beijing	December 5, 2011; August 1, 2013; July 21, 2016	Film director
CM3	Beijing	February 22, 2012; August 3, 2013	Production manager
CM4	Shanghai	February 6, 2012	Researcher
CM5	Shanghai	February 7, 2012	TV producer
CM6	Shanghai	February 7, 2012	Professor (International communication)
CM7	Shanghai	February 7, 2012	Media practitioner
CM8	Shanghai	February 7, 2012	Media practitioner
CM9	Shanghai	February 8, 2012	Professor (Sociology)
CM10	Shanghai	February 8, 2012	TV Producer
CM11	Shanghai	February 9, 2012	Professor (Media studies)
CM12	Shanghai	February 9, 2012	Professor (Chinese studies)
CM13	Shanghai	February 9, 2012	Public servant
CM14	Beijing	February 19, 2012	Media practitioner at a broadcasting station
CM15	Beijing	February 20, 2012	Researcher
CM16	Beijing	February 21, 2012	Reporter (Xinhua news agency)

(*continued*)

© The Author(s) 2018
C. S. Lee, *Soft Power Made in China*,
https://doi.org/10.1007/978-3-319-93115-9

Table A.1 (continued)

Code	Place	Date	Type
CM17	Beijing	February 23, 2012	Professor (Communication studies)
CM18	Shenzhen	February 26, 2012	Media practitioner
CM19	Shenzhen	February 27, 2012	Media practitioner
CM20	Shenzhen	February 28, 2012	Professor (Communication studies)
CM21	Shenzhen	February 28, 2012	Distribution manager
CM22	Shenzhen	February 28, 2012	Distribution manager
CM23	Shenzhen	February 28, 2012	Media practitioner at a broadcasting station in Shenzhen
CM24	Shenzhen	February 28, 2012	Reporter (*Nanhua zaobao*)
CM25	Shenzhen	February 29, 2012	Professor (International communication)
CM26	Beijing	March 5, 2012	Beijing Film Academy graduate
CM27	Shenzhen	June 14, 2012	Reporter
CM28	Shenzhen	June 14, 2012	Media practitioner
CM29	Hong Kong	June 16, 2012	Media practitioner
CM30	Hong Kong	June 17, 2012	Reporter (Xinhua news agency)
CM31	Hong Kong	June 18, 2012	Media practitioner
CM32	Shenzhen	June 19, 2012	Media practitioner
CM33	Shenzhen	June 19, 2012; July 21, 2016	Media practitioner
CM34	Shanghai	July 15, 2012	Media practitioner
CM35	Beijing	October 13, 2012; August 4, 2013	Professor (Communication studies)
CM36	Beijing	October 13, 2012; August 4, 2013	Research fellow (Communication studies)
CM37	Beijing	August 3, 2014; July 21, 2016	Media practitioner
CM38	Beijing	September 25, 2015	Media practitioner

Interviews in South Korea

Table A.2   South Korea: audiences

Code	Date	Gender	Age	Education level	Occupation/sector
KV1	November 19, 2011	Female	20s	University graduated	Educational sector
KV2	November 27, 2011	Female	20s	University graduated	International organization
KV3	November 27, 2011	Male	20s	University graduated	Bio industry
KV4	November 28, 2011	Female	20s	University graduated	Media company
KV5	November 29, 2011	Female	20s	Graduate student (MA)	Teacher
KV6	November 29, 2011	Female	20s	Graduate student (MA)	Teacher
KV7	November 29, 2011	Female	30s	Graduate student (MA)	Teacher
KV8	November 29, 2011	Female	30s	Graduate student (MA)	Teacher
KV9	November 30, 2011	Female	20s	University graduated	Fashion industry
KV10	December 5, 2011	Female	20s	University graduated	Law firm
KV11	December 8, 2011	Female	20s	University student	University student
KV12	December 8, 2011	Male	20s	University student	University student
KV13	December 8, 2011	Female	20s	University student	University student
KV14	December 8, 2011	Female	20s	University student	University student
KV15	December 9, 2011	Female	20s	University student	University student
KV16	December 9, 2011	Male	20s	University student	University student
KV17	December 9, 2011	Female	20s	University student	University student
KV18	December 9, 2011	Female	20s	University student	University student
KV19	December 10, 2011	Female	20s	University student	University student
KV20	December 11, 2011	Female	20s	University student	University student

(continued)

Table A.2 (continued)

Code	Date	Gender	Age	Education level	Occupation/sector
KV21	December 11, 2011	Female	20s	University student	University student
KV22	December 13, 2011	Female	20s	University student	University student
KV23	December 13, 2011	Female	20s	University student	University student
KV24	December 13, 2011	Female	20s	University student	University student
KV25	December 15, 2011	Male	20s	University student	University student
KV26	December 15, 2011	Male	20s	University student	University student
KV27	December 15, 2011	Female	20s	University student	University student
KV28	December 15, 2011	Male	20s	University student	University student
KV29	December 16, 2011	Female	20s	University student	University student
KV30	December 16, 2011	Female	20s	University student	University student
KV31	December 16, 2011	Male	20s	University student	University student
KV32	December 16, 2011	Male	20s	University student	University student
KV33	December 17, 2011	Female	40s	University graduated	Housewife
KV34	December 17, 2011	Male	20s	University student	University student
KV35	December 19, 2011	Female	20s	University student	University student
KV36	December 19, 2011	Female	20s	University student	University student
KV37	December 20, 2011	Female	20s	University student	University student
KV38	December 21, 2011	Female	20s	University graduated	Graduate student (MA)
KV39	December 21, 2011	Female	20s	University graduated	Graduate student (MA)
KV40	December 21, 2011	Female	20s	University graduated	Graduate student (MA)
KV41	December 21, 2011	Female	20s	University graduated	Graduate student (MA)

(continued)

Table A.2   (continued)

Code	Date	Gender	Age	Education level	Occupation/sector
KV42	December 21, 2011	Female	20s	University graduated	Graduate student (MA)
KV43	December 24, 2011	Male	20s	University student	University student
KV44	December 27, 2011	Male	30s	University graduated	Photographer
KV45	January 2, 2012	Female	20s	University student	University student
KV46	January 10, 2012	Male	30s	University graduated	Civil servant
KV47	January 10, 2012	Female	30s	University graduated	Company
KV48	January 11, 2012	Female	20s	University graduated	Office worker
KV49	January 24, 2012	Male	30s	University graduated	Working
KV50	January 26, 2012	Female	20s	University graduated	Civil servant
KV51	February 4, 2012	Female	30s	University graduated	Teacher
KV52	February 4, 2012	Female	30s	University graduated	Trade company
KV53	February 5, 2012	Female	30s	University graduated	Banker
KV54	February 16, 2012	Male	20s	University graduated	Trade company
KV55	February 16, 2012	Female	20s	University graduated	Banker
KV56	February 16, 2012	Female	20s	University student	University student
KV57	February 16, 2012	Male	20s	University student	University student
KV58	March 17, 2012	Male	20s	University student	University student
KV59	June 5, 2012	Female	20s	University graduated	Working
KV60	June 5, 2012	Male	20s	University student	University student
KV61	June 5, 2012	Male	20s	University student	University student
KV62	June 6, 2012	Male	20s	University student	University student
KV63	June 7, 2012	Female	20s	University student	University student
KV64	June 7, 2012	Female	20s	University student	University student
KV65	June 7, 2012	Female	20s	University student	University student
KV66	June 9, 2012	Female	20s	University student	University student
KV67	June 9, 2012	Male	20s	University student	University student

(*continued*)

Table A.2 (continued)

Code	Date	Gender	Age	Education level	Occupation/sector
KV68	June 26, 2012	Male	20s	University student	University student
KV69	June 26, 2012	Female	20s	University student	University student
KV70	June 26, 2012	Male	20s	University student	University student
KV71	June 28, 2012	Female	20s	University student	University student
KV72	June 28, 2012	Female	20s	University student	University student
KV73	June 29, 2012	Female	20s	University student	University student
KV74	June 29, 2012	Male	20s	University student	University student
KV75	June 30, 2012	Female	20s	University student	University student
KV76	June 30, 2012	Female	20s	University student	University student
KV77	July 2, 2012	Male	20s	University student	University student
KV78	July 2, 2012	Female	20s	University student	University student
KV79	July 3, 2012	Female	20s	University student	University student
KV80	July 3, 2012	Female	20s	University student	University student
KV81	July 4, 2012	Female	30s	University graduated	Office worker
KV82	July 10, 2012	Male	30s	MA	Graduate student (PhD)
KV83	July 20, 2012	Female	20s	MA	Graduate student (PhD)
KV84	February 6, 2013	Female	20s	University student	University student
KV85	February 24, 2013	Female	20s	University graduated	Designer
KV86	March 18, 2013	Male	30s	University graduated	Programmer
KV87	March 21, 2013	Male	20s	University graduated	Banker
KV88	November 29, 2013	Female	30s	PhD	University lecturer
CH1	October 26, 2017	Male	20s	University student	Part-time worker at Incheon airport

Table A.3 South Korea: media practitioners

Code	Place	Date	Type
KM1	Seoul	December 20, 2011; April 2, 2017	Freelance producer (China, Hong Kong, Taiwan, South Korea)
KM2	Seoul	December 22, 2011	Media company
KM3	Seoul	January 4, 2012	Reporter (*Kyōdō Tsūshinsha* (Kyodo News))
KM4	Seoul	January 19, 2012	TV Producer (KBS Media)
KM5	Ilsan	January 25, 2012	TV Producer (MBC)
KM6	Seoul	January 25, 2012	Distribution manager (China, Hong Kong, Taiwan, South Korea)
KM7	Seoul	January 26, 2012	Distribution manager at a broadcasting company
KM8	Seoul	March 15, 2012	Media practitioner at a broadcasting station
KM9	Seoul	March 17, 2012	Media practitioner at a broadcasting station (Junghwa TV)
KM10	Seoul	March 18, 2012	Distribution manager
KM11	Seoul	March 20, 2012	TV producer (MBC)
KM12	Ilsan	June 26, 2012	Media practitioner at a broadcasting station
KM13	Seoul	June 26, 2012	TV Producer (SBS)
KM14	Seoul	June 27, 2012	TV Producer (KBS)
KM15	Seoul	October 27, 2014	Media practitioner at a broadcasting station
KM16	Seoul	April 19, 2015	TV Producer (CJ E&M)
KM17	Seoul	January 7, 2016	TV Producer (MBC)

Interviews in Japan

Table A.4 Japan: audiences

Code	Date	Gender	Age	Education level	Occupation
JV1	February 13, 2012	Male	20s	University student	University student
JV2	February 14, 2012	Male	70s	High school graduated	Retried
JV3	February 14, 2012	Female	50s	High school graduated	Housewife
JV4	February 14, 2012	Female	50s	High school graduated	Housewife
JV5	February 14, 2012	Female	30s	High school graduated	Kindergarten teacher
JV6	February 14, 2012	Male	30s	University student	Teacher

Table A.4   (continued)

Code	Date	Gender	Age	Education level	Occupation
JV7	February 14, 2012	Male	60s	University graduated	Office worker
JV8	February 14, 2012	Female	50s	University student	University student
JV9	February 14, 2012	Male	20s	MA	Graduate student (PhD)
JV10	February 13, 2012	Male	20s	University student	University student
JV11	March 27, 2012	Female	20s	University student	University student
JV12	March 28, 2012	Male	30s	MA	Graduate student (PhD)
JV13	April 4, 2012	Male	20s	University student	University student
JV14	April 8, 2012	Female	40s	PhD	Civil servant
JV15	April 9, 2012	Male	30s	University graduated	Media company
JV16	April 13, 2012	Female	30s	MA	Service industry
JV17	April 13, 2012	Female	30s	MA	Japan International Cooperation Agency
JV18	April 13, 2012	Female	30s	MA	Teacher
JV19	April 13, 2012	Female	30s	MA	Research fellow
JV20	April 16, 2012	Female	30s	University graduated	Banker
JV21	April 16, 2012	Female	30s	University graduated	Office worker
JV22	April 16, 2012	Female	50s	High school graduated	Housewife
JV23	April 17, 2012	Female	20s	MA	Graduate student (PhD)
JV24	April 17, 2012	Female	20s	University student	University student
JV25	April 17, 2012	Female	20s	University student	University student
JV26	April 17, 2012	Female	20s	University student	University student
JV27	April 17, 2012	Female	20s	University student	University student
JV28	April 17, 2012	Female	20s	University student	University student
JV29	April 17, 2012	Female	20s	University student	University student
JV30	April 18, 2012	Male	20s	University graduated	Graduate student (MA)
JV31	April 21, 2012	Female	30s	University graduated	Civil servant
JV32	April 21, 2012	Male	30s	MA	Graduate student (PhD)
JV33	April 22, 2012	Male	20s	University graduated	Pharmaceutical company
JV34	April 22, 2012	Male	20s	University graduated	Transport company

(*continued*)

Table A.4   (continued)

Code	Date	Gender	Age	Education level	Occupation
JV35	April 23, 2012	Female	20s	University student	University student
JV36	April 23, 2012	Female	20s	University student	University student
JV37	April 23, 2012	Female	20s	University student	University student
JV38	April 23, 2012	Female	20s	University student	University student
JV39	April 24, 2012	Female	30s	University graduated	Flight attendant
JV40	April 24, 2012	Male	30s	University graduated	Trading company
JV41	April 25, 2012	Female	30s	University graduated	Banker
JV42	April 25, 2012	Male	20s	University graduated	Graduate student (MA)
JV43	April 27, 2012	Male	20s	University graduated	Graduate student (MA)
JV44	April 27, 2012	Female	30s	University graduated	Banker
JV45	April 27, 2012	Female	30s	University graduated	Banker
JV46	May 7, 2012	Male	20s	MA	Graduate student (PhD)
JV47	May 7, 2012	Female	40s	MA	Graduate student (PhD)
JV48	May 7, 2012	Male	20s	MA	Graduate student (PhD)
JV49	May 7, 2012	Male	60s	University graduated	Retired
JV50	May 7, 2012	Female	60s	High school graduated	Housewife
JV51	May 13, 2012	Female	30s	University graduated	Reporter
JV52	May 13, 2012	Male	30s	PhD	Faculty member
JV53	May 15, 2012	Male	20s	University graduated	Graduate student (MA)
JV54	May 15, 2012	Male	20s	University graduated	Graduate student (MA)
JV55	May 16, 2012	Female	30s	University graduated	Graduate student (MA)
JV56	May 16, 2012	Male	20s	University graduated	Graduate student (MA)
JV57	May 24, 2012	Male	30s	MA	Graduate student (PhD)
JV58	May 24, 2012	Female	20s	University graduated	Graduate student (MA)
JV59	May 24, 2012	Male	30s	University graduated	Graduate student (MA)

Table A.5   Japan: media practitioners

Code	Place	Date	Type
JM1	Tokyo; Singapore	April 9, 2012; August 27, 2013	Freelancer (Producer) (Taiwan, Japan)
JM2	Tokyo	April 13, 2012	Distribution manager
JM3	Tokyo	April 15, 2012	Media practitioner
JM4	Tokyo	May 8, 2012	Media practitioner
JM5	Tokyo	May 10, 2012	Distribution manager
JM6	Tokyo	May 10, 2012	A TV station
JM7	Tokyo	May 11, 2012	Government agency
JM8	Tokyo	May 14, 2012	Professor (Media studies)
JM9	Tokyo	May 15, 2012	Production
JM10	Tokyo	May 16, 2012	TV Producer
JM11	Tokyo	May 16, 2012	Media practitioner at a broadcasting station
JM12	Tokyo	May 18, 2012	Professor (Media studies)
JM13	Tokyo	May 22, 2012	TV Producer
JM14	Tokyo	May 22, 2012	Media practitioner
JM15	Tokyo	October 29, 2015	Media practitioner

APPENDIX B

Table B.1 Dataset for Chap. 3

First appeared on Korean TV	Title in English	Title in Korean	Title in Chinese	Originally from	Number of episode	Genre**	Broadcasted at (Korean TV station)
2001	The Long March	홍군대장정	红军长征	CCTV1	24	Premodern	AsiaN
2007	Butterfly Lovers	나비지애	梁山伯与祝英台	Guangzhou TV	41	Fantasy	Junghwa
2008	Tang Paradise	양귀비 의 대당부용원	大唐芙蓉园	CCTV8	30	Ancient (Tang)***	Junghwa
2009	The Qin Empire	대진제국	大秦帝国	CCTV	51	Ancient (Qin)***	Junghwa
2009	The Proud Twins	절대쌍교	小鱼儿与花无缺	Taiwan CTV		Martial arts	Ching
2009	The Spirit of the Sword	완화세검록	浣花洗剑录	Taiwan CTV	40	Martial arts	Ching
2009	Zhen Guan Chang Ge	정관장가	贞观长歌	CCTV1	82	Ancient (Tang)***	Ching
2009	Legend of the Condor Heroes	사조영웅전	射雕英雄傳	Xiamen TV	50	Martial arts	Ching
2009	Rose Martial World	메괴강호	玫瑰江湖	Guangdong TV	30	Ancient (Qing)***	Ching
2009	Records of the Grand Historian of China	한무제	汉武大帝	CCTV1	58	Ancient (Han)***	AsiaN
2010	Scheme of the Beauty (Beauty's Rival in Palace)	미인심계	美人心计	Shanghai TV	40	Ancient (Han)***	Junghwa

(continued)

Table B.1 (continued)

First appeared on Korean TV	Title in English	Title in Korean	Title in Chinese	Originally from	Number of episode	Genre**	Broadcasted at (Korean TV station)
2010	Journey to the West	신서유기	新西游记	Zhejiang TV	52	Fantasy	Junghwa
2010	The Myth	신화	神化	CCTV8	50	Ancient (Qin)***	Junghwa
2010	Confucius	공자춘추	孔子春秋	Hunan TV	38	Biography	Ching
2010	The Legend of Yang Guifei	양귀비비사	杨贵妃秘史	Hunan TV	49	Ancieyt (Tang)***	Ching
2010	Yong Zheng Dynasty	옹정황제	雍正王朝	CCTV	44	Ancient (Qing)***	AsiaN
2010	The Ultimate Master of War	손자병법	兵圣	CCTV	41	Biography	AsiaN
2010	The Vigilantes in Masks	괴협일지매	怪侠一枝梅	Jiangsu TV	36	Martial arts	AsiaN
2010	The Dream Of Red Mansions	홍루몽	红楼梦	Qingdao TV	50	Ancient (Qing)***	AsiaN
2011	Pretty Maid	미인애환	大丫鬟	Zhejiang TV	35	Ancient (Qing)***	Junghwa
2011	Unruly Qiao (Royal Johnson Physician)	따아오만아이	皇家娇医	CTV	38	Martial arts	Junghwa
2011	Jade Palace Lock Heart	궁쇄심옥	宫锁心玉	Hunan TV	39	Ancient (Qing)***	Junghwa
2011	The Last Night of Madam Chin	1948상하이, 금대반	金大班 (的 最后一夜)	Zhejiang TV	36	Modern	Junghwa
2011	Confucius	공자	孔子	CCTV	35	Biography	Junghwa
2011	Iron Masked Singer	장미저택	鐵面歌女	Shanxi TV	30	Premodern	Junghwa
2011	Butterfly and Sword	신유성호접검	新流星蝴蝶剑	CCTV	30	Martial arts	Junghwa
2011	The Romance Of Book & Sword	서검은구록	書劍恩仇錄	Hong Kong ATV	40	Martial arts	Junghwa

Year	English Title	Korean	Chinese	Channel	No.	Period/Genre	Broadcaster
2011	The Legend of Fong Sai-Yuk	방세옥	盖世英雄方世玉	CCTV		Martial arts	Junghwa
2011	Shaolin Temple Legend of the Hero	신소림사3	少林寺传奇3	CCTV8	60	Martial arts	Junghwa
2011	A Terracotta Warrior	진시황의 진용	古今大战秦俑情	CCTV	40	Ancient (Qin)***	Junghwa
2011	Fight and Love with a Terracotta Warrior (Ancient Terracotta Warrior)	천당수	天堂秀	CCTV	30	Contemporary	Junghwa
2011	Song of the Rising Wild	대풍가	大风歌	CCTV8	42	Ancient (Han)***	Junghwa
2011	Great General Han Xin	천하의 명장 한신	大将军韩信	N.A.	36	Ancient (Qin)***	Ching
2011	Painted Skin	화피	画皮	TVS4	34	Fantasy	Ching
2011	Treading on Thin Ice	보보경심	步步惊心	SBS	40	Timeslip	Ching
2011	Empresses in the Palace	옹정황제의 여인	后宫甄嬛传	BTV	38	Ancient (Qing)***	Ching
2011	Twin of Brothers	대당쌍룡전	大唐双龙传之长生诀	CCTV1	42	Ancient (Tang)***	Ching
2011	(New) My Fair Princess (Princess Pearl)	신환주격격	新还珠格格	Hunan TV	98	Ancient (Qing)***	AsiaN
2011	South Shaolin Temple*	남소림사	南少林荡倭英豪	Jiangsu TV	48	Martial arts	AsiaN
2012	The Kitchen	음식남녀	后厨	Dragon TV	32	Modern	Junghwa
2012	Beauty World	미인천하	唐宫美人天下	Anhui TV	35	Ancient (Tang)***	Junghwa
2012	Mystery in the Palace	심궁비사	深宫谍影	Hunan TV	97	Ancient (Qing)***	Junghwa
2012	Hong Kong Jade	신의천도룡기	新倚天屠龙记	Wenzhou News Channel	40	Martial arts	Junghwa

(continued)

Table B.1 (continued)

First appeared on Korean TV	Title in English	Title in Korean	Title in Chinese	Originally from	Number of episode	Genre**	Broadcasted at (Korean TV station)
2012	The Weaver	천애직녀도	天涯織女	Nanning News Channel	36	Fantasy	Junghwa
2012	The Glamorous Imperial Concubine	경세황비	傾世皇妃	Hunan TV	42	Ancient***	Junghwa
2012	A Weaver on the Horizon	의피천하	衣被天下	Taiwan CTV	36	Ancient (Song)***	Junghwa
2012	Chinese Detective	형명사야	刑名師爷	Taiwan CTV	30	Ancient (Ming)***	Junghwa
2012	The Emperor's Harem	후궁의 남자	后宫	Zhejiang TV	46	Ancient (Ming)***	Junghwa
2012	The Qin Empire 2	대진제국2	大秦帝国之纵横	CCTV1	51	Ancient (Qin)***	Junghwa
2012	Seven Variant Wu Yi Human Way	칠협오의	七俠五义人间道	Taiwan CTV	38	Martial arts	Ching
2012	Xiao Kongkong*	똥자스님! 소공공	聪明小空空	CCTV8	49	Martial arts	Ching
2012	Bu An	수사의신 이순풍	卜案	Shanghai TV	26	Martial arts	Ching
2012	Love Actually	사랑의 레시피	爱的蜜方	Hunan TV	30	Contemporary	Ching
2012	Love Amongst War	설평귀와 왕보천의 이런사랑	薛平贵与王宝钏	Jiangsu TV	48	Ancient (Tang)***	Ching
2012	Secret History of Princess Taiping	태평공주 비사	太平公主秘史	Hunan TV	45	Ancient (Tang)***	Ching
2012	Desperate Love	황릉비련	傾城绝恋	Henan TV	41	Ancient (Qing)***	Ching

2012	Judgment of Hong Wu	세상을 품진 거인! 주원장	洪武大案	Hebei TV	35	Ancient (Ming)***	Ching
2012	The Water Margin, the Outlaws of the Marsh	수호지	水浒传	CCTV	43	Martial arts	AsiaN
2012	Chu supremacy	초한쟁웅	楚汉争雄	Hunan TV	10	Ancient (Chu and Han)***	AsiaN
2012	Sui Tang Heroes	수당영웅	隋唐英雄传	Hunan TV	40	Ancient (Sui and Tang)***	AsiaN
2012	Three Kingdoms	삼국지	三国	CCTV	95	Ancient (Sanguo)***	AsiaN
2013	Heroes in sui and tang Dynasties	수당연의	隋唐演义	Dragon TV	62	Ancient (Tang)***	Junghwa
2013	The Demi-Gods and Semi-Devils	천룡팔부	天龙八部	Hunan TV	38	Martial arts	Junghwa
2013	The Legendary Swordsman	소오강호	笑傲江湖	TVB	40	Ancient (Han)***	Junghwa
2013	The King's woman	왕의 여인	王的女人	Jiangsu TV	32	Ancient (Chuhan)***	Junghwa
2013	Biography Of San Tsu	손자대전	孙子大传	CCTV	35	Ancient***	Junghwa
2013	Beauty without tears	산하련	美人无泪	Jiangsu TV	38	Ancient (Qing)***	Junghwa
2013	Turbulence of the Mu Clan (The Mu Saga)	목부풍운	木府风云	CCTV8	40	Historical subfield***	Junghwa
2013	Legend of Goddess Luo	삼국의 여인	新洛神	Jiangsu TV	65	Historical subfield***	Ching
2013	Women of the Tang Dynasty	여인천하	唐宫燕	Hunan Satellite TV	46	Ancient (Tang)***	Ching
2013	The Legend of Kublai Khan (Legend of Yuan Empire)	징기즈칸의 후예	建元风云	Hunan Satellite TV	55	Ancient (Yuan)***	Ching

(continued)

Table B.1 (continued)

First appeared on Korean TV	Title in English	Title in Korean	Title in Chinese	Originally from	Number of episode	Genre**	Broadcasted at (Korean TV station)
2013	The Empire Warrior	진룡황제	王者清風	Dongnan TV	38	Ancient (Qing)***	Ching
2013	King Lanling	난릉왕	兰陵王	Dragon TV	46	Ancient (Beiji)***	Ching
2013	Yangming Wang	철한의 계보 왕양명	王阳明	Guiyang TV	38	Ancient (Ming)***	Ching
2013	Prince of Lan Ling	난릉왕	兰陵王	Dragon TV		Ancient (Weijin Nanbeichao)***	AsiaN
2013	Swordsman	소오강호2013	笑傲江湖	Hunan TV	42	Martial arts	AsiaN
2013	New Detective	DBI특수사건전담반	新神探联盟	CCTV1	35	1940s	AsiaN
2013	Journey to the West	장기종의 서유기	张纪中西游记	TVS4	60	Martial arts	AsiaN
2014	Palace 3: The Lost Daughter	궁쇄연성	宫锁连城	Hunan TV	63	Ancient (Qing)***	Junghwa
2014	Jin Maoxiang*	가상의 길	金茂祥	CCTV	43	Ancient (Qing)***	Ching
2014	Assassinator Jingke	영웅	荆轲传奇	CCTV8	38	Ancient (Chunqiu)***	Ching
2014	The Sound of Desert	대막요 (풍중기연)	风中奇缘	Hunan TV	35	Ancient (Nanchao)***	Ching
2014	The Rudimentary Sun of Red Wall and Green Tile*	제국의 눈물	红墙绿瓦之残阳 (宫锁秘史)	N.A.	30	Ancient (Qing)***	Ching
2014	The Return of Condor Heroes	신조협려	神鵰俠侶	Hunan TV	52	Ancient (Song)***	Ching

Year	Title	Korean title	Chinese title	TV station	No.	Genre	Distributor
2014	*Step by Step Surprise*	보보경심2 (보보경정)	步步惊情	Zhejiang TV	41	Timeslip	Ching
2014	*Perfect Couple*	금옥량연	金玉良緣	Jiangsu TV	45	Historical subfiled***	AsiaN
2014	*The Mystery of Emperor Qian Long*	건륭전기	钱塘传奇	HBTV	48	Ancient (Qing)***	AsiaN
2014	*The Great Protector*	표문, 지켜야 할 것	镖门	Shenzhen Satellite TV	38	Martial arts	AsiaN
2015	*The Disguiser*	위장자: 감춰진 신분	伪装者	Hunan TV	48	Anti-Japanese	Junghwa
2015	*Nirvana in Fire*	랑야방: 권력의 기록	琅琊榜	BTV	54	Martial arts; Historical***; Political subfiled	Junghwa
2015	*Esoterica of Qing Dynasty*	풍운의 대가문 지수의 신	乾隆秘史	iQiyi	45	Ancient (Qing)***	Ching
2015	*Biography of Li Bing* *	이빙 전기	李冰传奇	N.A.		Ancient (Qin)***	Ching
2015	*Zhu Yuanzhuang and Liu Baiwen* *	주원장과 유백온	神机妙算刘伯温	BTV	40	Ancient (Ming)***	Ching
2015	*The Merchants of Qing Dynasty*	대청염상	大清盐商	CCTV8	34	Ancient (Qing)***	Ching
2015	*The Last Emperor Legend*	마지막 황제 (말대황제)	末代皇帝传奇	Wuhan TV	60	Ancient (Qing)***	Ching
2015	*The Patriot Fei Yue*	정충악비	精忠岳飞	Anhui TV	69	Ancient (Song)***	Ching
2016	*The Empress of China*	무미낭전기	武媚娘传奇	Hunan Satellite TV	96	Ancient (Tang)***	Junghwa
2016	*New Shadow Heroes*	신평종협영	新萍踪侠影	CCTV	37	Martial arts	Junghwa
2016	*The Qin Empire 3*	대진제국3	大秦帝国之崛起	CCTV8	40	Ancient (Qin)***	Junghwa

(continued)

Table B.1   (continued)

First appeared on Korean TV	Title in English	Title in Korean	Title in Chinese	Originally from	Number of episode	Genre**	Broadcasted at (Korean TV station)
2016	Legend of Miyue	미월전	半月传	Dragon TV	81	Ancient (Zhanguo)***	AsiaN
2016	The Legend of Bruce Lee	전설로 남은 영웅 이소룡	李小龙传奇	CCTV	50	Martial arts	AsiaN
Unclear	Mazu	마조	妈祖	CCTV8	38	Fantasy	Junghwa
Unclear	Incisive Great Teacher	서리인사	犀利仁师	Dragon TV	45	Historical subfield***	Junghwa
Unclear	My Amazing Bride	극품신낭	极品新娘	Jiangsu	40	Historical subfield***	Junghwa
Unclear	War of Desire	후궁쟁패	凤图腾	Hunan TV	49	Ancient (Tang)***	Junghwa
Unclear	Infernal Lovers	무간유애	无间有爱	Southeast TV	33	Premodern	Junghwa
Unclear	Love Me If You Dare	타래료, 정폐안	他来了，请闭眼	Dragon TV	24	Modern	Junghwa
Unclear	The Queen of SOP	승녀적대가	胜女的代价	Hunan TV	33	Modern	Junghwa
Unclear	Too Late to Say I Love You	래불급설아애니	来不及说我爱你	Hubei TV	36	Premodern	Junghwa
Unclear	Selected with a Kiss	천산모설	千山暮雪	Hunan TV	30	Modern	Junghwa
Unclear	My Sunshine	하이생소묵	何以笙箫默	Dragon TV	32	Modern	Junghwa

Source: Compiled by the Author

Notes: * refers to the English title that was not available and translated by the author. ** is combined SAPPRFT's guideline and audiences' responses. *** is categorized as a "historical" subfield

Table B.2 Television series mentioned by transnational audiences: Chaps. 3, 4, and 6

Title	Broadcasted at (Korean TV station)	First appeared on Korean TV	Originally from	Production date	Number of episode
Beauty World (美人天下 Meirentianxia, Miyinchenha)	Junghwa	September 9, 2012	Guangzhou TV	October 21, 2011	33
Confucius (孔子 Kongzi, Gongja)	Junghwa	September 26, 2011	Shandong TV	September 27. 2014	35
Dwelling Narrowness (蝸居 Wojin)	N.A.	N.A.	Shanghai TV	July 27, 2009	35
iPartment (爱情公寓 Aiqing gongyu)	N.A.	N.A.	Jiangxi TV	August 5, 2009	88
Journey to the West (西游记 Xiyouji)	N.A.	N.A.	CCTV	1986	25 (+16)
Justice Pao (包青天 Baoqingtian, Pocheongcheom)	N.A.	N.A.	CTS	February 23, 1993	236
New Journey to the West (新西游记 Shin Seoygi)	AsiaN	July 9, 2012	TVS4	July 28, 2011 July 9, 2012	60
New Justice Pao (新包青天 Baoqingtian, Shin Pocheongcheom)	OBS GyeconginTV	March 1, 2010	SDTV-2	February 4, 2009	61
My Fair Princess (还珠格格 Huanzhugege) (Season 1)	Junghwa	August 6, 2000	CTV	April 28, 1998	24
Old House Has a Joy (老房有喜 Laofang youxi, Nobbangyuhui)	N.A.	July 2000	Dragon TV	July 21, 1999	25
Ō no kōkyuuuuī (王の後宮)	Junghwa	September 24, 2012	Zhejiang TV	November 6, 2011	46
Futari no ōjo (二人の王女; 太平公主秘史 Taipinggongzhu mishi)	Ching	January 2, 2013	Hunan TV	March 27, 2012	45
Palace (宫锁珠帘, Gongsuozhulian, Gungsaesimok)	KBS	October 21, 2012	Hunan TV	January 20, 2012	37

Table B.2 (continued)

Title	Broadcasted at (Korean TV station)	First appeared on Korean TV	Originally from	Production date	Number of episode
Playful Kiss (恶作剧之吻 E'zuoju zhi wen)	SBS	January 5, 2007	Taiwan CTV	September 25, 2005	20
Princess Huaiyu (怀玉公主 Huaiyu Gongzhu, Hoeokgongju)	N.A.	N.A.	Taiwan CTS	April 5, 2000	118
Romance in the Rain (情深深雨蒙蒙 Qingshenshen yumengmeng, Angaebiyeonga)	iTV	June 2010	Taiwan CTV	April 3, 2001	46
Scarlet Heart (步步惊心 Bubujingxin)	CineonTV	October 5, 2011	Hunan TV	September 10, 2011	40
Schemes of a Beauty (美人心计 Meirenxinji)	Junghwa	August 2, 2010	Shanghai TV	March 15, 2010	40
Temptations (回家的诱惑 Huijia de youhuo)	Junghwa	February 28, 2013	Hunan TV	February 21, 2011	74
The Meteor Garden (流星花园 Liuxing Huayuan)	MBC	2002	Taiwan CTS	April 12, 2001	20
The Modern Family of China (家有儿女 Jiayou'ernv)	N.A.	N.A.	CCTV4	February 12, 2005	367
The Return of the Pearl Princess (新还珠格格 xin huanzhugege) (Season 2)	AsiaN	March 5, 2012	Hunan TV	July 16, 2011	98
Three Kingdoms (三国 Sanguo)	KBS 2	February 27, 2012	Jiangsu/Anhui/Chongqing/TianjinTV	May 2, 2010	95

Broadcasted at Korean TV station

Appendix C

Table C.1   TV series and celebrities affected by THAAD (2016)

Title	Main Korean actor/actress	Status	Broadcasting station	Number of episode
Anna's Sweetheart (安娜的爱人, Anna de airen)	Lee Seunghyun	Finished production, it was scheduled to be broadcasted this year.	It is scheduled to be broadcasted in 2018.	33
A Lover's Lie (恋人的谎言, Lianren de huangyan)	Jeong Ilwoo	It was started to produce in Suzhou in July 2016.	N.A.	50
A Woman's Dream is Like a Dream (女人花似梦, Nvren hua si meng)	Jeong Ilwoo	When to broadcast on air was not clear.	N.A.	30
August not the End (八月未央, Ba yue wei yang)	Rain	Being broadcasted.	N.A.	80
Bound at First Sight (最美不过初相见, Zui mei buguo chu xiangjian)	Lee Hyunwoo	Not broadcasted.	N.A.	36
Braveness of the Ming (锦衣夜行, Mianyi yexing)	Park Minyoung	Finished broadcasting.	N.A.	30
Dear Sorry (亲爱的对不起, Qinaide duibuqi)	Ju Jinmo	Finished production, it was scheduled to be broadcasted this year.	N.A.	24
Distressed Beauty (卿本佳人, Qingbenjiaren)	Kim Jeonghun	Being prepared for broadcasting.	It was broadcasted on December 13, 2016 in Hunan TV.	42
Hope Husband Success (望夫成龙, Wangfu Cheonglong)	Lee Taehwan	It was scheduled to be broadcasted in July 2016.	It was broadcasted on July 8, 2016 in Shenzhen TV.	66

(continued)

Table C.1   (continued)

Title	Main Korean actor/actress	Status	Broadcasting station	Number of episode
Fighter of the Destiny (择天记, *Zetianji*)	Ku Hyunho	Not broadcasted.	It was broadcasted on April 17, 2017 in Hunan TV.	56
Graduation Season (毕业季, *Biyeji*)	Jung Sujeong (Krystal)	Finished production, but not broadcasted.	N.A.	50
Happiness Chocolate (女汉子的进化论之幸福巧克力, *Nvhaizi de jinhualun zhi xingfu qiaokeli*)	Lee Seongmin	Finished production, but not broadcasted.	N.A.	N.A.
Jade Lover (翡翠恋人, *Beicui lianren*)	Lee Jong-suk	Finished production and being broadcasted.	It is scheduled to be broadcasted in Zhejiang Satellite TV (*Weishi*).	35
Love Express (爱情也包邮, *Aiqing ye baoyou*)	Ju Wan	Finished production, it was scheduled to be broadcasted this year.	N.A.	30
Memory Lost (美人为馅, *Meiren wei xian*)	Lee Geon	It was scheduled to be broadcasted in October 2016.	The first season broadcasted on October 24, 2016 via iQiyi.	12 (Season 1); 12 (Season 2); 12 (Season 3)
Mr. Right (我的男神, *Wo de nanshen*)	Ji Chang Wook	Finished production and being broadcasted.	N.A.	42
Return to Me (爱归来, *Ai guilai*)	Kwon Sangwoo	Finished production, it was scheduled to broadcast in November 2016.	N.A.	40
Shuttle Love Millennium (相爱穿梭千年2, *Xiangai chuanjun qiannian 2*)	Yoo In-na	It was scheduled to be broadcasted in September 14, 2016.	It was broadcasted on November 16, 2016 in Hunan TV.	28
The Fox's Summer (狐狸的夏天, *Huli de xiatian*)	Kim Taehwan	Just started to be produced, not broadcasted.	It was broadcasted on April 5, 2017 in Sichuan Satellite TV.	21 (Season 1); 23 (Season 2)

(*continued*)

Table C.1   (continued)

Title	Main Korean actor/actress	Status	Broadcasting station	Number of episode
The Lady in Cubicle (格子间的女人, *Gezijian de nvren*)	Lee Seunghyun	Finished broadcasting in 2014.	N.A	30
The Lee's Courtyard (李家大院, *Lijiadayuan*)	Chae Lim	Finished broadcasting.	N.A.	42
The Legendary Tycoon (传奇大亨, *Chuanqi da heng*)	Ku Hye-sun	Finished production, but not broadcasted.	It was broadcasted on October 9, 2017 in Zhejiang Satellite TV.	42
The Rhapsody of Summer Dream (夏梦狂诗曲, *Xiameng kuangshiqu*)	Go Junhee	Finished production, but not broadcasted.	N.A.	50
Time City (时光之城, *Shiguang zhi cheng*)	Park Minyoung	Not broadcasted.	N.A.	38
Turn into a Beautiful Man (变身花美男, *Bianshen hua meinan*)	Lee Shangyeob	Finished production, but not broadcasted.	N.A.	24
Undercover (卧底归来, *Wodigulai*)	Shin Min-hee	Not broadcasted.	It was broadcasted on April 17, 2017 in Jiangsu TV, but the Korean actress was not included.	42
The Happy Time of A Spicy Girlfriend (麻辣女友的幸福时光, *Mala nvyou de xingfushiguang*)*	Chu Jahyun	Finished broadcasting in 2012.	N.A.	30
Hunting Tiger 1946 (猎虎1946, *Liehu 1946*)*	Chu Jahyun	Finished broadcasting in 2015.	N.A.	35
The Song (恋恋阙歌, *Lianlian quege*)	Lee Seunghyun	Finished production, but when to broadcast on air was not clear.	It was broadcasted via iQiyi.	46

(*continued*)

Table C.1   (continued)

Title	Main Korean actor/actress	Status	Broadcasting station	Number of episode
Another Me in the World (世界上的另一个我, Shijieshang de ling yi ge wo)	Lee Seunghyun	Finished broadcasting in 2012.	It was broadcasted via iQiyi.	36
Hand in Hand (左手温暖右手, Zuoshou wenai youshou)	Chae Lim	Finished production, it was scheduled to be broadcasted early this year.	N.A.	47
My Goddess My Mother (我的女神我的妈, Wo de nvshen wo de ma)*	Lee Dahae	Started being produced and it was scheduled to be broadcasted in 2017.	N.A.	N.A.
Zhu Donghua, a 30-year-old Woman (女人三十朱冬花, Nv'ren sanshi wei donghua)*	Kim Jinwoo, Dennis Oh	Being prepared for broadcasting.	N.A.	30
The Hotel Family (酒店世家, Jiudian shijia)*	Lee Juhyun	Finished production in 2013, but not broadcasted.	N.A.	34
City Lover (城市恋人, Chengshi lianren)*	Choi Jiwoo	Being prepared for broadcasting.	It was broadcasted on August 19, 2016 in Zhejiang Satellite Television.	30
Rose's War (蔷薇的战争, Qiangwei de zhanzheng)*	Kim Sun-a	Finished production, but not broadcasted.	N.A.	34
Chong Er's Preach (重耳传, Chong er zhuan)*	Han Chaeyoung	Being filmed.	N.A.	80
Hundreds of Millions of Successors (亿万继承人, Yiwan jichengren)	Choi Siwon	Finished production, but not broadcasted.	N.A.	40
Cold Love Be Passionately in Love (冷爱热恋, Leng ai re ai)	Shin Min-hee	Finished production, but not broadcasted.	N.A.	42

(continued)

Table C.1 (continued)

Title	Main Korean actor/actress	Status	Broadcasting station	Number of episode
Good Wife (好妻子, *Hao qizi*)	Shin Min-hee	Finished production, but not broadcasted.	It was broadcasted in Dragon TV in 2016.	56
Saint Wang Xizhi (书圣王羲之, *Shushengwangxizhi*)*	Kim Taehee	Finished production, but not broadcasted.	Not yet broadcasted	40
Love in 1931 (1931年的爱情, *1931 nian de Aiqing*)*	Han Chaeyoung	Being prepared for broadcasting.	It is not possible to be broadcasted.	36
Winning (胜算, *Shengsuan*)*	Han Chaeyoung	Being prepared for broadcasting.	N.A.	50
A Single Wing Eagle (单翼雄鹰, *Dan yi xiong ying*)*	Jang Nara	Being prepared for broadcasting.	N.A.	38
I Loved You, Thinking of You Saddens Me (我曾爱过你, 想起就心酸, *Wo ceng ai guo ni, xiangqi jiu xinsuan*)*	Jang Donggeon	Being produced and filmed.	N.A.	40
Popcorn (爆米花, *Bao mihua*)	Park Haejin	Being prepared for broadcasting.	N.A.	35
Male Friends (男人帮朋友, *Nanrenbang pengyou*)	Park Haejin	Being prepared for broadcasting.	N.A.	40
Full House (幸福小镇之浪漫满屋, *Xingfuxiaozhen zhi langman manwu*)	Eli	Being prepared for broadcasting.	N.A.	35
A Wenzhou Daughter-in-Law in Friends' Circle (朋友圈儿之温州媳妇, *Pengyouquanr zhi Wenzhou xifu*)*	Kangta	Finished production, but not broadcasted.	N.A.	53
A Unique Place (异现场, *Yixianchang*)*	Han Jiseok	Finished production, but not broadcasted.	N.A.	N.A.

Source: Baidu Baike (n.d.), Sohu Yule (2016), Wangyi (2016). Translated by the author

Notes: (1) * refers to the English title that was not available and translated by the author. (2) The list of banned Korean TV series was from the following sources (Baidu Baike n.d.; Sohu Yule 2016; Wangyi 2016), but the information was compiled by the author

References

Baidu Baike. n.d. *Pengyouquanr zhi Wenzhou xifu [A Wenzhou Daughter-in-Law in Friends' Circle]*. Accessed March 19, 2018. https://baike.baidu.com/item/%E6%9C%8B%E5%8F%8B%E5%9C%88%E5%84%BF%E4%B9%8B%E6%B8%A9%E5%B7%9E%E5%AA%B3%E5%A6%87/1987886≤?fr=aladdin.
Sohu Yule [Sohu Entertainment]. 2016. Bao 'JinHanling' mingdan 42 ming yiren 53 bu ju shou yingxiang [The list of 'Korea Ban' Influences on 42 Celebrities and 53 Episodes of Television Series]. *Sohu*, August 7. Accessed August 6, 2017. http://yule.sohu.com/20160806/n462874682.shtml.
Wangyi. 2016. Bao 'Jinhanling' Mingdan 42 Ming Yiren 53 Bu Ju Shou Yingxiang ['The List of the Government's Ban of Korea' is Out Which Includes 42 Celebrities and 53 Dramas]. August 7. Accessed August 6, 2016. news.sina.com.cn/s/wh/2016-08-06/doc-ifxutfpc4637273.shtml.

INDEX[1]

A

Actors, 5, 8, 44n1, 54, 57, 59,
    73, 75n6, 99, 100, 132,
    137, 138, 140, 143, 144,
    182, 185, 188
Adam, Doug, 7
Africa, 10, 36, 40
Alibaba, 157
Americas, 5, 10, 33, 36
    Latin America, 33, 36
'Ancient' (*gudai*), 35
Artifacts (*yishupin*), 30
Asia
    Asia, East, 3, 9–15, 90, 113, 120,
        125, 135, 186, 187, 192
    Asian regions, 2, 11, 40, 126
    Asia, Southeast, 10, 36, 40,
        46n27, 126, 192
    Asia TV Forum, 58, 75n5
    Central, 33
    South, 33
Audience(s)
    external, 27, 30

Japanese, 6, 8, 13, 16, 17, 70, 72,
    82–88, 92, 98, 101, 121, 130,
    132, 133, 146, 147, 155, 177,
    182, 184, 186
potential, 6, 10, 65, 72, 158, 164
South Korean, 6, 8, 16, 17, 64, 72,
    82–84, 86, 87, 92, 98, 101,
    121, 143, 146, 147, 155, 177,
    182, 184, 186
target, 5, 96, 112, 122, 182, 184
transnational, 7, 8, 15, 25, 29, 82,
    83, 86, 87, 90, 91, 94–96, 99,
    113, 117, 118, 129, 144, 155,
    156, 160, 164, 167, 175, 176,
    179–181, 185, 188
Audio-visual products (*yingxiang*), 30
Authoritarian regime, 2, 27, 192
Authoritarianism
    competitive, 28
    consultative, 28
    resilient authoritarianism, 28
    responsive authoritarianism, 28
    soft authoritarianism, 3

---

[1] Note: Page numbers followed by 'n' refer to notes.

C. S. Lee, *Soft Power Made in China*,
https://doi.org/10.1007/978-3-319-93115-9